THE FILMS AND CAREER OF AUDIE MURPHY

by
Sue Gossett

Published by
Empire Publishing, Inc.
Box 717
Madison, NC 27025-0717
(336) 427-5850

Other Western movie books published by Empire Publishing, Inc:

The Roy Rogers Reference-Trivia-Scrapbook by David Rothel
The Gene Autry Reference-Trivia -Scrapbook by David Rothel
More Cowboy Shooting Stars by John A. Rutherford and Richard B. Smith, III
An Ambush of Ghosts by David Rothel
Tim Holt by David Rothel
Whatever Happened to Randolph Scott? by C. H. Scott
Randolph Scott / A Film Biography by Jefferson Brim Crow, III
Saddle Pals by Garv Towell and Wayne E. Keates
Saddle Gals by Edgar M. Wyatt and Steve Turner
The Round-Up by Donald R. Key
Trail Talk by Bobby J. Copeland
Riding the Silver Screen Range by Ann Snuggs
B-Western Boot Hill by Bobby Copeland
Richard Boone, A Knight without Armor in a Savage Land by David Rothel
Bill Elliott, the Peaceable Man by Bobby Copeland
Roy Barcroft, King of the Badmen by Bobby Copeland
Those Great Cowboy Sidekicks by David Rothel
Silent Hoofbeats by Bobby Copeland
Audie Murphy: Now Showing by Sue Gossett
So You Want to See Cowboy Stuff? by Boyd Magers
Charles King: We Called Him "Blackie" by Bobby Copeland

Empire Publishing, Inc.
Box 717
Madison, NC 27025-0717
(336) 427-5850

ISBN Number 0-944019-22-6
Library of Congress Catalog Card Number 96-85103

Manufactured in the United States of America

Cover Design by Patrick Downey

First Printing: 1996
Second Printing: 1997
Third Printing: 2003
1 2 3 4 5 6 7 8

DEDICATION

This book is dedicated to all the friends, and past, present and future fans of Audie Murphy.

ACKNOWLEDGMENTS

Many thanks to everyone involved in getting this book written. My sincere appreciation goes to my friend, Stan Smith, who, without his consummate help and cooperation, this book could have never been achieved.

To Scott Shoemaker, for his countless hours of taping and editing films. To Budd Boetticher, director of THE CIMARRON KID and A TIME FOR DYING, who gave support and encouragement. To Audie's sisters and my friends, Billie Murphy Tindol and Nadene Murphy, for their wonderful stories.

To Pat Downey, owner of Good News Graphics, in Dayton, Ohio, for putting me in touch with Donald R. Key, publisher of Empire Publishing, Inc. To Don Key, for believing in this book, my thanks.

A very special thank you to Neil Summers, actor/stuntman who worked on ARIZONA RAIDERS and A TIME FOR DYING with Audie, for loaning all the beautiful and unique stills. Audie and Neil were good friends.

To Captain Carl Swickerath, Ret. U.S. Army, whose immense contribution regarding Audie's military background, I give my utmost gratitude. Without his expertise and knowledge, this book would not be complete.

Other contributors who offered their services and assistance include Sharon Young, Jade B. Krug, Mike West, Wayne Cutshaw, and Margaret Kelley, all members of the Audie Murphy National Fan Club. Also, thanks to Perry Robertson, long-time collector on Audie. A nod of recognition also to Hubert Claeys whose valuable input on Western genre is remarkable with his additional facts..

To my family, friends and co-workers for their love and support. Special appreciation to my husband, Dave, for putting up with leftovers on many occasions.

To the late David "Spec" McClure, Audie's friend throughout his life, who supplied so much of the detailed descriptions and background for the films. "Spec" also convinced Audie to write his famous autobiography, *To Hell and Back.*

To Universal-International, Columbia, Paramount, United Artists, 20th Century Fox, Allied Artists, American International, Metro-Goldwyn-Mayer and FIPCO Productions, for their photographs and films of Audie.

My sincerest gratitude to Larryann Willis and Terry Murphy who took the time to answer my questions and reviewed the book's accuracy.

Finally, last, but not least, to my brother, John LaMartine, who did all the fine editing, I give my thanks. His unique touch makes him invaluable to me and to this book.

CONTENTS

Introduction 7

Foreword 20

Filmography
- Beyond Glory 22
- Texas, Brooklyn and Heaven 24
- Bad Boy 26
- The Kid from Texas 29
- Sierra 32
- Kansas Raiders 35
- The Red Badge of Courage 37
- The Cimarron Kid 41
- The Duel at Silver Creek 44
- Gunsmoke 47
- Column South 50
- Tumbleweed 53
- Ride Clear of Diablo 56
- Drums across the River 59
- Destry 62
- To Hell and Back 66
- World in My Corner 71
- Walk the Proud Land 74
- The Guns of Fort Petticoat 77
- Joe Butterfly 80
- Night Passage 83
- The Quiet American 87
- Ride a Crooked Trail 91
- The Gun Runners 94
- No Name on the Bullet 98
- The Wild and the Innocent 101
- Cast a Long Shadow 105
- The Unforgiven 108
- Hell Bent for Leather 113
- Seven Ways from Sundown 116
- Posse from Hell 119
- Battle at Bloody Beach 123
- Six Black Horses 126

Showdown 129
Gunfight at Comanche Creek 132
The Quick Gun 135
Bullet for a Badman 138
Apache Rifles 141
Arizona Raiders 145
Gunpoint 148
Trunk To Cairo 151
The Texican 154
40 Guns To Apache Pass 157
A Time For Dying 160

Television Appearances 164
The Flight 165
The Man 169
Whispering Smith-Stakeout 173

Military Heritage-War Years 178

Songs and Poetry 183

Photo Gallery 185

Complete Filmography 195

Selected Bibliography 196

About the Author 197

INTRODUCTION

On July 16, 1945, Audie Murphy's picture appeared on the cover of *Life* Magazine. Among the millions who saw that picture was film star James Cagney. Cagney immediately saw the potential for the young war hero as a movie idol, and invited him to Hollywood, with the idea of casting him in a Cagney Productions film. As things turned out, Audie's first film appearance would be three years away, when Cagney loaned out his services to Paramount Studios for a small part in BEYOND GLORY. But, unlike many Hollywood hopefuls who never achieved fame, Audie persevered and became the star that Cagney and others knew he could be.

* * *

Rising up from the lowest level of poverty, Audie Murphy was to become the soldier most decorated for valor in the history of World War II before he was old enough to vote.

He was born to Emmett and Josie Bell Murphy, on a sharecropper's farm on June 20, 1924, near the little town of Kingston, Texas. The very early years had Audie strapped in a baby swing while his mother worked in a cotton patch nearby. From the time he could walk, his world was one of hard work—by carrying wood to the house and, at an early age, shooting game for the dinner table. Sometimes he could only afford a single shell in his rifle to supply meat for his family of nine brothers and sisters. His accuracy had to be exact or they didn't eat. Later in combat, that on-target precision would pay off in saving not only his life but those of his buddies throughout his war years.

His sister, Billie tells a rather humorous story during Audie's growing up years. She let's us know that Audie was fond of practical jokes. She recalls how, one day, Audie had offered his siblings some little pieces of "candy." When they tasted the "candy", they discovered that he had cut up a bar of Lifebouy soap and offered it to them.

When Audie was twelve, his father deserted the family. Audie quit school after only completing the fifth grade and went to work as a farm hand. In 1941, when Audie was sixteen, his mother passed away. This was catastrophic for Audie as he adored his mother. Shortly thereafter, he went to work in a combination general store, garage and filling station in Greenville. Since there was no one to care for the three younger children, the extremely difficult decision of placing them in an orphanage was made. Audie mourned his mother's passing for the rest of his life.

The Japanese bombing of Pearl Harbor in December 1941 prompted many Americans to volunteer for military service. Audie tried to enlist on June 20, 1942, his 18th birthday into the marines. They turned him down because he didn't weigh enough. Then he tried to enlist in the paratroopers because he thought they were tough. Again he was rejected for being underweight. Finally, he tried the infantry. They asked no questions and let him in. They said he was light on his feet and that he'd make a good soldier.

Audie had never been over 100 miles from home so off he went on a bus to the induction center. During a training session of close order drill at Camp Wolters, Texas, he fell flat on his face, passed out cold. The company commanders tried to have him transferred to cook and bakers school because of his baby-faced youthfulness, but Murphy persisted in becoming a fighting soldier. (In his own words, "he hated his own cooking.") After thirteen weeks of basic training, he was sent to Fort Meade, Maryland, for advanced infantry training. In February of 1943, Casablanca in North Africa was to be his first tour of duty as a replacement. He was assigned to Company B, 1st Battalion, 15th Infantry Regiment, 3rd Infantry Division at Port Lyautey. Audie stayed with this outfit throughout the war. Less than two and one half years later, he would be promoted to commander of his unit.

Upon arrival in Sicily, he had his first encounter with death. He killed two Italian soldiers as they tried to escape on their magnificent white horses. When questioned by his platoon leader why he did it, he replied, "It was my job."

Audie contracted malaria while in Sicily. It put him in the hospital for several days while in Salerno, and on an occasional basis during the remainder of the war.

Before his 21st birthday, and after more than two years overseas, most of it front line duty, Audie Murphy returned home at the end of World War II with every decoration for valor this country could bestow, including three Purple Hearts. He participated in nine battle campaigns including the assault landings at Sicily and Southern France. His fame earned him the title of "The most decorated combat soldier of World War II."

Audie's homecoming to Farmersville, Texas, in 1945 was sheer excitement. His family and friends all gave him a hero's welcome upon his arrival. Audie never enjoyed talking in public and shied away from a lot of attention. On one occasion, while a formal ceremonial dinner was being held in his honor in San Antonio, Audie quietly settled into a local hotel room and slept through the whole thing.

Once when he was in New York, they even had an Audie Murphy Day at Ebbet's Field. He was overwhelmed with America's gratitude. He went to hospitals where he visited with the soldiers. He wasn't comfortable with the civilians yet and spent much of his time with those with whom he could relate. Like them, soldiering was deep within his heart and remained there with him over the years. He returned to Europe in 1948 on behalf of the army and paid his respects to those who had fallen. While there, he had mixed emotions, those being saddened by the futility of war and then being with the children of which he was so fond. He loved kids and it showed.

Here is a little note of interest from Audie's younger sister, Billie, shortly after Audie came home from the war. She relates how Audie purchased a two-story home for his oldest sister Corinne to live in along with her husband and children. This enabled the three youngest children to be taken from the orphanage and reunited with the rest of the family. Audie had vowed before going in the Army he would get them out and he fulfilled that promise. Also, while he was home, Billie recalls that Audie bought her her first pair of nylons, Sunday shoes of black patent leather and the most beautiful dress in the world. This is something she has remembered for all these many years, and will never forget. Audie loved doing things for other people.

Audie moved to California in the summer of 1945 and lived with James Cagney for over a year. Since nothing substantial materialized from a movie contract offered by Cagney, Audie left. After leaving the Cagneys, Audie spent many nights sleeping in a gym owned by his friend, Terry Hunt. He finally landed a small role in his first movie, BEYOND GLORY, starring Alan Ladd and Donna Reed. Although his role was small in this film, he achieved his first critical write-up: "Audie Murphy makes his debut and does right well for himself. You'll recognize him. He's the one with the southern drawl."

One day, Audie saw a picture of Wanda Hendrix on the March 1946 cover of *Coronet* magazine. She was a rising star under contract to Paramount at that time. She said that she went to the studio front office and asked that Audie be cast in BEYOND GLORY. While working in his first movie, Audie had another *Life* magazine photo layout. The theme covered the Murphy film debut, his romance with Wanda, and her recent movie, RIDE THE PINK HORSE. They were married on January 8, 1949.

He then got his second movie offer in TEXAS, BROOKLYN AND HEAVEN, with the help of his longtime friend, David "Spec" McClure. "Spec," through his association with Hedda Hopper, was helpful in obtaining a small part for Audie in the film. Audie appreciated the help but was becoming frustrated that he couldn't obtain better movie roles. Afterward, he announced that he would never be in another picture unless he had the starring role. Soon after, his big break finally came when he starred in BAD BOY with Jane Wyatt and Lloyd Nolan.

In the fall of 1948, Audie got that break, thanks to James "Skipper" Cherry and producer Paul Short, both connected with Interstate Theatres, Inc. He had come back to Texas for a visit and, as usual, spent much time with Skipper, his advisor and close friend. At that time, Short was looking to cast BAD BOY in Hollywood. Cherry contacted Short and asked if he would consider giving Audie a part in the film. Over some objection from the president of Allied Artists, Audie screen-tested for, and got, the starring role.

The world premiere of the film was held on February 16th, 1949, at the Majestic Theatre in Dallas. Audie was present for the big occasion, along with Wyatt, Nolan, and other cast members. Following the premiere, Audie embarked on

Audie and Wanda Hendrix (circa 1950)

an extensive tour of the Southwestern United States, promoting the picture and attending autograph parties for his newly published autobiography, *To Hell and Back.*

Audie's acting in BAD BOY was good enough for one of the major Hollywood studios to invest in his name and talents. Universal International offered him a seven year contract at $2,500 per week. It became a package arrangement with producer Short purchasing five stories in which Audie was to star.

Of the five, only THE KID FROM TEXAS made it to the screen, as Audie's second starring role and first Western. Like BAD BOY, KID was heavily promoted in Texas. Short announced the "world premiere" for the same theater in Dallas for March of 1950. The film broke the attendance records set by BAD BOY the previous year, playing to full houses.

Before he made another film, the radio show, "This Is Your Life," hosted by Ralph Edwards, had Audie in the spotlight. It focused on his growing up years, went back to his school days and shared with the audience his war exploits. He was reunited with war buddies he had not seen in four or five years. He was visibly moved by seeing his friends, not only from the war but from his hometown as well.

With his long term contract in place, Audie decided to buy out Short's multi-picture arrangement. However, the two never worked together again. He quickly plunged into two more Westerns—KANSAS RAIDERS and SIERRA. During the filming of SIERRA, Audie and Wanda announced their marriage was over and the divorce became final on April 20, 1951.

After these films, Audie announced that he would probably go back into the army. The Korean War broke out in June 1950. In July, Audie returned to Dallas to join the 36th Infantry Division (Texas National Guard). If that division was re-activated as regular army, Murphy would again find himself with a combat outfit. He had considered volunteering for direct military service, but the "police action"—which the war was called —indicated a short term of combat, and Audie had little desire to pull a full-time hitch in a peace-time army.

Two other factors were to affect his decision. He was up for the starring role in THE RED BADGE OF COURAGE, and he had a great desire to play in that movie even if it was his last one. Also, in July 1950, Audie met Pamela Archer. She was a Braniff Airline hostess who had seen Audie's picture on the cover of *Life* magazine. A serious romance resulted and they were married three days after his divorce became final the following year.

Following his marriage to Pamela Archer on April 23, 1951, Audie returned to Universal and his Western movie career. Audie very much wanted a family. His post-war life had been virtually rootless. He thought that a family of his own might give him the stability he desperately needed. Then on March 14, 1952, Terry Michael, made his debut and just a little over two years later, James Shannon (Skipper), was born on March 23, 1954. The boys were named after Audie's close friends, Terry Hunt and James "Skipper" Cherry.

But a family costs money; and about the only way Audie could earn good money was through motion pictures. KANSAS RAIDERS was the first movie he made under a new contract with Universal Studios. However, Audie still thought that he was too poorly paid, and in a sense he was right. As the star of the pictures, he actually made less money than some of the better character actors who had been brought in to give the still-green Murphy a solid backing.

On occasion, Audie, in an attempt to panic the studio into raising his salary, would announce his intentions of quitting pictures altogether and leaving Hollywood. Nobody could have forced him to make more movies. But his contract would have made it impossible for him to go to other studios in search of more money.

When it was announced that John Huston was going to make THE RED BADGE OF COURAGE for Metro-Goldwyn-Mayer, "Spec" McClure suggested Audie for the part of the "Young Soldier." The film was starcrossed from the beginning. Louis B. Mayer did not want to do the film at all, and there was further objection to casting Audie. Huston prevailed, however, with promotional help from Hedda Hopper's column. She went to bat for Audie and thought very highly of him. Huston liked Audie tremendously, and called him "his gentle-eyed little killer."

Originally, Huston envisioned authentic outdoor scenes shot in Virginia and Tennessee. However, the approved budget forced the director to shoot all the footage within California, some of it even on Huston's ranch. Immediately

Audie Murphy, who starred with Bill Mauldin in Metro-Goldwyn Mayer's THE RED BADGE OF COURAGE, played the role of "The Youth" in the Stephen Crane classic of the Civil War.

after the shooting schedule was finished, Huston was off to Africa to direct THE AFRICAN QUEEN, leaving the editing of RED BADGE entirely to the studio. Lacking Huston's final touches in the editing room, RED BADGE suffered at the box office.

However, Huston was convinced that Audie had the capability of becoming a fine actor, getting two of the finest performances from Murphy that the Texan gave in his entire movie career—THE UNFORGIVEN and THE RED BADGE OF COURAGE. "He's got the ability to win audiences. He arouses the maternal instinct in women and the fraternal instinct in men. Not many actors can do that." (*Audie Murphy, American Soldier*)

NOTE: To read about John Huston, Metro-Goldwyn-Mayer, and the actual making of THE RED BADGE OF COURAGE, the book *Picture* by Lillian Ross offers a detailed account of this film.

Later in the 1950s, Audie bought an estate in Dallas, Texas, but he never lived in it. His younger brother, Joe, occupied and took care of the house for a few years. In May of 1980, the house was converted into a restaurant which is called Dovie's. It stayed mostly unchanged with the exception of an addition of a large courtyard room. Dining rooms have been made from what used to be the four upstairs bedrooms. Downstairs rooms remain the same with the porch having been enclosed and the original kitchen being increased in size using the garage and other original buildings.

Three years and eight films later, having convinced Universal he was mature enough to handle a big-budget starring role, the production of his autobiography, TO HELL AND BACK, moved into high gear. Audie was able to make an impact on this movie and served as the source of material for the script, costumes, acting, sets, props, casting, and unofficial technical advisor. Audie had reservations abouth having to relive the war, but was convinced by producer Aaron Rosenberg and director Jesse Hibbs to perform the part himself.

Audie often reminisced about his actual battles in Europe between takes on the set, recalling his army buddies. Many had been killed in action and he was always deeply respectful of their memory.

Director Hibbs had to cope with one problem, which he found hard to solve. The picture had several prolonged battle scenes. "To start a battle was a cinch," Hibbs said, "I just fired the first shot and guns went into action. But stopping the battle was another matter." His loudspeaker could not be heard above the din and roar of the action. In desperation, Hibbs hit upon a logical solution to the problem. He had a flag pole erected on his observation post behind the cameras. When he wanted to "cut" the action, he merely ran up the white flag of surrender and all firing ceased.

Audie was somewhat amused that the army at Fort Lewis, the site of the movie, could only supply five working tanks for a scene which authentically called

Audie Murphy, wiping out German-infested hill shortly after buddy is killed by sniper in a scene from TO HELL AND BACK (1955)

for six German tanks to advance on his army company.

A succession of premieres were held during August 1955 in four Texas cities: San Antonio, Houston, Dallas and Fort Worth. Most of the theaters set attendance records during its run. The box-office grosses from the Majestic Theatre in Dallas were second only to GONE WITH THE WIND.

While doing an appearance tour for the film in Washington, DC, Audie was invited to sit in the gallery of the senate chamber by Senator Price Daniel of Texas. While being seated, Senator Daniel broke into the floor debate and introduced him. Audie stood up, waved and smiled, and was loudly applauded by the senators and the gallery observers.

TO HELL AND BACK grossed almost ten million dollars during its initial theatrical release, and, at the time, became Universal's biggest hit movie in the 43-year history of the studio. This film would not be released until October, 1955, but Universal believed the movie would be a big hit, so the studio gave Audie latitude in choosing roles as long as they required a lot of action. Terry Murphy, who played Joe Preston Murphy (at 4) is Audie's oldest son. Corinne, Charles Emmett (Buck), Vernon, June, Oneta, J.W., Richard, Eugene, Nadene, Billie and Joseph Murphy were the names of Audie's brothers and sisters in real life.

Following this major success, Audie took on a different characterization as a professional boxer in WORLD IN MY CORNER. To prepare for the role, he began a strenuous training program. Several sparring partners wound up as on-screen opponents, resulting in some of the most realistic boxing scenes ever filmed.

Murphy picked the prize fight part in an attempt to break away from Westerns. He, Aaron Rosenberg, and Jesse Hibbs were again teamed as star-producer-director. This was the combination that made TO HELL AND BACK.

WORLD IN MY CORNER was well-received, but Audie and Universal understood that his fans still wanted to see him in Westerns. However, his next film, WALK THE PROUD LAND, portraying the life of John Clum, the U.S. Government agent who persuaded Geromino to surrender, fared poorly. Based on the results, Universal turned down Audie's next project, a movie based on Western artist Charles Russell.

JOE BUTTERFLY was Audie's only real try at slapstick comedy. There was a "sneak" preview at a theater in Manhattan and it seemed to go over quite well with the audience. It also did quite well at the box office, however, there were some critics who just gave Audie faint praise. Obviously, he wasn't meant to be a lover or comedian on the big screen. His best work was certainly in Westerns where he felt comfortable.

The only picture in which he didn't receive exclusive top billing was NIGHT

Boxer and the Lady—Audie Murphy and Barbara Rush, romantic co-stars of Universal-International's WORLD IN MY CORNER.

PASSAGE, in which he co-starred with the popular and talented James Stewart. He also had a strong supporting role in THE UNFORGIVEN with Burt Lancaster and Audrey Hepburn. His first two minor roles in BEYOND GLORY with Alan Ladd and Donna Reed, and TEXAS, BROOKLYN AND HEAVEN with Guy Madison and Diana Lynn, allowed him to establish himself as an actor. Audie gave some of his best performances with these highly respected actors.

Audie had a long standing interest in film production. Murphy-Brown Productions made THE GUNS OF FORT PETTICOAT at Columbia. MCR Productions (Audie Murphy, John Champion and Paul Ross), produced THE TEXICAN for Columbia. Audie was a producer on CAST A LONG SHADOW and acted as a producer on TO HELL AND BACK. The last film he was to produce was A TIME FOR DYING in 1969.

Another out of character role for Audie was his role as THE QUIET AMERICAN. He had been called by the Academy Award winning director, Joseph Mankiewicz. Audie didn't hesitate. He packed his bags and began reading the book in his hotel room. He felt that anything Mankiewicz did would be good. Audie and Pam celebrated their seventh wedding anniversary in Rome after shooting the interiors for the picture.

THE GUN RUNNERS was yet another try to keep Audie from being type cast. This story was based on Ernest Hemingway's novel *To Have and Have Not.* The 1944 version starred Humphrey Bogart and Lauren Bacall.

Whenever Audie was cast in a movie, one of two things were evident. He wore a uniform or was given a horse. Naturally, he was at ease with either one. Many southwesterners are born to the saddle and Audie was no exception. He was comfortable with the six-gun as he was with a carbine, rifle or machine gun. He was also fond of playing the good guy, a straight-forward part, but once in a while, as a change of pace, equally liked the challenge of a psychological role such as the killer in NO NAME ON THE BULLET. Assurance and self-confidence shows a very intense side of Audie. As he played this part, he meant business. This was his portrayal of a man everyone feared because, he was a hired killer and all thought he had come to kill them.

A little lighter side of Westerns came in the form of THE WILD AND THE INNOCENT with Sandra Dee as his female counterpart. Audie actually did his own singing in this film, doing a fine job with a pleasant harmony.

Audie took a little time out of his busy schedule to try his hand at some television productions. In the late 1950s and early 1960s Audie appeared in three productions. In February, 1958 he starred in the G.E. Theater doing "The Incident;" in 1959, Suspicion in "The Flight" and in 1960 for Ford Startime Theater, "The Man." Then in 1961, he made twenty-six episodes of "Whispering Smith" along with Guy Mitchell. However, only thirteen of them were shown and since the production schedule was canceled, Audie went back to making movies.

Audie had a love of life which showed particularly when he was outdoors. Animals and children seemed to be near him for the most part. After the war, he also raised purebred Quarter Horses, his most famous horses being Depth Charge and Joe Queen. Audie liked to ride good Quarter Horses in his movies to give them recognition. Audie had other interesting horses that he worked with also. His horse in TUMBLEWEED, is an ungainly creature who turns out to be a life-saver and hero of this film. He is able to hike over mountain crags, find water in the alkali desert and plays dead to fool Indians.

Audie went on to make ten more Westerns for Universal between the years 1957 and 1965. However, one of the best acting performances he gave outside of THE RED BADGE OF COURAGE was that as a supporting actor in THE UNFORGIVEN in 1960, starring Burt Lancaster and Audrey Hepburn. Again, he was directed by John Huston who always got a top-notch performance from Audie.

In 1963, Audie did the foreword for a film entitled WAR IS HELL. This was a picture that revolves around a medal-happy non-commissioned officer who will do anything to add to his battlefield record, even stooping to kill his superior officer. This film was showing on the screen at the Texas Theater on

November 22, 1963. Lee Harvey Oswald was in the theater and was arrested by the police shortly after the assassination of John F. Kennedy.

Some later films were shot overseas. TRUNK TO CAIRO was filmed entirely in Israel and THE TEXICAN, filmed in the Barcelona, Spain, area. The remaining two movies, 40 GUNS TO APACHE PASS and A TIME FOR DYING, were shot back in the States.

The final film that Audie made and also produced was A TIME FOR DYING, directed by Budd Boetticher, who also directed him in THE CIMARRON KID in 1953. In this movie Audie plays an aging Jesse James, a role he played once before in KANSAS RAIDERS. He plays this older Jesse with such feeling that the audience has to be aware that this is indeed one of the finest acting roles Audie ever did. His last was his best. Audie was a very good actor, but unfortunately, he never got the chance to show just how talented he really was.

During a business trip, Audie died as the result of a plane crash on May 28, 1971, in a rainstorm near Galax, Virginia, some twenty miles southwest of Roanoke. How ironic it was that he was killed on his mother's birthday.

Due to the remoteness of the area, it took several days to find the plane and its passengers. Audie Leon Murphy was laid to rest on June 7, 1971, in Arlington National Cemetery with full military honors. Among the dignitaries was George Bush, then Ambassador-at-Large to the United Nations. His engraved headstone reads as follows: Audie L. Murphy, Texas. Major Infantry, World War II, June 20, 1924 - May 28, 1971, Medal of Honor, DSC - SS & OLC; LM - BSM & OLC; PH & 2 OLC. (DSC-Distinguished Service Cross; SS-Silver Star; LM-Legion of Merit; BSM-Bronze Star Medal; OLC; Oak Leaf Cluster; PH-Purple Heart).

Since Audie's death, there have been many tributes honoring him. The most impressive of those being the Audie L. Murphy Memorial Veterans Hospital in San Antonio, Texas. It was dedicated on November 17, 1973. A one-ton bronze, eight-foot statue of Audie is the fine work of sculptress, Jimilu Mason, who was one of Audie's many admirers. He is dressed in battle fatigues holding a rifle with bayonet. Inside the hospital, is a museum that depicts Audie's life and has items including a uniform, other clothing, books and pictures. The museum has been remodeled in recent years and is definitely worth visiting. Prior to and after the dedication of the hospital, there have been numerous memorials, statues, poems and songs written to honor this truly humble man.

The most recent accolade for Audie occurred on March 16, 1996, when The National Cowboy Hall of Fame and Western Heritage Center located in Oklahoma City, Oklahoma, honored Audie as being deserving of the recognition for his great contribution to the Western film. Audie was inducted posthumously into the "Hall of Great Western Performers." He will be joining other such famous men and women of the large and small screen including John

Wayne, Gregory Peck, Barbara Stanwyck and others in this prestigious Hall of Fame.

This recognition is mainly attributed to Audie's many fans who had written requesting that he be so honored. The center has preserved and interpreted our nation's rich Western heritage and was founded to honor outstanding individuals whose lives epitomize the values of honesty, integrity and self-sufficiency.

On this, the "35th Annual Western Heritage Awards," Audie's sisters, Billie Murphy Tindol and Nadene Murphy accepted the award. "Audie could bring a tear to a glass eye" relates Nadene in her speech. This caused the audience to laugh and to know that Audie did have a tremendous sense of humor. "Where but in America could an uneducated young man go to war, become a world hero and a movie star but in these great United States?" concludes Nadene.

Audie has portrayed powerful roles throughout his motion picture career. His appearance as the solid, young gunslinger, mostly on the side of justice showed in his films as part of the American Western. He handles complex and difficult assignments with self assurance and an ease borne of his own exploits on the battlefields. His fellow officers have tagged him "the soldier's-soldier." Audie had such a love of the army that in the mid-50s, he made a Public Service Announcement promoting a six-month reserve program to all eligible young men.

Audie was a very private person and modest individual who did not disclose a lot of his inner feelings. Something he once said about himself was that "he was blessed with an over abundance of luck."

This book will, hopefully, keep Audie Murphy's name alive for another generation to come and for the future generations yet to come. We must never forget this man who gave so much for his country, for if even one person remembers him, he will never be forgotten.

FOREWORD
by
NEIL SUMMERS

In my 30 years as a professional stuntman, I worked on quite a few of Audie Murphy's films. In fact, it was on ARIZONA RAIDERS that I got my membership into the Screen Actor's Guild by doing a stair fall on location at Apache Junction, Arizona. Although Mr. Murphy and I did not socialize between film assignments, I stayed in touch and received employment on other films culminating with a role as one of the gang members on A TIME FOR DYING, directed by Audie's long-time friend, Budd Boetticher. Other films were planned but, sadly, this was to be Audie's last appearance on screen.

Audie Murphy with Neil Summers on the set of A TIME FOR DYING

During my life on film sets, I have met and worked with almost every major star there has been in the last three decades, but there was a special feeling working on one of Audie's sets. I suppose a lot of the fascination had to do with Audie's war exploits. The other stuntmen and I would discuss at length what it must have been like for Audie to have gone through during the war....what he'd seen, what he'd experienced and what he'd had to do to survive, while all others around him were being killed. All this, before he was eighteen years old!!! We all knew he was deeply affected by the war, but watching him goof around on the sets, you would never have known it.

Audie was well liked by the crew and fellow actors and everyone gave him the utmost respect. He was a friendly man, although naturally reserved with people he didn't know, and he was not a man to be crossed. He worked hard on his films and he expected others around him to do the same. He knew his weapons; he knew his dialogue; he knew his stunts; and he knew his horses. It all shows in the finished product as Audie's films, for the most part, stand up exceptionally well in today's screenings.

A lot of Audie's co-workers, co-stars and directors have passed away and his long time stunt double, Jim Sheppard, was killed doing a drag on COMES A HORSEMAN a few years ago.

I can still remember exactly where I was when word came of Audie's tragic plane crash. We were on location at Tucson, Arizona, for scenes in DIRTY LITTLE BILLY when word came out to the set. It got quiet for a while, then the set started to come back to life when one of the crew members, who knew Audie, blurted out that "it took a lousy plane wreck to do what the whole German Army couldn't do." With this announcement, we all cheered and clapped for Audie. When the day's work was done, some of us were still shaken and headed for the bar to talk over our memories of Audie. We laughed at some of his practical jokes, (one of his favorites was to put rubber snakes in the pouches on the sides of other actor's chairs), and we talked about how we would miss this true American hero.

Audie Murphy was not an actor trying to be a man. Audie was a man who was an actor. We are sorely lacking for men in this country, and there is hardly a day goes by that I don't think of Audie and how he impressed me and how kind he was to me. Audie Leon Murphy was the real thing and I am very proud to have known him.

NEIL SUMMERS
Sherman Oaks, California

BEYOND GLORY

STUDIO: PARAMOUNT

PRODUCER: Robert Fellows
DIRECTOR: John Farrow
ORIGINAL SCREENPLAY BY: Jonathan Latimer, Charles Marquis Warren and William Wister Haines
DIRECTOR OF PHOTOGRAPHY: John F. Seitz, A.S.C.
ART DIRECTORS: Hans Dreier and Franz Bachelin
PROCESS PHOTOGRAPHY: Farciot Edouart, A.C.E.
SET DIRECTION: Sam Comer and Ray Moyer
ASSISTANT DIRECTOR: William H. Coleman
MUSIC SCORE: Victor Young
EDITORIAL SUPERVISION: Eda Warren
COSTUMES: Edith Head
MAKE-UP SUPERVISION: Wally Westmore
SOUND RECORDING BY: Hugo Grenzbach and Walter Oberst

DATES OF FILMING: Early October 1947 to November 25, 1947
LOCATION OF FILMING: Paramount Studio in Hollywood

CAST:

Rockwell (Rocky) Gilman .. Alan Ladd
Ann Daniels .... Donna Reed
Maj. Gen. Bond .... George Macready
Lew Proctor .... George Coulouris
Raymond Denmore, Sr Harold Vermilyea
Pop Dewing .... Henry Travers
Captain Harry Daniels .... Tom Neal
Raymond Denmore, Jr .... Conrad Janis
Cadet Sgt. Eddie Loughlin .. Dick Hogan
Miller .... Paul Lees
Thomas .... Audie Murphy
Mrs. Daniels .... Geraldine Wall
Dr. White .... Luis Van Rooten
Mr. Julian .... Charles Evans
Cora .... Margaret Field
Barney .... Sean McClory
General Presscott .... Steve Pendleton
John Craig .... Vincent Donahue
Colonel Stoddard .... Harlan Tucker
Cadet .... Russell Wade

RUNNING TIME: 82 minutes
RELEASE DATE: September 1948

SYNOPSIS:

Rocky Gilman blacked out during a key battle in Tunisia and is convinced that this lapse was responsible for the death of his commanding officer. After his discharge, the incident continues to haunt him. He meets his CO's widow and they fall in love. With her encouragement, he enters West Point and is doing well in his studies when he is called before a board of inquiry. His lapse of duty is investigated as a reprisal by a wealthy financier, whose son, a spoiled plebe, resented Rocky's involvement in his forced resignation from the academy. Under great pressure from the inquiry, he leaves the Point and a court martial is ordered.

As the trial continues, a young soldier, Hogan, who witnessed Rocky's blackout, tells the court that Rocky was innocent of any wrongdoing, losing consciousness due to an artillery bombardment before the CO was killed. At the end, a relieved Rocky says, "Why didn't you say this before?" Hogan replies, "You never would let me talk about it, Rocky, remember?"

BACKGROUND:

Audie is cast as a cadet roommate, Thomas, and appears in several scenes with Ladd. In his most prominent scene, Thomas talks with another roommate as a romantic letter arrives for Rocky. They speculate about the contents of the letter. Thomas offers his opinion that the letter could be a "Dear John," which, in fact, turns out to be the case.

Although his role was small in this film, he achieved his first critical write-up: "Audie Murphy makes his debut and does right well for himself. You'll recognize him. He's the one with the southern drawl."

For BEYOND GLORY, Audie was paid $300 a week with a guarantee of ten weeks work—or $3,000 for the picture.

Audie always said that he was fortunate in having Alan Ladd as the star of BEYOND GLORY. Ladd told him to just relax, do his work, and get away from the studio. He especially advised Audie not to get upset over the pressures and temperaments found in the movie business. In reflection years later, Audie said, "Alan Ladd gave me the best advice I ever got in Hollywood."

Alan Ladd and Audie Murphy at the Christmas plebe dance in a scene from BEYOND GLORY (1948)

TEXAS, BROOKLYN AND HEAVEN

STUDIO: UNITED ARTISTS (Release)

PRODUCER: Robert S. Golden
DIRECTOR: William Castle
BASED ON THE SATURDAY EVENING POST STORY BY: Barry Benefield
ASSOCIATE PRODUCER: Lewis J. Rachmil
SCREENPLAY BY: Lewis Meltzer
DIRECTOR OF CINEMATOGRAPHY: William Mellor, A.S.C.
ART DIRECTION: Jerome Pycha, Jr.
SET DIRECTION: George Sawley
PRODUCTION ASSISTANT: Larry Witten
MUSICAL DIRECTOR: Emil Newman
MUSICAL SCORE: Arthur Lange
SONG - "Texas, Brooklyn and Heaven" by Ervin Drake and Jimmy Shirl
FILM EDITOR: James Newcom
ASSISTANT DIRECTOR: Harold Godsoe
SOUND: John Carter
WARDROBE: Earl Moser
GOWNS: Mary Grant
HAIRDRESSING: Helen Lierley
MAKE-UP: Mel Berns

DATES OF FILMING: Mid-January 1948 to February 19, 1948
LOCATION OF FILMING: General Service Studios in Hollywood

CAST:

Eddie Tayloe .... Guy Madison
Perry Dunklin .... Diana Lynn
Mike .... James Dunn
The Bellhop .... Lionel Stander
Mandy .... Florence Bates
Gaboolian .... Michael Chekhov
Ruby Cheever ..... Margaret Hamilton
Pearl Cheever .... Moyna Magill
Opal Cheever .... Irene Ryan
MacWirther .... Colin Campbell
Capt. Bjorn .... Clem Bevans
The Agent .... William Frawley
Bernie .... Alvin Hammer
Carmody .... Roscoe Karns
Dr. Dunson .... Erskine Sanford
McGonical .... John Gallaudet
Policeman .... James Burke
Thibault .... Guy Wilkerson
Copy Boy .... Audie Murphy
Bartender .... Tom Dugan
Customer .... Jesse White
Barker .... Frank Scannell
Sergeant .... Dewey Robinson
Cop On Phone .... Ralph Peters
Man In Subway .... Herb Vigran
Lady ....Jody Gilbert
Wife .... Mary Treen
Reporter .... Charles Williams

RUNNING TIME: 76 minutes
RELEASE DATE: July 16, 1948

SYNOPSIS:

This movie is a comedy about two Texans—Guy Madison and Diana Lynn—who meet on their way to New York and become involved with some very zany characters.

Guy is a newspaper editor in Dallas, who very much wants to write a play. To be successful as a playwright, he must go to New York. Upon learning of his grandfather's death, he receives a small inheritance from the estate where he sees a chance to realize his dream.

He meets Diana on the way to New York and gives her a lift in his car as she has no transportation. Her heart is set on going to Brooklyn in hopes of finding fame and fortune. In the course of their travels, they meet several interesting and unusual people, one being a lady pick-pocket. Diana befriends her, finds out she has no place to go and gets her a place to live in a house she rents a room from three spinster sisters. Eventually, Diana finds a job at Coney Island in a girlie show but when Guy finds out about it, he drags her away from the looks of the unsavory folk.

Guy finds a rather unique business nearby which offers patrons rides on mechanical animals as well as a boat for an old retired sailor. The place is not doing very well so Guy buys it and puts Diana in charge. She makes some changes and helps promote it. The attraction makes money and eventually Diana and Guy decide that they really want to move back to Texas and purchase the ranch they have wanted all along.

BACKGROUND:

Early in the film, Audie appears in one scene as a newspaper copy-boy. He delivers copy to Madison, an obituary notice, which turns out to be about Madison's grandfather. Audie asks if he receives an inheritance, and Madison tells him he will get $6,000. This scene over, the movie's plot moves from Texas to Brooklyn. Audie's name was included in a general comment as one of "an interesting subordinate cast."

Audie was paid $500 for three days work and was given four shirts for posing for an advertisement in connection with the picture. After this movie, Audie said that he would never work in another picture unless he had the starring role. Offered $500 for three days of work in a third movie, Audie turned it down. True to his word, he did not appear in another picture until he got the starring role.

Unfortunately, research has shown that there are no known photographs of Audie since his role in this film was so small.

Publicity photo of Guy Madison and Diana Lynn in TEXAS, BROOKLYN AND HEAVEN (1948)

BAD BOY

STUDIO: ALLIED ARTISTS (Release)

PRODUCER: Paul Short
DIRECTOR: Kurt Neumann
SCREENPLAY BY: Robert D. Andrews
ADDITIONAL DIALOGUE BY: Karl Kamb
STORY BY: Robert D. Andrews and Paul Short
ASSOCIATE PRODUCER: George Bertholon
DIRECTOR OF PHOTOGRAPHY: Karl Struss, A.S.C.
PRODUCTION DESIGNED BY: Gordon Wiles
ART DIRECTOR: Theobold Holsopple
SET DECORATOR: Raymond Boltz, Jr.
SUPERVISING FILM EDITOR: Otho Lovering
FILM EDITOR: William Austin
PRODUCTION MANAGER: Allen K. Wood
ASSISTANT DIRECTOR: Frank Heath
DIALOGUE DIRECTOR: Clarence Marks
TECHNICAL ADVISOR: William O'Donnell
TECHNICAL COORDINATOR: James O. Cherry
COSTUME SUPERVISION: Lorraine MacLean
MAKEUP: Charles Huber
HAIRDRESSER: Lela Chambers
MEN'S WARDROBE: Courtney Haslam
LADIES' WARDROBE: Esther Krebs
SOUND ENGINEER: Earl Sitar
MUSICAL SCORE BY: Paul Sawtell

DATES OF FILMING: Mid-October to November 8, 1948
LOCATION OF FILMING: Monogram Studios, Hollywood; Janns Ranch at Conejo, California

CAST:

Marshall Brown .... Lloyd Nolan
Mrs. Brown .... Jane Wyatt
Danny Lester ....Audie Murphy
Chief .... James Gleason
Bitsy .... Stanley Clements
Miss Strawn .... Martha Vickers
Arnold Strawn ....Rhys Williams
Judge Prentiss ....Selena Royale
Ted ....James Lydon

RUNNING TIME: 86 minutes
RELEASE DATE: February 22, 1949

SYNOPSIS:

BAD BOY is based on a true case history derived from the files of Variety Clubs International, which, among other charitable work, worked with juvenile offenders to rehabilitate them outside a standard prison environment. The film is set at the club's "Boys Ranch" in Texas.

The film bridges a chronological and cinematic theme between the release of BOYS TOWN and a more realistic look at dysfunctional youths of the 1950s, as shown in James Dean's REBEL WITHOUT A CAUSE. Danny Lester is definitely a young man somewhat out of control. At first, his violent and criminal behavior seems to occur for no reason. Gradually, we become aware of Danny's deep psychological problems, which stem from arguments with his step-father, and the death of his mother, apparently from a dose of sleeping pills Danny has given her.

Captured during a robbery attempt, Danny is brought before a juvenile court and finally released to Marshall Brown who runs the Boys Ranch. Although the court is skeptical that Danny can stop being a delinquent youth, Brown feels that the ranch environment may help Danny's attitude. Perhaps he can find out what is troubling Danny.

At first, Danny appears to adjust to ranch life, doing chores willingly. Soon, however, he is sneaking out to commit another burglary, breaking into a local jewelry store. There are further confrontations at the ranch. In the meantime, Brown manages to trace Danny's family history, and eventually discovers why Danny is so violent at times, particularly when anyone addresses him as "son."

Five years before, Danny was working for a local pharmacist, and had brought home pills for his sick mother. He gets into an argument with his step-father, who does not take his wife's illness seriously. The step-father attempts to assert his parental authority over Danny, referring to him as "son." Danny resents this and says so. Afterwards, he gives some pills to his mother. Next day, she is dead and his step-father accuses Danny of being a murderer. Danny explodes, beats up the step-father and runs away.

Brown talks to the doctor who treated Danny's mother. Seems she died of natural causes and the sleeping pills did not cause her death. Before Brown can get back to the ranch, the police discover that Danny has committed another robbery in a gun shop. They confront him. He manages to get away briefly, but the car he is driving crashes. He is injured and surrounded by the police but refuses to surrender. Brown arrives on the scene to tell him about his mother and convinces Danny he did not cause her death.

Eventually, Danny recovers from his injuries, and gets another chance to live at the ranch. At the end of the film, Danny has enrolled as an engineering student at Texas A&M.

BACKGROUND:

With two forgettable bit parts under his belt, and a growing frustration with the powers-that-be in Hollywood, Audie Murphy let it be know publicly that he would not accept another part in any more movies unless he had a starring role.

While some veterans of the movie industry probably found his attitude and resolve unacceptable, this was post-World War II America, Audie Murphy was that war's most famous fighting soldier, and he looked good in front of a camera. Good attitude or bad, Audie was a potential box-office draw, which was something Hollywood usually couldn't pass up. Allied Artists offered Audie the lead in

BAD BOY, resulting in the real beginning of his movie career.

In his third movie, Audie played the role of a young felon who was rehabilitated by the work of Variety Clubs International with juvenile delinquents. The motion picture was described by one critic as "standard film drama."

Another critic wrote: "Audie Murphy is surprisingly effective in his role of the teen-age, trigger-happy, baby-faced thug who resists every attempt to reshape him into a solid and respectable citizen."

A third critic wrote: "Audie Murphy wants to be a good actor and gives a good promise of achieving his aim."

Except for several months in a Hollywood drama school and small parts in two previous movies, Audie had no acting experience when he took over the title role of BAD BOY. He did so with much confidence. He believed that most professional actors did not know their jobs either. But producer Paul Short did not exactly agree with the Murphy viewpoint. He surrounded Audie with veteran players who could cover for his inexperience. This policy was followed by other producers in several succeeding films. Audie quickly learned anything in which he had a particular interest. He learned to act by actually starring in motion pictures.

BAD BOY was extremely important to the Murphy screen career. Many theater exhibitors belonged to Variety Clubs International. Because of this factor, the film was almost certain to get wide circulation and Class-A treatment. And so would Audie Murphy as a promising new movie actor. This was a gamble which Murphy took. The gamble paid off. BAD BOY led to starring roles in forty future movies.

During the filming, Audie came up with one of his famous quips. He apparently had a difficult time getting through a certain scene and consequently several retakes had to be made. Finally, the director of the film, Kurt Newmann, became agitated and complained about the delay of getting through the scene. Audie answered him by saying, "You must remember that I am working under a great handicap." "What handicap?" asked Newmann. "No talent," replied Audie with a smile.

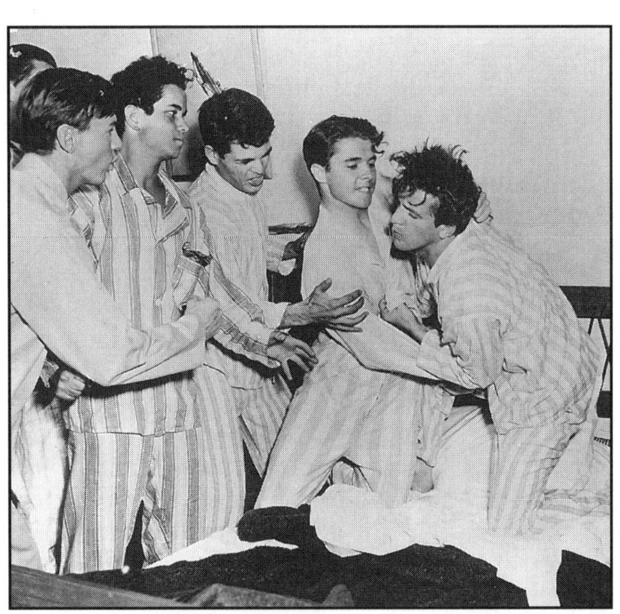

James Lydon, Audie Murphy and Stanley Clements in a scene from Audie's first starring role, BAD BOY

THE KID FROM TEXAS

STUDIO: UNIVERSAL-INTERNATIONAL

PRODUCER: Paul Short
DIRECTOR: Kurt Neumann
STORY BY: Robert Hardy Andrews
SCREENPLAY BY: Robert Hardy Andrews and Karl Kamb
DIRECTOR OF PHOTOGRAPHY: Charles Van Enger
TECHNICOLOR COLOR CONSULTANT: William Fritzsche
ART DIRECTION: Bernard Herzbrun and Emrich Nicholson
SET DECORATIONS: Russell A. Gausman and Oliver Emert
SOUND: Leslie I. Carey and Robert Pritchard
FILM EDITOR: Frank Cross
MUSIC: Milton Schwarzwald
MAKE-UP: Bud Westmore

DATES OF FILMING: May 26, 1949, to June 29, 1949
LOCATION OF FILMING: Idyllwild, California, area

CAST:

Billy The Kid .... Audie Murphy
Irene Kain .... Gale Storm
Alexander Kain .... Albert Dekker
Jameson .... Shepperd Strudwick
O'Fallon .... Will Geer
Minninger .... William Talman
Morales .... Martin Garralaga
General Wallace ...... Robert H. Barrat
Crowe .... Walter Sande
Pat Garrett .... Frank Wilcox
Major Harper .... Dennis Hoey
Sheriff Rand .... Ray Teal
Morgan .... Don Haggerty
Copeland .... Paul Ford
Sid Curtis .... John Phillips
Matt Curtis .... Harold Goodwin
Lucas .... Zon Murray
Denby .... Tom Trout
Maria .... Rosa Turich
Lupita .... Dorita Pallais
Marguarita .... Pilar Del Ray

RUNNING TIME: 78 minutes
RELEASE DATE: March 1950

SYNOPSIS:

The setting is New Mexico, circa 1880. The governor of the territory is trying to discourage a range war between ranchers. Billy is caught up in the middle of the war, and soon becomes a wanted man.

Billy is hired as a ranch hand by Roger Jameson, who is subsequently killed by gunfighters from a rival ranch. Billy makes a vow to seek revenge and kill the men responsible for Jameson's death. A killing spree follows as Billy becomes an outlaw.

The governor tries to convince Billy to give himself up. He refuses. Soon after, he is captured by Pat Garrett, convicted of murder and sentenced to hang. However, he escapes from jail. A $10,000 reward is posted as a massive manhunt begins. Eventually, Garrett finds Billy again and kills him in a shootout.

With 21 notches on his guns, Billy the Kid was just 21 years, four months and five days old when he died. Historians have called him a bandit, ballad makers a "Robin Hood," but after 70 years the fairest verdict was probably that of the humble Mexicans who buried him, who called him simply "el chivito," the kid, and left his final judgment to God.

BACKGROUND:

Paul Short was proving himself to be a shrewd, but cautions showman. For Audie's second starring role, he chose Billy the Kid. The story of the young outlaw had been filmed many times over the years. Practically all versions had made money. In casting Audie as Billy, Short had a new angle. He saw the young outlaw as a victim of circumstance. He called Billy "the original juvenile delinquent," and this was how Audie portrayed the character.

When Short gave him the title role in BAD BOY, he also put Audie under a personal, multi-picture contract. This meant that the two would be working as a star-producer team for several movies.

BAD BOY had been a financial success. Hollywood was impressed. Murphy and Short were now able to move to Universal, one of the major studios with excellent distribution facilities. At Universal, the Short-Murphy movies were certain to get wide circulation.

On the first day of shooting, Audie's double broke his collar bone and Audie had to do his own riding throughout the picture. Subsequently, Audie did most of his own stunt work, even in dangerous situations. During his movie career, he used only two stand-ins.

BAD BOY had finally made Audie Murphy visible on the Hollywood map. THE KID FROM TEXAS placed him firmly on the "Western" side of that map. From this point on, Audie's career was to be mostly associated with movies that also featured horses, saloons, six-shooters and frontier women in need.

The plot was considered by one critic a "complicated story which slows down the action," although an off-screen narrator notes that, true to the legend, Billy, at the tender age of 21, has notched 21 kills.

When he was selected to star in THE KID FROM TEXAS, an expert was hired to teach Audie the fast draw. It was not long before Audie was outdrawing the expert. Wanda Hendrix said that Audie constantly practiced before a mirror so that he could correct his faults. (*Audie Murphy, American Soldier*)

One of the advantages of being able to film at a studio like Universal was the availability of set crews to construct authentic-looking buildings. The crew built an eight-room, two-story mansion on the back lot for a climatic scene. The house served as a fortress for "Billy" when he was surrounded by the posse. The home was so well designed that movie stars inspecting the residence said that they would enjoy living in a house like it. The life of the building was short-lived, however, and went up in flames in about twenty minutes.

Publicity photo of Audie Murphy from THE KID FROM TEXAS

SIERRA

STUDIO: UNIVERSAL-INTERNATIONAL

PRODUCER: Michel Kraike
DIRECTOR: Alfred E. Green
SCREENPLAY: Edna Anhalt
ADDITIONAL DIALOGUE BY: Milton Gunzburg
BASED ON A NOVEL BY: Stuart Hardy
DIRECTOR OF PHOTOGRAPHY: Russell Metty, A.S.C.
TECHNICOLOR COLOR CONSULTANT: William Fritzsche
FILM EDITOR: Ted J. Kent
ART DIRECTION BY: Bernard Herzbrun and Robert F. Boyle
SET DECORATIONS: Russell A. Gausman and John Austin
SOUND: Leslie I. Carey and Glenn E. Anderson
HAIR STYLIST: Joan St. Oegger
MAKE-UP BY: Bud Westmore
MUSIC: Walter Scharf
SONGS: "End of the Road," "Hideaway," "Black Angus McDougal," "Drift Along" by: Arnold Hughes and Frederick Herbert
"The Whale Song," "Sarah the Mule" by: Burl Ives

DATES OF FILMING: August 30, 1949 to October 3, 1949
LOCATION OF FILMING: Kanab, Utah, area and Universal Studio

CAST:

Riley Martin .... Wanda Hendrix
Ring Hassard .... Audie Murphy
Lonesome .... Burl Ives
Jeff Hassard .... Dean Jagger
Big Matt .... Richard Rober
Brent Coulter .... Anthony Curtis
Sam Coulter ...... Houseley Stevenson
Duke Lafferty .... Elliott Reid
Dr. Robbins .... Griff Barnett
Aunt Susan.............. Elisabeth Risdon
Sheriff Knudsen .... Roy Roberts
Hogan........................... Gregg Martell
Mrs. Jonas....................... Sara Allgood
Judge Prentiss .... Erskine Sanford
Jed Coulter .... John Doucette
Little Sam .... Jim Arness
Jim Coulter......................... Ted Jordan
Snake Willens .... I. Stanford Jolley
Al.. Jack Ingram

RUNNING TIME: 83 minutes
RELEASE DATE: June 1950

SYNOPSIS:

Audie stars as Ring Hassard, who makes a living as a mustanger, rounding up wild horses to be tamed and sold. He lives with his father, Jeff, played by veteran character actor Dean Jagger, at an isolated mountain cabin. Years before, Jeff had been falsely accused of murdering another man and since then Jeff has avoided contact with people and the authorities.

Ring meets a woman lawyer, Riley, played by Audie's real-life new bride, Wanda Hendrix. Jeff is injured while attempting to tame one of the mustangs. Ring and Riley ride into town to get a doctor for him. Complications arise quickly: Riley is bitten by a rattlesnake, but recovers; Ring encounters a gang of cowboys who have stolen his recently acquired mustangs.

After attempting to get his mustangs back, Ring is overpowered and brought to town to stand trial for horse stealing (which, as any true Western fan knows, subjected a guilty prisoner to a sentence of hanging). Riley defends Ring, but the judge now wants to find out where Ring's father is. Ring, of course, won't talk. Later, Ring manages to escape from jail (Audie Murphy would, in the course of his movie career, escape from jail and all sorts of confinement seemingly dozens of times), to bring a doctor back to the cabin and attend to his father.

A posse is formed to find Jeff. Riley finds out that Jeff is not the killer people think he is. As the climax of the movie nears, the mustangs stampede. Riley is rescued by Ring (again). Another man confesses that he was the real murderer. Jeff is exonerated; Ring and Riley fall in love and settle down.

BACKGROUND:

Universal took advantage of what was seen as a real life love affair between Audie Murphy and Wanda Hendrix. During their courtship days, they had been publicized as "America's most romantic young couple." They were married on January 8, 1949. The public, as interpreted by Hollywood publicity agents, smiled upon the union and declared it "ideal."

Audie Murphy, taking Wanda Hendrix to his hideout in the hills in this scene from SIERRA

While Universal was pondering ways to get Audie more acting experience and screen exposure, somebody came up with a brainstorm: "Why not co-star the young lovers in a movie?" The advantage of the arrangement would lean heavily to Murphy. Wanda, a skilled actress and good screen name, could likely carry the picture even if Audie stumbled dramatically.

A critic noted that "Audie and Wanda make a cute couple." Another complimented Murphy on his "terrific job" of horse-back riding.

Through the years, several Murphy movies featured little known actors who went on to fame on their own. SIERRA included two obscure players who were destined to become big stars. One was Anthony Curtis, who soon shortened his first name to Tony. Also, Jim Arness became a household name as Marshall Dillon in the long-running television series "Gunsmoke."

In a story appearing in a Los Angeles paper, datelined September 28, 1950, Kanab, Utah, it was reported that Audie and Wanda had almost drowned on the set of SIERRA. The Murphys, on location, had camped in the bed of Kanab Creek, which normally carries but a trickle of water. However, a thirty minute cloudburst "sent a four foot deep flood of water rushing down the narrow draw of Kanab Creek." The two were almost trapped between the steep walls of the draw, but Audie, the story said, "leaped on the back of his horse, grabbed Miss Hendrix and rode up the canyon-side to safety." It was reported by Fred Barker, publicity man for Universal-International Studios, that Wanda "was badly shaken up by the wild, bareback 150 yard gallop." Fortunately, the 500 horses corraled in the draw near where Wanda and Audie were camping did not stampede, although they were badly frightened by the onrushing water." (*Audie Murphy, American Soldier*)

Audie plays a hard-riding, straight-shooting young mountain boy in SIERRA.

KANSAS RAIDERS

STUDIO: UNIVERSAL-INTERNATIONAL

PRODUCER: Ted Richmond
DIRECTOR: Ray Enright
STORY AND SCREENPLAY BY: Robert L. Richards
DIRECTOR OF PHOTOGRAPHY: Irving Glassberg, A.S.C.
TECHNICOLOR COLOR CONSULTANT: William Fritzsche
ART DIRECTION: Bernard Herzbrun and Emrich Nicholson
MUSICAL DIRECTION: Joseph Gershenson
FILM EDITOR: Milton Carruth
SET DECORATIONS: Russell A. Gausman and Ruby R. Levitt
SOUND: Leslie I. Carey and Glenn E. Anderson
COSTUMES: Bill Thomas
HAIR STYLIST: Joan St. Oegger
MAKE-UP: Bud Westmore

DATES OF FILMING: May 22, 1950, to June 24, 1950
LOCATION OF FILMING: Idyllwild, California, area

CAST:

Jesse James .... Audie Murphy
Quantrill .... Brian Donlevy
Kate Clarke ..... Marguerite Chapman
Bill Anderson .... Scott Brady
Kit Dalton .... Tony Curtis
Union Captain .... Richard Arlen
Frank James .... Richard Long
Cole Younger .... James Best
Red Leg Leader .... John Kellogg
James Younger .... Dewey Martin
Willie .... George Chandler
Pell .... Charles Delaney
First Lieutenant............. Richard Egan
Tate .... Dave Wolfe

RUNNING TIME: 80 minutes
RELEASE DATE: November 1950

SYNOPSIS:

Audie portrays a young Jesse James in this Western set in the 1860s. He and his brother Frank become new members of Quantrill's Raiders, who consider themselves Confederate sympathizers, but are best known for the bloody attack and looting of Lawrence, Kansas. In the film, the raiders include other famous outlaw gang members, Cole Younger and two Dalton brothers. Although Jesse joins to help the Confederate cause, he soon realizes that others in the group are simply bandits and killers, out to line their own pockets.

Jesse is drawn to the strong leadership of Quantrill, but is bothered by the often senseless killings. He considers quitting the raiders, but stays because of Quantrill's beliefs. Also, Jesse feels drawn toward Quantrill's girlfriend, Kate.

Jesse eventually becomes Quantrill's second-in-command after a savage knife fight with another raider, who turns out to be a Union spy. But he continues to have strong feelings against the bloody raids.

During one raid, Quantrill is blinded,

creating confusion among the raiders. They hide out at a farmhouse they have previously attacked. Eventually they are tracked down by Union troops. Quantrill knows there is a back way out where they can escape the soldiers, but he decides to stay and fight, sacrificing his life so Jesse, Kate and the others can get away.

BACKGROUND:

Critics said that "Audie delivers strongly as Jesse James" and that his performance was "topnotch." Audie's acting continued to improve with this role, although the movie was not considered a critical success.

KANSAS RAIDERS was the first movie he made under a new contract with Universal Studios. This was also the first film where Audie had an on-screen kiss, with co-star Marguerite Chapman.

Audie's research of Jesse James found him to be almost identical with the proportions of James. "James," according to Audie, "was exactly my height and weight and he even wore a size nine shoe and seven hat, which is me from head to foot."

Left to right: Scott Brady, Brian Donlevy, and Audie Murphy in KANSAS RAIDERS

THE RED BADGE OF COURAGE

STUDIO: METRO-GOLDWYN-MAYER

PRODUCER: Gottfried Reinhardt
DIRECTOR: John Huston
STORY BY: Based on the Stephen Crane novel *The Red Badge of Courage*
SCREEN PLAY BY: John Huston
ADAPTATION BY: Albert Band
DIRECTOR OF PHOTOGRAPHY: Harold Rosson, A.S.C.
ART DIRECTORS: Cedric Gibbons and Hans Peters
FILM EDITOR: Ben Lewis
MUSIC BY: Bronislau Kaper
RECORDING SUPERVISOR: Douglas Shearer
SET DECORATIONS: Edwin B. Willis and Fred MacLean
SPECIAL EFFECTS: Warren Newcombe
MAKE-UP CREATED BY: William Tuttle

DATES OF FILMING: August 25, 1950 to October 11, 1950
LOCATION OF FILMING: Chico, California, area and the John Huston Ranch in the San Fernando Valley (Southern California)

CAST:

Henry Fleming .... Audie Murphy
The "Loud" Soldier .... Bill Mauldin
The "Tall" Soldier .... John Dierkes
The Tattered Man .... Royal Dano
The "Cheery" Soldier .. Andy Devine
Thompson .... Robert Easton Burke
The Lieutenant .... Douglas Dick
The General .... Tim Durant
Bill Porter .... Arthur Hunnicutt

RUNNING TIME: 69 minutes
RELEASE DATE: September 1951

SYNOPSIS:

The Red Badge of Courage was written by Stephen Crane in 1894. From the moment it was published, it was accepted by critics and public alike as a classic story of war, and of the boys and men who fought. His story is of a frightened boy, Henry Fleming, who went into battle and came out of it a man with courage. More than that, it is a story of many frightened boys who went into a great civil war and come out as a nation of united, strong and free men.

Voiceover narrative:

> Spring 1862: the bloody War Between the States, great movement shook the land, marches, sieges, conflicts but for the untried army on the Rapahannock, war simply a matter of waiting, waiting and endless drilling. There was a youthful private who was deeply troubled by the talk of his comrades. They were so sure of their courage. They are all afraid, since it will be the first battle for many of them, including the youth. He's really scared on the inside but talks tough on the outside. Too much drilling makes them want to fight.

The unit begins its march slowly heading up river.

> They were at last going to fight. Tomorrow, perhaps, there would be a battle and he would be in it. Was it possible that he would be a part of a great battle in a great war? In the darkness he saw visions of a thousand-tongued fear who would babble at his back and cause him to flee.

Fording the river, the sounds of gunfire are heard for the first time. The men come upon the body of a Union soldier which causes the youth to see the horrors of war. As they get closer to the fighting, they take up their positions. Some of the soldiers start to run while the officers try to make them stay. As the rebels charge the front lines, they are told to hold and they beat back the initial assault.

> He felt alone in space. No one else seemed to be wrestling with such a terrific personal problem. He was a mental outcast. So it was over at last. The supreme trial had been passed. The red formidable difficulties of war had been vanquished. He felt that he was a fine fellow.

> Again the enemy returns with more men and determination. The youth stared. Surely, he thought, this impossible thing was not about to happen. He waited as if he expected the enemy to suddenly stop, apologize and retire bowing. It was all a mistake. It becomes too much and the youth runs. He is panic stricken and heads away from battle towards the trees. He hears the general giving orders to the men and learns that his regiment had won, and so felt like a coward. The youth cringed as if discovered in a crime. So his regiment had won after all. His imbecile comrades had remained and their very ignorance had brought them victory. He felt betrayed. He wondered what they would remark when later he appeared in camp. His mind heard howls of derision.

> Coming down the path, he sees the wounded coming from battle and he regarded the wounded soldiers in an envious way. He conceived persons with torn bodies to be peculiarly happy. He wished that he too had a wound, a red badge of courage.

Henry sees his friend Jim who has been mortally wounded and watches him die. He is devastated and visibly shaken. As he goes off by himself, he hears gunfire. More Union soldiers are running and in an effort to find out what is happening, he is knocked out by one of them. When found later that evening by a sentry, he is taken back to camp and tells them that he got separated from his unit and "shot."

> He had performed his mistakes in the dark; he was still a man.

Audie Murphy played a Union soldier in this stirring film of the Civil War.

There is another skirmish and this time Henry advances to an insecure position.

> The youth was not conscious that he was erect upon his feet. He lost every sense but his hate. For the first time in his life he was possessed by a great passion, the passion to destroy the enemy. He felt the power of an army within himself. He was a battle cry, a bullet, a sword.

Henry's unit advances once again rushing forward into battle. He grabs the colors and leads the men on an aggressive attack that defeats the Confederates. He meets the enemy color bearer and grabs his flag to keep it from hitting the ground as the bearer falls. Henry is later recognized by the general for leading the charge.

The troops regather and head back down the road with Henry proudly carrying the flag.

> So it came to pass that as he trudged from the place of blood and wrath, his soul changed. He had been to touch the great death and found that after all, it was but the great death. Scars faded as flowers and the youth saw that the world was a world for him. He had rid himself of the red sickness of battle. The sultry nightmare was in the past. He turned now with a lover's thirst to images of tranquil skies, fresh meadows, cool brooks and an existence of soft and eternal peace.

BACKGROUND:

Metro-Goldwyn-Mayer announced plans for filming THE RED BADGE OF COURAGE in the spring of 1950. A few friends, including Hollywood columnist Hedda Hopper, began to push Audie Murphy for the starring role. However, they ran into much opposition. John Huston favored Audie, but the studio planned to use one of its contract players. It was argued that Murphy had too little acting experience to handle such a dramatically demanding role. Eventually, the pro-Murphy people finally won.

In this movie, Audie gave what many thought was an Academy Award performance. Both he and the picture received high critical praises. One critic wrote: "Audie Murphy behaves with the soldierly competence that might be expected from our most decorated soldier." Another critic said: "Audie Murphy gives a sensitive performance, wonderfully conveying, in the end, the dead somnambulistic feel of a man in combat."

A couple of humorous stories concerning the picture: one scene in the picture called for Audie, as "The Young Soldier" to confess his fear of battle to Bill Mauldin, who played "The Loud Soldier." Audie kept avoiding this scene, causing several retakes. Finally he said, "I'll be damned if I can confess my fear to this rear echelon inkslinger (cartoonist)." Consequently, director, John Huston had to stop the shooting and re-write the scene on the spot. As re-written, Mauldin had to confess his fear first, then Audie admitted that he too was afraid. This was satisfactory to Audie and the shooting continued.

One of the areas in the San Fernando Valley where a battle scene was being filmed was adjacent to a large orange grove. It was a hot day, Audie was thirsty and at the first opportunity he slipped into the orange grove and proceeded to stuff his Union private's blouse with oranges. Suddenly, he heard a loud, rasping voice call out "Thief! Thief! Thief!" Audie could not see anyone but he hastily retreated from the grove with oranges spilling out of his blouse as he ran. He fully expected to be peppered with birdshot at any moment. As Murphy emerged from the grove he noted a goodly number of the cast standing there laughing and pointing behind him. Turning around he saw a "beautiful parrot fluttering from one orange tree to another shrieking "Thief! Thief! Thief!" The owner found (and with reason) a parrot more effective than a dog in guarding his grove against trespassers. (*Audie Murphy, American Soldier*)

Audie Murphy, holding a Union flag as his company wins the battle in this scene of THE RED BADGE OF COURAGE

THE CIMARRON KID

STUDIO: UNIVERSAL-INTERNATIONAL

PRODUCER: Ted Richmond
DIRECTOR: Budd Boetticher
SCREENPLAY BY: Louis Stevens
STORY BY: Louis Stevens and Kay Lenard
DIRECTOR OF PHOTOGRAPHY: Charles P. Boyle, A.S.C.
TECHNICOLOR COLOR CONSULTANT: William Fritzsche
ART DIRECTION: Bernard Herzbrun and Emrich Nicholson
SET DECORATIONS: Russell A. Gausman and Joe Kish
SOUND: Leslie I. Carey and Corson Jowett
MUSICAL DIRECTOR: Joseph Gershenson
FILM EDITOR: Frank Gross, A.C.E.
COSTUMES: Bill Thomas
HAIR STYLIST: Joan St. Oegger
MAKE-UP: Bud Westmore

DATES OF FILMING: May 17, 1951 to June 15, 1951
LOCATION OF FILMING: Sonora, California, area

CAST:

Bill Doolin .... Audie Murphy
Carrie Roberts .... Beverly Tyler
Bitter Creek .... James Best
Rose .... Yvette Dugay
Dynamite .... John Hudson
Red Buck....................... Hugh O'Brian
Pat Roberts .... Roy Roberts
Swanson.......................... David Wolfe
Bob Dalton .... Noah Beery
Marshal Sutton .... Leif Erickson
George Weber .... John Hubbard
Stacey Marshall............ Frank Silvera

RUNNING TIME: 84 minutes
RELEASE DATE: January 1952

SYNOPSIS:

THE CIMARRON KID seemed almost to be a sequel to KANSAS RAIDERS, based on the locale and the main character's involvement with the Dalton Gang. Audie plays another real-life outlaw, Bill Doolin, who has been recently released from jail. Doolin is traveling by train when it is held up by the Daltons. He is recognized and assumed to be a member of the gang. He is forced to flee and become a fugitive. The local marshal finds him working on a cattle ranch, and wants to know the whereabouts of the gang. Doolin refuses to tell him, escapes, and decides to join the gang again.

Soon after, the gang raids two Coffeyville, Kansas, banks. But the robbery does not go as planned. Several gang members are killed. However, Doolin escapes back to the hideout. There he argues with another gang member, Red, who wants to go back to Coffeyville to seek revenge. Doolin thinks that is too risky and won't go along with the plan. The rest of the gang agree with Doolin, essentially making him the new leader.

What's left of the gang regroups and

Jack Ingram is accusing Audie Murphy of being a train robber in THE CIMARRON KID.

begins a spree of robberies. Doolin and Red get into a fight, with Doolin wounded and Red killed. While recovering from his wound, Doolin's girlfriend, Carrie, tries to persuade him to give up the outlaw life.

Doolin hears about a large shipment of gold bullion from gang member Dynamite, and decides on one more major train robbery, and then plans to flee to Argentina with Carrie and the money. The plan calls for switching the gold with lead bars while on the train. As the train leaves the station, Doolin and Dynamite are on board. Dynamite begins exchanging the gold bars for the lead ones, and tosses them off the train at various intervals for pick-up by gang members.

However, the marshal has been told about the scheme. Gang members are in place to collect the gold from the train, but are intercepted and killed by the marshal and his deputies.

Doolin receives a telegram from Rose, a girlfriend of another gang member. She warns him of the trap waiting for him. Doolin now realizes that he has been double-crossed, and forces Dynamite to change clothes with him before they reach the station. Mistaken for Doolin, Dynamite is killed. Doolin escapes, but without the gold.

At the end, Carrie persuades Bill to give himself up and do his time in prison. Afterward, they will be able to start a new ranching life together.

BACKGROUND:

A critic described THE CIMARRON KID as a movie "between a conventional sagebrusher and the exalted Western." In show-business slang, a "sagebrusher" usually refers to a Class-B Western. In this picture, Audie Murphy plays the real-life outlaw Bill Doolin. The storyline follows him joining the notorious Dalton gang.

By this, his eighth movie, critics got used to Audie's deliberately underplaying his roles. They understood it as a manner of acting that Murphy had developed, and not the hesitation of one who did not know his job. Typically one critic wrote: "Murphy turns in an even, soft-spoken performance".

Shooting on THE RED BADGE OF COURAGE was completed seven months before filming began on THE CIMARRON KID. But Murphy, still under contractual obligations to Universal, could not wait for the reviews on RED BADGE. He and Pamela Archer had been married on April 24, 1951 and after a brief honeymoon in Texas, came home to Hollywood where they moved into an unpretentious apartment on Fountain Avenue. Audie and Pamela had already planned to start having children soon so he could not get far away from the popular Westerns in which he was already typed.

Audie and Pam had only been married for a few days when filming began. Audie wasn't about to let her stay home alone in Hollywood, so they packed their bags and flew back to the west coast. They went to Sonora, California, where the picture was shot. Pam stayed in town while Audie was on location, and he joined her when the shoot was over. The last day on location, Pam got poison ivy very badly. What a way to end a honeymoon!

Audie Murphy is shooting it out in this scene from THE CIMARRON KID.

THE DUEL AT SILVER CREEK

STUDIO: UNIVERSAL-INTERNATIONAL

PRODUCER: Leonard Goldstein
DIRECTOR: Don Siegel
STORY BY: Gerald Drayson Adams
SCREENPLAY BY: Gerald Drayson Adams and Joseph Hoffman
DIRECTOR OF PHOTOGRAPHY: Irving Glassberg, A.S.C.
TECHNICOLOR COLOR CONSULTANT: William Fritzsche
COLOR BY TECHNICOLOR
ART DIRECTION: Bernard Herzbrun and Alexander Golitzen
SET DECORATIONS: Russell A. Gausman and Joe Kish
SOUND: Leslie I. Carey and Corson Jowett
MUSICAL DIRECTION: Joseph Gershenson
FILM EDITOR: Russell Schoengarth, A.C.E.
COSTUMES: Bill Thomas
HAIR STYLIST: Joan St. Oegger
MAKE-UP: Bud Westmore

DATES OF FILMING: November 26, 1951 to December 29, 1951
LOCATION OF FILMING: Greater Los Angeles area and Universal Studio

CAST:

Silver Kid .... Audie Murphy
Opal Lacey .... Faith Domergue
Lightning Tyrone .. Stephen McNally
Dusty Fargo .... Susan Cabot
Rod Lacey .... Gerald Mohr
Johnny Sombrero ...... Eugene Iglesias
Ratface Blake .... Kyle James
Pete Fargo .... Walter Sande
Tinhorn Burgess .... Lee Marvin
Jim Ryan .... George Eldredge

RUNNING TIME: 77 minutes
RELEASE DATE: August 1952

SYNOPSIS:
A vicious gang of claim jumpers forces miners to sign away their claims through fear of torture or death. The claims are then transferred over to one of their own men or sold to innocent miners who just arrived in the territory, looking for new claims to work. The jumpers' plan is simple and foolproof because no one knows who they are. Since their victims either disappear or are found dead, there isn't anyone who can put their finger on the culprits.

Luke Cromwell and his father find gold in a stream by their shack. While Luke takes the dust to town to be assayed, the jumpers move in, threaten the father to sign the deed over to them, then kill him and scatter. Luke, hearing the shots, turns back only to find his father's body.

When the jumpers rob and kill another miner, the sheriff, Lightning Tyrone, forms a posse. While chasing the jumpers, Tyrone is shot by the outlaws but has the posse continue the hunt. However, the jumpers get away and the posse heads back to town.

Meanwhile, a severely wounded

miner is brought into Silver City. It is hoped he can identify the jumpers. About the same time, there is a new arrival in town: Opal Lacey, to whom Lightning is attracted. Opal is accompanied by her "brother" Rod, supposedly a mining engineer. Rod is actually the boss of the claim jumpers. Opal sees the miner and knows he could cause trouble for them. She pretends to be a nurse, and offers to tend to the miner's wounds. However, when left alone with the miner, she kills him and thus ends the threat of him talking and revealing the description of the jumpers.

While Lightning is recuperating at a nearby fort, his long-time deputy and friend, Dan, is shot and killed. Upon learning about the death of his friend, Lightning goes looking for Johnny Sombrero, a prime suspect, but Johnny has an alibi.

Opal is at the assay office with Rod and suggests to Lightning that the Silver Kid may have had something to do with Dan's death. After his father's death, Luke takes on the guise of the Silver Kid in hopes of finding the ones who murdered him. He also has a reputation of being fast with his guns. Lightning talks with the Kid and realizes that he also has a solid alibi for the night Dan was killed. Lightning offers the Kid a job as his new deputy. He's going to need someone with a fast draw while his shoulder and trigger finger heal.

During dinner, at the home of Dusty and her father, Lightning reveals that he is going to Opal's place. Dusty has been very interested in Lightning but he considers her too young for any romantic involvement. This gives the Kid a chance to pay more attention to her.

Opal lures Lightning to her house, but she is setting him up for an ambush. Blake, one of Rod's henchmen, gets set to gun him down as he leaves, but the Kid has been watching and is one step ahead. He quickly subdues Blake,

Stephen McNally, Susan Cabot, and Audie Murphy in a scene from DUEL AT SILVER CREEK

knocking him out, and saving Lightning's life. Instead of putting Blake in jail, they hide him in a safe place where no one can get at him to keep him from talking.

Thinking Blake is in jail, Johnny Sombrero distracts Lightning while Rod's gang dynamites the jail looking for him. Finding that they have been tricked, Opal tries another scheme to find out where Blake is. She convinces Lightning that her house has been broken into and Rod kidnapped by outlaws. Lightning and the Kid go to her house but find nothing. Opal overhears Lightning and the Kid talking outside her bedroom and realizes that Lightning has a bad gun hand and can't pull a trigger. Up until now, this has been a fact known only by the two of them.

Johnny learns about Lightning's injury from Opal, but Lightning thinks the Kid blabbed it around town. He fires the Kid and orders him out of town. The Kid leaves and Lightning challenges Johnny, who calls his bluff. As they are getting ready to draw, Lighting is shot by the Kid, grazing his wrist. The Kid tells Johnny he's taking over for Lightning. Johnny draws, but not fast enough. The Kid is faster and shoots Johnny. Johnny then confesses, before he dies, that Opal was his girl and that she killed Dan.

Lightning goes to Opal's where she tries to lie about Dan's death. She finally confesses to him and tells him that she is part of Rod's gang of claim jumpers. She then takes Lighting to the hideout. The outlaws see the posse coming with Opal and scatter to hold them off. Rod confronts and kills Opal for bringing the posse. A gunfight ensues where Lightning kills Rod. The Silver Kid and Dusty finally get together.

BACKGROUND:

Of his performance in THE DUEL AT SILVER CREEK, critics said: "Murphy socks over his gunhand role in expert fashion;" and "Audie's fast gunplay whets the appetite."

Although RED BADGE OF COURAGE allowed Audie to expand his acting and attempt to appeal to a broader audience, he continued to be best known as a Western movie hero, and immediately returned to the genre. THE DUEL AT SILVER CREEK was the first of seven Westerns in a row before he would again turn to a wartime movie setting.

Audie was more relaxed for this film as his confidence began growing. When asked how he liked the idea of getting the girl for the first time in a picture and going into a clinch for the film's fadeout, Audie scratched his head and replied, "It's a nice change, I guess."

Although becoming a screen veteran, Audie was still somewhat embarrassed when kissing before a camera. He has done it only once before, and that kiss lasted only a second or two and then he made his famous sunset ride. A solid pal of laborers and technicians around the sound stages, Audie took a prolonged ribbing from the boys about that first screen kiss. Audie's romantic scene with Susan Cabot was filming on the final shooting day and Audie handled the scene like a trouper. "What the heck," he told a co-star," I was getting in a rut."

GUNSMOKE

STUDIO: UNIVERSAL-INTERNATIONAL

PRODUCER: Aaron Rosenberg
DIRECTOR: Nathan Juran
SCREENPLAY BY: D.D. Beauchamp
FROM THE NOVEL *Roughshod* by Norman A. Fox
DIRECTOR OF PHOTOGRAPHY: Charles P. Boyle, A.S.C.
TECHNICOLOR COLOR CONSULTANT: William Fritzsche
COLOR BY TECHNICOLOR
ART DIRECTION: Alexander Golitzen and Robert F. Boyle
SET DECORATIONS: Russell A. Gausman and Ray Jeffers
SOUND: Leslie I. Carey and Robert Pritchard
MUSICAL DIRECTION: Joseph Gershenson
FILM EDITOR: Ted J. Kent, A.C.E.
COSTUMES: Rosemary Odell
HAIR STYLIST: Joan St. Oegger
MAKE-UP: Bud Westmore
ASSISTANT DIRECTOR: William Holland

DATES OF FILMING: June 12, 1952 to July 11, 1952
LOCATION OF FILMING: Big Bear, California, area and Universal Studio

CAST:

Reb Kittredge .... Audie Murphy
Rita Saxon .... Susan Cabot
Dan Saxon .... Paul Kelly
Johnny Lake .... Charles Drake
Cora Dufrayne .... Mary Castle
Curly Mather .... Jack Kelly
Professor .... Jesse White
Matt Telford .... Donald Randolph
Brazos .... William Reynolds
Doc Farrell .... Chubby Johnson

RUNNING TIME: 79 minutes
RELEASE DATE: March 1953

SYNOPSIS:

Chased by Union soldiers, two friends, Reb Kittredge and Johnny Lake, depart in different directions. As Reb heads for town, he is bushwhacked. He tries to find out who it is but finds only empty shells for his trouble. He hitches a ride on the stage to town where he encounters Rita Saxon, who's not impressed with him. Reb's a gunfighter and she is afraid he's out to kill her father. He owns the last ranch in the basin that Matt Telford, a ruthless land baron, is trying to purchase. When Telford has Saxon's ranch, he will own all the land in the area. Rita tells her father that Kittredge is in town. Dan Saxon confronts him and Reb shoots him in self defense, wounding him.

After Reb checks in at the hotel, Rita decides it might be better to work with Reb, and tries to persuade him to help her father keep his cattle ranch from Telford. Reb gives her a hard time because Telford had offered him a job. She attempts to seduce him but he doesn't fall for her little game. Reb then goes to Telford's saloon where he meets an old friend, Cora Dufrayne.

They talk for a while when Matt comes in. He wants Reb to get Saxon to sell the ranch. Reb wants more money than Telford is offering and walks out. Telford tells Cora to send for her boyfriend, Johnny Lake, who is also a hired gun.

Dan Saxon is broke. Rita thinks that with Reb's help, they can complete the cattle round-up, and the ranch could be saved. At first, Reb refuses, but, in the saloon, Saxon engages Reb in a card game, literally betting the ranch on a cut of the cards. Usually, Dan has never lost a cut, but this time he purposely loses letting Reb think he won, thus transferring the ownership of the ranch. Saxon figures he can win it back later. However, Reb doesn't know that Dan doesn't have any money and hasn't paid his ranch hands recently. The hands are hostile to Reb, but he persuades them to work one more round-up.

With the round-up in progress, the cattle are stampeded and scattered by Telford's men. The ranch hands have to begin herding the steers back onto Saxon's land, but they need more supplies. Rita goes into town for the supplies only to find that Telford has closed the general store to them. Reb heads to town with Rita to get the needed supplies but is intercepted by Telford's thugs again, who beat Reb and injure his gun hand. This damage puts him out of action temporarily. Reb and Rita also discover that another attack of the round-up is imminent. They are thwarted driving the cattle through the valley by Telford's men who have set brushfires. They decide to drive the cattle over the mountains.

Curly, who is part of the cattle drive, is trying to regain Rita's affection. At one time they were sweethearts but now she realizes he was the one who tried to ambush Reb and will have nothing to do with him. Reb and Curly have it out and Reb orders Curly to leave. Curly heads straight for Telford's to join up with his gang. Reb knows Telford will try again to keep them from getting the cattle and so sets up a trap for them which results in a surprise ambush. Several of Telford's men, including Curly, are killed.

Reb finally gets the cattle to market and heads for Telford's. Johnny is there to stop Reb and kill him if necessary. However, Johnny sees Telford try to shoot Reb in the back and kills Telford instead. Reb, Johnny and Cora have a final drink after which Reb and Rita leave together.

BACKGROUND:

GUNSMOKE was described by a critic as being "a conventional blend of sagebrush and six shooters." Another critic wrote: "Murphy, who gets better with each picture, turns in a top performance, playing the role with a sardonic humor that is very effective."

GUNSMOKE united Audie Murphy and Aaron Rosenberg as a producer-star team that would prove to be highly successful. Rosenberg would produce five more pictures together for Audie, including the successful TO HELL AND BACK and NIGHT PASSAGE.

For this movie, Audie used the kind of clothes a regular cowhand would wear. He was used to wearing darker clothing or more rugged outfits. He always wanted to achieve the most authentic look for his films and did so with the help of the studio wardrobe department. The majority of the hats Audie wore in many of his Westerns were usually the kind with the sweat around the band to make it look authentic and used.

Audie Murphy is bushwhacked and takes cover from his attacker in this scene from GUNSMOKE (1953).

COLUMN SOUTH

STUDIO: UNIVERSAL-INTERNATIONAL

PRODUCER: Ted Richmond
DIRECTOR: Frederick de Cordova
STORY and SCREENPLAY BY: William Sackheim
DIRECTOR OF PHOTOGRAPHY: Charles P. Boyle, A.S.C.
TECHNICOLOR COLOR CONSULTANT: William Fritzsche
COLOR BY TECHNICOLOR
ART DIRECTION: Alexander Golitzen and Hilyard Brown
SET DECORATIONS: Russell A. Gausman and Ruby Levitt
SOUND: Leslie I. Carey and Glenn E. Anderson
TECHNICAL DIRECTION BY: Col. Paul R. Davison, U.S.A. Ret.
MUSICAL DIRECTION: Joseph Gershenson
FILM EDITOR: Milton Carruth, A.C.E.
COSTUMES: Rosemary Odell
HAIR STYLIST: Joan St. Oegger
MAKE-UP: Bud Westmore
ASSISTANT DIRECTOR: Fred Frank

DATES OF FILMING: July 20, 1952 to August 27, 1952
LOCATION OF FILMING: Apple Valley, California, area

CAST:

Lt. Jed Sayre .... Audie Murphy
Marcy Whitlock .... Joan Evans
Capt. Lee Whitlock .. Robert Sterling
Brig. Gen. Storey .... Ray Collins
Menguito .... Dennis Weaver
Chalmers .... Palmer Lee
Corp. Biddle .... Russell Johnson
Trooper Vaness .... Jack Kelly
Lt. Posick .... Johnny Downs
Sgt. McAfee .... Bob Steele
Primrose .... James Best
Joe Copper Face .... Ralph Moody
Trooper Chavez .... Rico Alaniz

RUNNING TIME: 84 minutes
RELEASE DATE: June 1953

SYNOPSIS:

Fort Union—Territory of New Mexico, January 1861. The breach between the North and South was rapidly widening. A grim specter of civil war hovered over the land. It was a time of crisis...a time for choosing sides.

While Lt. Jed Sayre is a loyal Unionist, many of the troops in the fort are southern sympathizers. Fights erupt among the men, anticipating the outbreak of war. Jed tries to keep an uneasy peace between them, the troops and the surrounding Indian tribes. However, the new authority at the fort, Captain Whitlock, has little or no love for the Indians.

Although the Indians have remained peaceful, the fort receives orders to move the Navajo tribe to a remote inhospitable area. Jed is assigned to be in charge of the relocation and reluctantly begins the task. Most of the troops are called to duty, leaving the

Audie Murphy and Joan Evans in COLUMN SOUTH

fort with only a few men to protect it.

When a prospector is found killed and scalped, Whitlock is convinced Indians are responsible. However, Jed finds out that the man was actually killed by a rival prospector out to get his gold, who scalped his victim to make it look like an Indian ambush. When the two men return to the fort, they find the troops out looking for the Indians. Jed convinces the captain to meet with the Indians after he tells him that a white man killed the prospector, not an Indian. Whitlock then determines the Indians are not interested in war.

The Indians come to the fort to trade and Jed invites them to eat with the officers. Marcy, Whitlock's sister, is outraged and stalks out with Jed in hot pursuit. He confronts her behavior as being insulting to the chief. Jed is very protective of the Indians since his father was involved in a massacre that he witnessed when he was a little boy. Thus Jed has been trying to make up for the unnecessary killing ever since. Marcy learns this from another officer and feels a sense of sadness for Jed and apologizes to him for her behavior.

The Civil War is starting to heat up with Mississippi seceding from the Union. An order is issued to move the Navajoes to Yellow Springs. While the relocation is happening, a renegade Apache, Menguito, takes advantage of the situation and leads his braves into attacking the fort and nearby town. Menguito is angry because his Apaches have been unfairly accused of stealing army rifles. One of the troopers has found the rifles hidden under a waterfall. Now the army has no choice but to send the Indians to Yellow Springs and this shatters Jed's faith because the Indians have been friendly up until now.

Jed then becomes aware that the accusations against the Apaches have been fabricated by Whitlock's superior, General Storey. Storey is apparently trying to cause disruption among the territory's citizens as a way to help the Confederates in their effort to gain more land as the war breaks out. This sets the lie and the officers believe that the Indians will attack. Jed is appointed to taking most of the men from the fort, thus leaving it unprotected. What few soldiers remain are waiting for reinforcements, which, as it happens, won't be coming.

Menguito begins his attacks on civilians and towns since there are no soldiers to stop him. Still the soldiers on the trail see no Indians, no Apaches on the warpath.

The column of soldiers rest. Jed finds a letter that tells of the plot to keep the North from winning the war. Jed and his troops eventually fight their way back to the fort and recapture it. Jed and some of the men get inside the fort and, using the ammunition that has been stored there, force the Indians to give up. Menguito captures Storey who confesses that they planted the rifles on the reservation. Jed and Menguito establish peace again.

Mississippi secedes from the Union, soon followed by other states. Southern troops in the territory begin resigning to join the Confederate Army. Whitlock resigns his commission and turns command of the fort back over to Jed.

BACKGROUND:

Audie plays a Union Cavalry lieutenant in temporary charge of an army post in New Mexico, just before the start of the Civil War When a new commander takes over the post, he antagonizes the Indians. It was then up to Audie to unmask the villainy and restore peace.

Murphy got favorable reviews for his performance in the picture. One critic wrote "Murphy is best among the players." Another said: "Audie is the most believable player in the cast."

Although featured in this film as an Apache, Dennis Weaver was to become famous as the limping "Chester" in the long-running television series "Gunsmoke," before branching out in a diversity of roles.

TUMBLEWEED

STUDIO: UNIVERSAL-INTERNATIONAL

PRODUCER: Ross Hunter
DIRECTOR: Nathan Juran
SCREENPLAY: John Meredyth Lucas
FROM A NOVEL BY: Kenneth Perkins
DIRECTOR OF PHOTOGRAPHY: Russell Metty, A.S.C.
TECHNICOLOR COLOR CONSULTANT: William Fritzsche
ART DIRECTION: Bernard Herzbrun and Richard H. Riedel
SET DIRECTION: Russell A. Gausman and John Austin
MUSICAL DIRECTION: Joseph Gershenson
SOUND: Leslie I. Carey and Glenn E. Anderson
FILM EDITOR: Virgil Vogel
COSTUMES: Bill Thomas
HAIR STYLIST: Joan St. Oegger
MAKE-UP: Bud Westmore
ASSISTANT DIRECTOR: John Sherwood

DATES OF FILMING: March 11, 1953 to April 12, 1953
LOCATION OF FILMING: Red Rock Canyon (Southern California) and Universal Studio

CAST:

Jim Harvey .... Audie Murphy
Laura .... Lori Nelson
Sheriff Murchoree .... Chill Wills
Nick Buckley .... Roy Roberts
Lam Blandon .... Russell Johnson
Louella Buckley .... K.T. Stevens
Sarah Blandon .... Madge Meredith
Marv .... Lee Van Cleef
Ted .... I. Stanford Jolley
Aguila............................ Ralph Moody
Seth Blandon .... Ross Elliott
Tigre .... Eugene Iglesias
Trapper Ross .... Phil Chambers
Weber .... Lyle Talbot
Wrangler .... King Donovan
Prospector .... Harry Harvey

RUNNING TIME: 79 minutes
RELEASE DATE: December 1953

SYNOPSIS:

Jim Harvey comes across an injured Indian and saves his life by treating his wounds. Jim later finds out that the wounded Indian is Tigre, son of Aguila, Chief of the Yaquis. Jim, who has been hired on as guard of a wagon train, is on his way to town. While on the trail, Jim takes off to scout the territory. He finds evidence of a shod pony and sees Indian smoke up ahead. Jim knows that Indian ponies aren't shod and this gives him the idea that a white man was perhaps the one who wounded Tigre. He races back to the wagon train and has them head for cover from an impending Yaqui attack.

After the first attack, Jim takes a flag of truce and looks for Aguila, in hopes of keeping him from attacking again. Since Jim once helped Tigre, he is optimistic that Aguila will have compassion to leave the wagons alone. However, Aguila doesn't believe Jim; he is captured and left to die. The Indians attack the wagons and eventually all the men are killed. The women are saved because Jim found a way to hide them earlier. Tigre's mother, who is grateful for saving her son's life, saves Jim.

Back in town, Jim is accused of deserting the wagon train. After explaining what happened, no one believes his story and the townspeople are ready to hang him for treason. Murchoree, the sheriff, puts him in jail for his own protection. Somehow, Tigre finds out about Jim, breaks into the jail and kills the guard. While they are trying to escape, Tigre is killed and Jim is wounded.

Jim wanders onto the Buckley ranch looking for a horse. He is confronted by a ranch hand and escorted to Mr. Buckley. Jim explains to Buckley that he needs to find out about the white man who set up the ambush of the wagon train. But before Jim can find out anything, he passes out from his injury. After Mrs. Buckley treats his wound, the posse turns up looking for Jim. The Buckley's protect Jim by giving him Tumbleweed, their best pack horse and telling the posse they have not seen him around.

Before long, Jim finds a hidden cache of tools and some silver ore hidden on Lam Blandon's land. Not knowing who the land belongs to, Jim takes the ore and rides off again in search of Aguila to clear his name. Murch finally finds Jim's trail and goes after him alone with the rest of the posse fanning out. Jim is headed for Coy-

On a sun-baked outdoor set, Chill Wills has to have a swig from the water canteen before he feels up to going on with his performance of a man dying of thirst by a dried-up desert waterhole. Scene is the set of the Technicolor adventure drama, TUMBLEWEED, starring Audie Murphy, Lori Nelson and Wills.

Murphy finds a mangy little cayuse loaned to him to be almost a human companion in this scene from TUMBLEWEED.

ote Springs, but upon arriving at the water hole, finds that is it is dry. Jim is about spent but Tumbleweed begins digging in the soft alkali and finds water. This sustains Jim and as he is about to head out, Murch stumbles onto the dry water hole. Jim returns to Murch and gives him water as the rest of the posse catches up with them. They knock Jim out and plan to string him up then and there.

However, Aguila and his warriors are on the warpath in the area. Jim and the posse are close to being seen and attacked. Thinking quickly, Jim urges Tumbleweed and the rest of the posse to play "possum" and let the Yaqui's think that they are all dead. When the Yaqui's get close, the posse opens up with gunfire. Aguila is mortally wounded but Jim manages to get him to talk before he dies. Aguila names Lam as a traitor to his people and tells Murch that Jim had nothing to do with the wagon train ambush. Lam takes off with Jim in hot pursuit. They fight; Lam goes over a cliff and in the end, Jim gets the horse and the girl.

BACKGROUND:

TUMBLEWEED was described by critics as a "lively, fast-moving Western" in which a "relaxed Audie Murphy handled his role flawlessly" and "lent realism to his character."

A publicity release from Universal-International to promote Audie in this film has the title of an article, "Guns Have Been Good To Me." Audie explained in the article why guns were so important as a part of his life. As a Western star, his skill with six guns was a significant component of his success.

All the intricate shooting and riding stunts in the movie were performed by Audie, who shunned the use of a stunt double.

RIDE CLEAR OF DIABLO

STUDIO: UNIVERSAL-INTERNATIONAL

PRODUCER: John W. Rogers
DIRECTOR: Jesse Hibbs
SCREENPLAY BY: George Zuckerman
ADDITIONAL DIALOGUE BY: D.D. Beauchamp
STORY BY: Ellis Marcus
DIRECTOR OF PHOTOGRAPHY: Irving Glassberg, A.S.C.
TECHNICOLOR COLOR CONSULTANT: William Fritzsche
COLOR BY TECHNICOLOR
ART DIRECTION: Bernard Herzbrun and Robert Boyle
SET DECORATIONS: Russell A. Gausman and Julia Heron
SOUND: Leslie I. Carey and Richard DeWeese
MUSICAL DIRECTION: Joseph Gershenson
FILM EDITOR: Edward Curtiss, A.C.E.
COSTUMES: Rosemary Odell
HAIR STYLIST: Joan St. Oegger
MAKE-UP: Bud Westmore
ASSISTANT DIRECTOR: Fred Frank

DATES OF FILMING: July 15, 1953 to August 11, 1953
LOCATION OF FILMING: Victorville, California, area

CAST:

Clay O'Mara .... Audie Murphy
Laurie Kenyon .... Susan Cabot
Whitey Kincade .... Dan Duryea
Kate .... Abbe Lane
Jed Ringer .... Russell Johnson
Fred Kenyon .... Paul Birch
Tom Meredith .... William Pullen
Tim Lowerie .... Jack Elam
Reverend Moorehead .... Denver Pyle

RUNNING TIME: 80 1/2 minutes
RELEASE DATE: March 1954

SYNOPSIS:

Clay O'Mara works for the railroad in Denver. He receives a telegram about the killing of his father, brother, and cattle being rustled off the family ranch and leaves for home immediately. He finds Sheriff Kenyon's niece, Laurie, who directs him to the cantina where he finds the sheriff and Tom Meredith, his father's lawyer.

Clay asks to be deputized since the rustlers haven't been caught. The sheriff is reluctant to make Clay a deputy, convinced he is out for revenge. Clay assures Kenyon that he only wants to talk to the people involved. Finally, the sheriff obliges and gives Clay a badge. When Clay asks who might be responsible for the deaths, he is informed that the prime suspect is Whitey Kincade, a ruthless killer.

Clay tracks down Kincade at the Diablo saloon, gets the drop on Whitey and arrests him for murder. Kincade protests that he is innocent, but Clay does not believe him. In this case, however, Whitey is telling the truth. They make it back to town and Whitey is put in jail. Kenyon and Meredith are the real killers and they had hoped that Kincade would kill Clay.

Kenyon slips a gun to Kincade, giving him a chance to break out of jail. Kenyon wants Whitey to kill Clay during his escape. While Clay is sleeping, Whitey has his chance to kill Clay but can't bring himself to shoot him in the back. Clay wakes up and the two men talk about his family's

Audie Murphy and Dan Duryea play captor and prisoner who wind up on the same side of a fight in RIDE CLEAR OF DIABLO.

killings. Whitey warns Clay about "certain people" in town who may be responsible, but he will not reveal names.

Whitey is tried for the crimes and found innocent. As he leaves town, he warns Clay not to turn his back on the sheriff or his henchman, Jed Ringer, who had testified and lied at the trial.

Meanwhile, Clay has become romantically involved with Laurie since she has broken off her engagement to Meredith. As Clay assumes more responsibilities as deputy, he begins to strike up a friendship with Whitey. He finds out from a rancher that a white stallion has been stolen from him. Clay goes to Diablo to find Whitey and the two of them ride off to check out the territory. Whitey has an idea where the horse might be and takes Clay to the Lowerie ranch, where they find the stallion. Whitey holds the Loweries at bay while Clay takes the horse back to town. As soon as Clay clears the property line, Whitey lets them go after Clay. He gets shot but makes it back to town, recuperating under Laurie's care.

Ringer and Meredith decide to attack a Wells Fargo bullion shipment, after which Ringer double-crosses Meredith who hides the bullion for himself. The sheriff, covering for Meredith, once again tries to throw his deputy off the trail, telling Clay that Ringer killed his father and brother. Whitey is on his way to see Clay while he is with Laurie only to find out from her that Clay has gone after Ringer. Whitey then goes after Clay to help him.

Clay searches the nearby territory and finds the empty Wells Fargo wagon. Whitey catches up with him and they trace the wagon tracks back to Ringer's hiding place in an old mine shaft. During a shootout Ringer wounds Whitey. Clay then kills Ringer.

Kenyon and Meredith ride to the Loweries' place to go after Clay. It is likely Clay will soon find out the truth about their attack on the ranch. Clay takes Whitey back to Diablo where Whitey finally tells him about Kenyon and Meredith and how they killed his family.

The sheriff arrives in Diablo but before Clay can go after him, Whitey tries to shoot it out with Kenyon who kills Whitey. Clay kills the sheriff then goes after Meredith. After a short fight, Clay arrests Meredith for murder. Soon, Clay and Laurie are married and go back to Denver.

BACKGROUND:

For this movie, Audie got unusually good reviews. The picture was described as "a suspenseful Western." Another critic called the picture "a well-plotted Western action movie with emphasis on characterizations."

Newsweek magazine reviewed the film and made this remarkable comment: "It is very difficult for Murphy to appear unnatural in anything he does, whether it be a first-class motion picture like THE RED BADGE OF COURAGE or a routine Western like this." The reviewer further praised it as one of the best Murphy Westerns.

DRUMS ACROSS THE RIVER

STUDIO: UNIVERSAL-INTERNATIONAL

PRODUCER: Melville Tucker
DIRECTOR: Nathan Juran
SCREENPLAY BY: John K. Butler and Lawrence Roman
STORY BY: John K. Butler
COLOR BY TECHNICOLOR
DIRECTOR OF PHOTOGRAPHY: Harold Lipstein, A.S.C.
TECHNICOLOR COLOR CONSULTANT: Monroe W. Burbank
ART DIRECTION: Bernard Herzbrun and Richard H. Riedel
SET DECORATIONS: Russell A. Gausman and Julia Heron
SOUND: Leslie I. Carey and Richard DeWeese
MUSICAL DIRECTION: Joseph Gershenson
FILM EDITOR: Virgil Vogel, A.C.E.
COSTUMES: Jay Morley, Jr.
HAIR STYLIST: Joan St. Oegger
MAKE-UP: Bud Westmore
ASSISTANT DIRECTOR: Tom Shaw

DATES OF FILMING: October 8, 1953 to October 31, 1953
LOCATION OF FILMING: Kernsville, California, area

CAST:

Gary Brannon ....Audie Murphy
Sam Brannon ....Walter Brennan
Frank Walker .... Lyle Bettger
Jennie .... Lisa Gaye
Morgan .... Hugh O'Brian
Sue Randolph .... Mara Corday
Taos .... Jay Silverheels
Nathan Marlowe............ Emile Meyer
Sheriff Jim Beal ....Regis Toomey
Chief Ouray .... Morris Ankrum
Billy Costa .... Bob Steele
Jed Walker .... James Anderson
Les Walker..................George Wallace
Ralph Costa.................Lane Bradford
Stilwell .... Howard McNear
Fallon...............................Gregg Barton

RUNNING TIME: 78 minutes
RELEASE DATE: June 1954

SYNOPSIS:

Audie's character, Gary Brannon, runs a freight business with his father, Sam. The Western town they live in is located near Ute Indian territory which is supposed to be off-limits to whites. But, prospectors want to cross the river which separates them from the Utes in search of gold.

Gary agrees to provide freight wagons and accompany some prospectors to help save the town from going broke. Sam knows the expedition will break the treaty. He goes to the sheriff to plead with him to stop the men. Since the sheriff is not interested in helping, Sam sets off alone.

Two of the prospecting agents, Walker and Malone, have already crossed the river to scout the territory and are soon attacked by the Utes. Malone is taken prisoner but Walker gets away. Gary starts off to rescue Malone, who is the father of his girlfriend, Jennie. Malone is distracted by Sam's arrival, and is attacked by an Indian. During the struggle, Gary gets the upper hand and is about to kill his attacker when Sam intervenes. Gary has a strong hatred for the Utes, as one of them had killed his mother years before.

Sam attempts to make a deal with the Utes, as a trade for Malone. He succeeds, but Walker, who wants trouble for his own benefit, soon stirs up a shooting war. Several whites, including Walker, want to provoke the Utes into an all-out fight, which will eventually bring in the U.S. Cavalry, pushing them out of the territory and onto a reservation. After that, the men can lay claim to all the gold in the nearby mountains.

Sam is shot and unable to go to the chief's camp to continue treaty negotiations. Gary must go in his place. Still carrying the hatred in his heart, Gary knows he must try to keep the peace. He will explain to the chief that the attack on the Utes has come from a small group of outsiders, not the townspeople.

Gary approaches the camp and is almost killed, but is saved by the chief's son, Taos. Gary has a chance to talk to the old chief, who is dying. He is able to let out some of the anger over his mother's death. The chief tells him that the brave who killed his mother was put to death for his crime. After the chief dies, Taos becomes

Audie Murphy and Hugh O'Brian, who is giving the orders in this scene from DRUMS ACROSS THE RIVER

leader. He also tells Gary that the brave who killed his mother was the chief's son. Gary now feels more sympathetic towards the Indians. He is invited to attend the chief's funeral and told by Taos to never return. Upon Gary's promise, Taos tells him there will be no war with the whites.

A posse has been formed to look for Gary and is ready to move across the river when he comes back. Gary and Walker disagree about dealing with the Utes, but Gary prevails for the moment. But Walker isn't finished yet. He spreads a rumor that the Brannons have struck a secret deal with the Utes and sends for a hired gun named Morgan to go after Gary.

Walker and Morgan kidnap Sam. They tell Gary he must cooperate with them to get his father back and Gary reluctantly agrees. The men want his freight rig to steal a safe from the stage and make it look like the Utes were responsible. After the robbery, Walker tells Morgan to kill Gary after they hide the safe.

After Walker's men set the stage on fire with flaming arrows, Gary tricks Morgan by telling him something is wrong with one of the mules. Morgan is distracted and Gary kills him. Unfortunately, Morgan dies before Gary can get any information as to where his father is being held.

Gary hides the safe and gets back to town to find out that one of the stage drivers survived to tell the sheriff that the Brannon rig was involved in the robbery. Since neither Brannon has been seen all day, the sheriff thinks that they have a secret deal going with the Utes. Gary is arrested for armed robbery and murder. He won't defend himself because he fears Walker will kill his father if he talks. Without a defense, he is found guilty and sentenced to hang.

Jennie visits Gary in jail and through her, he arranges a deal with Walker. He will reveal the location of the safe in exchange for Walker getting him out of jail and letting Sam go.

Just before he is to be hanged, Walker arrives with Sam. He persuades the sheriff to take both men to out to look for the gold and the safe. Gary tells them the safe is hidden across the river. Once across, the party is attacked by the Utes. Gary and Walker fight. Gary is almost killed by one of the Indians, but is saved by Taos. As Walker flees, Gary soon catches up with him and along with the rest of the gang and kills him. He gets the rest of the gang and rescues Sam. He then assures Taos the peace will be preserved. Gary and Sam head back to town where he is reunited with Jennie.

BACKGROUND:

Besides Walter Brennan, the cast included such notables as Hugh O'Brian (pre-"Wyatt Earp"), Jay Silverheels (better known as "Tonto"), Regis Toomey, perennial Western sidekick/villain Bob Steele, and Howard McNear, who later gave numerous haircuts to every citizen in the town of Mayberry, as "Floyd the Barber" on "The Andy Griffith Show."

DRUMS ACROSS THE RIVER was described as a "surprising, vital sort of Western." One critic wrote: "Audie Murphy puts on a great show of action in his role."

DESTRY

STUDIO: UNIVERSAL-INTERNATIONAL

PRODUCER: Stanley Rubin
DIRECTOR: George Marshall
SCREENPLAY BY: Edmund H. North and D.D. Beauchamp
FROM A STORY BY: Felix Jackson
SUGGESTED BY MAX BRAND'S NOVEL, *Destry Rides Again*
DIRECTOR OF PHOTOGRAPHY: George Robinson, A.S.C.
TECHNICOLOR COLOR CONSULTANT: William Fritzsche
ART DIRECTION: Alexander Golitzen and Alfred Sweeney
SET DECORATIONS: Russell A. Gausman and John P. Austin
SOUND: Leslie I. Carey and Glenn E. Anderson
FILM EDITOR: Ted J. Kent, A.C.E.
DANCES BY: Kenny Williams
COSTUMES: Rosemary Odell
HAIR STYLIST: Joan St. Oegger
MAKE-UP: Bud Westmore
ASSISTANT DIRECTOR: Frank Shaw
MUSIC SUPERVISION BY: Joseph Gershenson
"Bang! Bang!," "If You Can Can-Can," "Empty Arms"
WORDS & MUSIC BY: Frederick Herbert and Arnold Hughes

DATES OF FILMING: Early May 1954 to June 15, 1954
LOCATION OF FILMING: Universal Studio and Greater Los Angeles area

CAST:

Tom Destry .... Audie Murphy
Brandy .... Mari Blanchard
Decker .... Lyle Bettger
Rags Barnaby .... Thomas Mitchell
Mayor Sellers .... Edgar Buchanan
Martha Phillips .... Lori Nelson
Doc Curtis .... Wallace Ford
Bessie Mae Curtis .... Mary Wickes
Jack Larson .... Alan Hale, Jr.
Curly .... George Wallace
Mac .... Richard Reeves
Henry Skinner .... Walter Baldwin
Eli Skinner .... Lee Aaker
Professor .... Mitchell Lawrence
Dummy .... Frank Richards
Sheriff Bailey .... Trevor Bardette
Bartender .... Ralph Peters
Cowhand .... John Doucette

RUNNING TIME: 95 minutes
RELEASE DATE: November 1954

SYNOPSIS:

In the town of Restful, a high-stakes poker game finds rancher Henry Skinner sitting with a sure winning hand. He bets all his money and ranch deed to match the bet of saloon owner (and resident bad guy) Phil Decker. Decker signals his girlfriend, Brandy, to spill hot coffee on Skinner, diverting his attention at which time his hold card is switched. Of course, Skinner loses the poker hand and his ranch and accuses Decker of cheating him. Decker shrugs it off as Skinner goes to find the sheriff, and attempts to get the deed back. However, what he winds

Audie Murphy, having a chat with Mari Blanchard in DESTRY

up getting is shot, but to everyone in the saloon, Decker blithely announces that the sheriff died of a "heart attack."

Restful now needs a new sheriff. The mayor appoints the town drunk, Rags Barnaby, whose main claim to fame was riding with the famous lawman, Destry, now deceased. Rags decides he needs help and sends for Destry's son, Tom. However, when Tom arrives, instead of a gun-toting lawman, he gets off the stage carrying a birdcage and parasol to help a young lady. Naturally both Rags and Tom are the laughing stock of the town, which puts Rags in a very embarrassing position.

Young Tom soon finds himself pitted against the town's baddest citizen. Decker informs Tom that he collects guns as a hobby, and would like to have Tom's. Tom calmly informs Decker that he doesn't carry a gun. Later, Rags urges Tom to strap on his father's guns. Tom declines, explaining that his father was shot in the back while wearing his guns. Rags feels that Tom should leave because he's not going to clean up Restful with a pocket full of rocks and doesn't want him to get hurt.

Rags is not encouraged by Tom's way of doing things, resigns as sheriff and returns to drinking. Meanwhile, Tom is apprised of the suspicions of Decker's involvement with the previous sheriff's demise, has himself sworn in as the new sheriff. He then gets Rags back on his feet and sets out to find the truth.

Out at the ranch, Henry Skinner is defending his home against Decker and his men. Destry arrives but, unfortunately, the paper Skinner signed over to Decker at the poker game is valid and he must turn the ranch over to him. Even though Decker's claim is legal, the townsfolk still turn against Tom.

Tom needs proof about how Sheriff Bailey really died. He tricks Brandy into getting him that proof. He then gets the doctor to examine the body and dig for the bullet. Tom hears gunfire coming from Decker's saloon. Some of the hands are having some fun doing a little promiscuous shooting. After borrowing some guns from Decker's men, Tom puts on a display of trick gunplay, that shows that first impressions are mighty important. Just because he doesn't carry a gun doesn't mean he can't shoot. He then proceeds to dig the bullets out of the wall. When questioned what he's doing, Destry explains to Decker that he collects old, used bullets. He really needs them to compare the bullet found in Bailey to the ones from Decker's boys.

Tom realizes that the bullet that killed Bailey came from Curly's gun and so Tom arrests him. Tom tries to get Curly to talk telling him that if he doesn't, he'll hang alone. Just as Curly is about to tell Tom what he knows, Mayor Sellers informs Tom that he will be trying the case. Tom won't have any of that. He's waiting for a territorial judge with a real jury, not a hand picked bunch of two for a nickel gunslingers and barflys.

While Tom is being distracted by Brandy, Curly escapes from jail. Rags is shot and dies shortly afterward. Incensed by this, Tom, finally puts on his father's guns and goes after Decker. Brandy tries to warn Tom that Decker has a trap set for him. She is killed by shielding Tom with her body as Tom gets Decker. The town of Restful is again at peace as Tom and Martha finally get together.

BACKGROUND:

Following earlier cinematic versions of Max Brand's popular novel (Tom Mix in 1932, and James Stewart with Marlene Dietrich—DESTRY RIDES AGAIN—in 1939), Audie stars in his first "comedy", while remaining in his familiar action-Western genre.

The story has the people in a small Western town derisively appointing a local souse as sheriff. In the Murphy version this role was played by Thomas Mitchell. The old drunk sent for the son of a famous marshal to be his deputy. The son, played by Audie Murphy, seemed to be a sissy through about three-fourths of the story. He believed in keeping order by proper legal procedure. Toward the end, the Murphy character turned out to be a "hell on wheels" as he brought law and order to the town with fists and guns.

In one of the picture's many expertly staged climaxes, Audie puts on a sudden demonstration of marksmanship, shooting down everything in sight in the saloon. All this doing it with borrowed guns, for up to that point, he doesn't carry one of his own.

A reviewer described DESTRY as a fast-paced action picture. It was highly successful with both critics and the public. One reviewer wrote: "Audie Murphy was an amazingly apt bit of casting. He fits the original Max Brand concept better than either Tom Mix or James Stewart." Another critic said: "Audie seems to have come into his own, with sure ease underplaying his role." Another said: "Murphy does exceptionally well. The ease with which he handles his part is a big asset to the show."

Such critical opinions were the best Audie had received since THE RED BADGE OF COURAGE. And this was his first try at comedy, which was directly opposite in nature to RED BADGE.

Universal had started pre-production on TO HELL AND BACK in 1953, but would not start shooting until September, 1954. The studio had correctly guessed that it would be a big picture, so it wanted to give Audie a build-up and a change in image. For these reasons, DESTRY was carefully selected as a sure-fire formula picture. Universal also experimented with the sex appeal that Murphy might project on the screen. He was given two leading ladies, Mari Blanchard and Lori Nelson.

Having demonstrated his increasing versatility as an actor, Universal decided Audie was now ready to play the most dramatic role of his career—as Audie Murphy, celebrated war hero.

Audie Murphy, trying to get George Wallace to confess who killed Rags Barnaby in DESTRY

TO HELL AND BACK

STUDIO: UNIVERSAL-INTERNATIONAL

PRODUCER: Aaron Rosenberg
DIRECTOR: Jesse Hibbs
WRITTEN FOR THE SCREEN BY: Gil Doud
BASED ON AUDIE MURPHY'S AUTOBIOGRAPHY, *To Hell and Back*
DIRECTOR OF PHOTOGRAPHY: Maury Gertsman, A.S.C.
TECHNICOLOR COLOR CONSULTANT: William Fritzsche
ART DIRECTION: Alexander Golitzen and Robert Clatworthy
SET DECORATIONS: Russell A. Gausman and John P. Austin
SOUND: Leslie I. Carey and John A. Bolger, Jr.
FILM EDITOR: Edward Curtiss, A.C.E.
HAIR STYLIST: Joan St. Oegger
MAKE-UP: Bud Westmore
ASSISTANT DIRECTOR: Tom Shaw
TECHNICAL ADVISORS: Major Leonard J. Murray, Infantry, U.S.A.; Colonel Michael Paulick, Infantry, U.S.A.
MUSIC SUPERVISED BY: Joseph Gershenson
"Dogface Soldier," WORDS AND MUSIC BY: Bert Gold and Ken Hart

DATES OF FILMING: Early September, 1954 to October 28, 1954
LOCATION OF FILMING: Yakima, Fort Lewis, Washington, area and Universal Studio

CAST:

Audie Murphy .... Audie Murphy
Johnson .... Marshall Thompson
Brandon .... Charles Drake
Kerrigan .... Jack Kelly
Lieutenant Manning ... Gregg Palmer
Valentino .... Paul Picerni
Lieutenant Lee .... David Janssen
Kovak .... Richard Castle
Captain Marks .... Bruce Cowling
Colonel Howe .... Paul Langton
Sanchez .... Art Aragon
Swope .... Felix Noriego
Thompson .... Denver Pyle
Saunders .... Brett Halsey
Maria .... Susan Kohner
Helen .... Anabel Shaw
Mrs. Murphy .... Mary Field
Audie As a Boy .... Gordon Gebert
Steiner .... Julian Upton

RUNNING TIME: 105 minutes
RELEASE DATE: October 1955
LOS ANGELES PREMIER: Wiltern Theatre on October 12, 1955

SYNOPSIS:

At age 12 on a sharecropper's farm, Audie Murphy struggles to keep his younger brothers and sisters together after his father's desertion of the family. He quits school and goes to work full time on a neighboring farm. Shortly after his 16th birthday Audie's beloved mother passes away. America is at war and Audie decides to join the service.

After rejection by the navy, marines and paratroopers for being underweight, he is accepted into the army, sent to Casablanca and assigned to Baker Company. The day after his arrival, the company commander tries to have him reassigned from the rifle company to a less hostile environment. Apparently, they feel he is too frail to fight. Murphy protests, stating he wants no special treatment and learns he is only trying to do him a favor. The captain finally relents and allows him to stay, stating he feels every man should be given a chance.

The company is told that the Germans have been driven out of North Africa and the men begin to celebrate, expecting that they will now be sent home. The celebration is short-lived however, with the news of reassignment to invade the island of Sicily.

The initial landing on Sicily goes fairly smoothly. Shortly after their trek inland, a German machine-gun nest attacks, killing the lieutenant. Apparently only one gun is on the hill so Audie tosses a grenade, killing the Germans. This is Audie's first encounter with the enemy. Shortly after this, he is promoted to corporal and put in charge of his squad.

Week after week, the men advance through tough opposition until, at last, all of Sicily is free of the enemy. Company B is now headed for Salerno, facing fierce resistance from the Germans.

Upon arriving at the Volturno River, a combat patrol is ordered to stir up the Germans. Close to dawn, the big guns on both sides of the river begin firing. The Seventh Army is ready to cross when Murphy and Baker Company arrive. The men are getting edgy and fights break out. Audie gets promoted to sergeant during the course of more fighting along the way. The unit finally gets some R & R after two months solid in the field and they head for Naples.

Later on, Audie's squad is trying to capture a two-story farmhouse for observation purposes, but the price they pay is high. The men begin clearing the farmhouse, room by room. As they continue their search for the enemy, Audie sees what he thinks is a German soldier, and fires his weapon. What he actually sees is his own dirty reflection in a mirror. This prompts one of his own men to remark, "man, that's the first time I ever saw a Texan beat himself to the draw." Audie threatens to turn his gun loose on the soldiers that witnessed the event if they ever relay this back to any of his men. A little humor never hurts once in a while.

With the fields near the farmhouse muddy, the German tanks can't advance. However, when the rain doesn't come, the fields begin to dry up. One tank, that has been hit by mortar fire, is being repaired by the Germans. Audie takes three men with him and blows the treads off so the tank is immobile. For this, he earns a decoration and an offer to take a battlefield commission. Audie refuses because he doesn't want to be transferred from his men, which is the rule. The next day, with the fields drying out, the tanks once again fire upon the farmhouse, blasting the Americans back to the open fields. One by one the men in Audie's unit are killed.

The Third Division lands in Southern France, pushing the Germans back. Audie's unit is again pinned down. Audie and Brandon toss the grenades to destroy the machine gun nest, but

Brandon is killed by a German soldier. Audie is overcome with grief and single-handedly wipes out the Germans on the hill, making is easier for the advancing Americans to move up. Audie goes back down to where Brandon is lying, sits down beside the body and bawls like a baby.

Audie is offered an opportunity to go to West Point and this time he accepts a commission as 2nd Lieutenant. Due to a shortage of officers, he is told he won't have to transfer and the rule has been waived. His platoon heads for the Colmar area to eradicate a German observation post. Again, the Germans attack viciously and the fire is returned by our tanks.

Audie receives the following orders: "The Germans are defending the town of Holtzwihr, which is their last foothold in France. It is heavily fortified and when that town is reduced, there is nothing between them and the German border. It must be taken at all costs." Our tanks are in place and the platoon is on their objective.

Audie and his men get ready. The tanks are ready but one of them sustains a direct hit and begins to burn. Audie orders his men to fall back while he stays in a forward position directing artillery fire. His deadly aim is accurate and the German tanks head for cover. Audie orders the artillery to keep after the German infantry, and as he uses the last of his ammunition, he sees a perfectly good machine gun on top of the burning tank destroyer. He pulls the trigger and the clatter of the gun is like music to his ears. As Audie mows down the Germans, the tank is hit by mortar shells but Audie stands his ground, and for almost an hour, fires on the enemy. They can't see him through all the smoke so he is more or less protected. At last, after the ammunition is exhausted, Audie climbs down off of the burning tank. Seconds later, it explodes. Murphy heads back to the woods to regroup his men and refuses medical attention. For this action, Audie receives the highest decoration this country can bestow, The Congressional Medal of Honor. His dreams of going to West Point have been shattered because of the serious nature of his wounds. He watches the men as they march past him in formation and thinks of his buddies who didn't make it.

BACKGROUND:

Since Murphy had become an accomplished actor by the time this movie was made, he's able to do something rather unusual in Hollywood. He gets to play himself. He also had other input in the production, advising on the script, action, sets, props, costumes and the casting. This project meant a lot to him personally.

In addition to starring in the picture, Audie also served as the chief technical advisor, but he was not given screen credit for this job. Colonel Michael Paulick was a credited technical advisor. During World War II, Paulick was the commanding officer of the 1st Battalion, 15th Infantry Regiment, 3rd Infantry Division. The 1st Battalion included Company B, which Audie joined as a private and ended as the company commander. Colonel Paulick recommended Audie for his first Silver Star and The Legion of Merit.

The movie rights on TO HELL AND BACK were sold to Universal for

$25,000. Of this amount, Murphy got 60%. He was paid $100,000 for playing the lead and acting as technical advisor on the movie. In addition, he received 10% of the net profits. Rumor and conjecture have sometimes wildly exaggerated the amount Audie received for the net profits.

In a legal statement made in October 1966, Murphy said that he had received exactly $387,745.17 for his 10% share of the net profits of TO HELL AND BACK. This amount plus the $100,000 added up to $487,745.17 in October 1966.

While this sum is considerable, it was no more than many movie stars made for merely acting in a single picture. In Murphy's case, he furnished the story, served as technical advisor, and starred in the movie. He used much of the money he received from the motion picture to buy a ranch (known as A.M. Farms) near Perris, California.

Readers of the book version of *To Hell and Back* will find that it often differs radically from the film version. This was because of two different viewpoints. The book strove for realism; and the movie, for idealism. Sometimes the realism had to be sacrificed. For example, the death of Brandon was first filmed realistically but it came out so brutally on the big screen that studio officials thought it might repel audiences. The scene was toned down considerably and re-shot.

Audie Murphy, giving the order to cross the river in this scene from TO HELL AND BACK

Audie, as was his custom when he could, got several personal friends in the cast. Among them was Tommy Hart, a former longshoreman and fight referee in real life. Art Aragon was an ex-professional pugilist known in fight circles as "The Golden Boy." Volney Peavyhouse, a flyer in World War II, was Audie's stand-in.

Audie got a case of the "jitters" when facing the movie camera. "Funny thing that I should get stage fright doing all those things in front of the cameras," he admits. "I didn't have it 'way back when.'"

He had repeated several of the heroic moments at least a dozen times in front of the cameras before he got them right. "I'm glad I made the mistakes during the making of the movie," Audie told the director, Jesse Hibbs. "When these things first happened, there were no allowances for re-takes." He blushingly admitted that he got a worse case of the jitters re-enacting his World War II heroics for a movie camera then he did at the time they were actually performed.

While the film was being shot, wife Pam and son Terry visited the set on several occasions. In fact, Terry had a small part in the picture, as one of Audie's younger brothers in an early scene. Once while Terry was watching the shooting of a combat scene and Audie was dodging through machine gun fire and artillery bursts, the little fellow yelled out, "Look out, Dad!" (*Audie Murphy, American Soldier*)

While the cameras were rolling, Audie climbed up on the burning tank destroyer and started firing the machine gun. The gun jammed and the director yelled "Cut!" Audie, with his dry sense of humor said, "If that had happened during the real thing, we wouldn't have to bother making this picture at all."

One last interesting note of information was the amount of ammunition used in the film. A total of 50,000 rounds of ammunition, 300 pounds of TNT, 600 pounds of blasting powder and 10 cases of 40 percent dynamite were required for the filming of the battle scenes.

Audie Murphy, receiving the Congressional Medal of Honor in the last scene from TO HELL AND BACK

WORLD IN MY CORNER

STUDIO: UNIVERSAL-INTERNATIONAL

PRODUCER: Aaron Rosenberg
DIRECTOR: Jesse Hibbs
SCREENPLAY BY: Jack Sher
BASED ON A STORY BY: Jack Sher and Joseph Stone
DIRECTOR OF PHOTOGRAPHY: Maury Gertsman, A.S.C.
ART DIRECTORS: Alexander Golitzen and Bill Newberry
SET DIRECTORS: Russell A. Gausman and Julia Heron
SOUND: Leslie I. Carey and Robert Pritchard
TECHNICAL ADVISORS: Frankie Van and H. Tommy Hart
FILM EDITOR: Milton Carruth, A.C.E.
GOWNS: Bill Thomas
HAIR STYLIST: Joan St. Oegger
MAKE-UP: Bud Westmore
ASSISTANT DIRECTOR: Joseph E. Kenny
MUSIC SUPERVISION BY: Joseph Gershenson

DATES OF FILMING: June 1, 1955 to June 29, 1955
LOCATION OF SHOOTING: Universal Studio and Los Angeles area

CAST:

Tommy Shea .... Audie Murphy
Dorothy Mallinson ...... Barbara Rush
Robert T. Mallinson .... Jeff Morrow
Dave Bernstein .... John McIntire
Ray Kacsmarak .... Tommy Rall
Harry Cram .... Howard St. John
Al Carelli .... Chico Vejar
TV Announcer .... Steve Ellis
Fighter .... Art Aragon
Doris .... Dani Crayne
Ring Announcer ...... James F. Lennon
Parker .... Cisco Andrade
Stretch Caplow .... H. Tommy Hart
Mrs. Mallinson ....Sheila Bromley

RUNNING TIME: 82 minutes
RELEASE DATE: March 1956

SYNOPSIS:

Tommy Shea is a tough, young boxer from the "wrong side of the tracks." Although he loses a local fight, several people see the potential for Tommy to become a serious contender in his weight class. His trainer thinks his career will improve quickly if Tommy signs a contract with a well-connected but crooked fight manager, Harry Cram. Tommy refuses. One person who approaches Tommy is Dave Bernstein, a former fight manager who feels Tommy has potential and leaves his card for the young pugilist.

Tommy loses his job at the factory and out of desperation winds up at the address given to him by Dave at the arena. Tommy meets Robert Mallinson, a rich industrialist interested in promoting young boxers. Soon, Mallinson's daughter, Dorothy, begins to take a personal interest in Tommy. Mallinson sends Dave after Tommy to train at the house. Since he has nowhere else to go, Tommy decides it may not be a bad idea.

Tommy trains and Dave finds him a fight which he wins through sheer determination. He is also being watched by Harry Cram, who tries to proposition Tommy into some fights. However, Tommy and Dave won't go along with Cram. Ray, Tommy's former trainer, decides to work for Cram, basically for the money.

After winning his next fight, Tommy takes Dorothy to the area where he grew up. He explains to her that he has chosen a boxing career because it seems to be a fast way to make money and escape from the slums. Dorothy tells him that money isn't everything. She is resentful of her father, convinced her mother was driven to a sanitarium by his rigid money-is-everything way of living. She expresses fear that Tommy will end up the same way. He assures her that won't happen, but he needs to make enough money so they can live comfortably without relying on her father.

A non-title fight is lined up with the welter-weight champion, arranged by Tommy's trainer and Cram. The deal calls for Tommy to lose the fight. However, Tommy never agreed to take a dive. Once in the ring, he takes a bad pounding from the champion, but eventually wins in a split decision.

Mallinson offers Tommy the opportunity to stay on at the house. He asks about his feelings for Dorothy and tells Tommy he wants to help him. Tommy agrees. When he tells Dorothy she becomes upset and doesn't want her father working with Tommy. Tommy feels he can handle her father and tells her not to worry.

Tommy is soon caught between Dorothy's idealism, her father's greed, and his own fierce desires. With Mallinson pushing him, he first agrees to throw a rematch with the champ and take the money. Dorothy finds out about this and leaves. Tommy realizes he can't have Mallinson controlling his life anymore.

Audie Murphy with John McIntire, refusing an offer from crooked fight promoter Howard St. John in this scene from WORLD IN MY CORNER

Mallinson brings his wife home from the sanitarium knowing that it will also bring Dorothy back. Tommy finds Dave packing after he reads about the upcoming fight with Carelli. Tommy tries to explain why he's fighting Carelli but Dave thinks Tommy has sold him out to fight for Cram, which he hasn't. Tommy goes back to the house only to find that Dorothy is leaving and taking her mother with her. She has also found out about the "fix." Tommy wants to marry her but feels that he can't without the money to support her in the proper manner. After Dorothy leaves, Tommy comes to his senses and tells Mallinson off. He insists that the fight will be fought fair and square, and that he won't be taking a dive.

The day before the fight in his hotel room, Tommy tells Cram he won't throw the fight. Cram agrees to allow a fair fight, but later has three henchmen beat him, badly injuring his ribs. His manager tries to talk him out of the fight, but Tommy insists on going through with it telling them that there are some things he won't do for money.

The fight is brutal for Tommy with the champ pounding on his damaged ribs. The manager wants to have the fight stopped. Tommy refuses, but he can't last much longer. In desperation, his manager suggests Tommy switch to his early left-handed style of fighting, confusing the champ. It works with Tommy knocking him out and becoming the new champion. Back in the locker room, the doctor warns Dave that Tommy should never fight again. However, in Dave's eyes, Tommy is a real champion. After the fight, he reunites with Dorothy, giving up his boxing career. Tommy has finally gotten out of the slums.

BACKGROUND:

For two solid weeks, Audie slugged it out in the ring against such accomplished professional opponents as Chico Vejar, Cisco Andrade, Baby Ike and Frank Muche. Los Angeles boxing experts, invited to the studio to watch Murphy go against Vejar, were amazed at the rugged nature of the cinematic ring warfare. Never before had they seen two "actors" exchange such solid blows for the sake of movie cameras.

"I knew they would be impressed," commented director Jesse Hibbs. "Audie is the most conscientious screen actor I've ever known. He trained like a pro for eight weeks for this part because he was determined to look like an expert in the ring, no matter how many hard punches he had to take in order to deliver one."

During the making of this film, Audie had a real life boxer train him. Chico Vejar also played the role of the welter-weight champion. Audie was a stickler for reality. He was in top condition and was still slugging after three hard days of fight scenes. During one of the rounds with Chico, he managed to land a few blows—enough to give Chico an eye cut. The fighting was so real and authentic looking that even the extras watching this particular fight scene were applauding as the round ended.

The movie was described as a "serviceable, if not original, prize-fight film." Of Audie's performance, a critic wrote: "Murphy's skill and charm as an actor increases in every picture."

WALK THE PROUD LAND

STUDIO: UNIVERSAL-INTERNATIONAL

PRODUCER: Aaron Rosenberg
DIRECTOR: Jesse Hibbs
SCREENPLAY: Gil Doud and Jack Sher
BASED ON A BIOGRAPHY BY: Woodworth Clum
PRINT BY TECHNICOLOR
DIRECTOR OF PHOTOGRAPHY: Harold Lipstein, A.S.C.
TECHNICOLOR COLOR CONSULTANT: William Fritzsche
ART DIRECTION: Alexander Golitzen and Bill Newberry
SET DECORATIONS: Russell A. Gausman and Ray Jeffers
SOUND: Leslie I. Carey and Frank H. Wilkinson
FILM EDITOR: Sherman Todd, A.C.E.
COSTUMES: Bill Thomas
HAIR STYLIST: Joan St. Oegger
MAKEUP: Bud Westmore
ASSISTANT DIRECTOR: Phil Bowles
SPECIAL PHOTOGRAPHY: Clifford Stine, A.S.C.
MUSIC SUPERVISION BY: Joseph Gershenson

DATES OF FILMING: December 1955 to January 6, 1956
LOCATION OF FILMING: Tucson, Arizona, area

CAST:

John P. Clum .... Audie Murphy
Tianay .... Anne Bancroft
Mary Dennison .... Pat Crowley
Tom Sweeny .... Charles Drake
Taglito .... Tommy Rall
Eskiminzin .... Robert Warwick
Geronimo .... Jay Silverheels
Tono .... Eugene Mazzola
Disalin .... Anthony Caruso
Santos .... Victor Millan
Captain Larsen .... Ainslie Pryor
Chato .... Eugene Iglesias
General Wade .... Morris Ankrum
Governor Safford . Addison Richards
Alchise .... Maurice Jara
Stone .... Frank Chase
Naylor .... Ed Hinton
Pica .... Marty Carrizosa

RUNNING TIME: 88 minutes
RELEASE DATE: September 1956

SYNOPSIS:

In 1874, John P. Clum arrives as the new Indian agent for the Apaches. The Interior Department has taken over responsibility for the Indians from the War Department. Clum sees how his new charges are treated by the army, being chained and worked hard. Clum orders them freed, allows them to return to the reservation and sends the army away. He encourages the Apaches to return to their traditional customs and incorporates a police force who make the rules that everyone must follow.

An Indian woman, Tianay, is in mourning for her dead husband but is sent to be Clum's housekeeper. She tends to him with her little son, Tono. It is a nice arrangement for her but Clum has a fiancee and asks Tianay to leave before his future wife gets there. Tianay is wanting to stay on but he tells her that his fiancee wouldn't like it if she remained.

Meanwhile, white men are caught poaching on Indian land with scalps in their possession. Clum turns the men over to the local sheriff for trial. However, the poachers are soon released. Apparently the sheriff doesn't find anything wrong with whites gathering Indian scalps. Clum and his friend Sweeny, a retired Union soldier, are enjoying a drink at the saloon where the poachers find them. A fight ensues with Clum and Sweeny who soon head back to the reservation a little bit battered and bruised.

Clum employs Sweeny to head his police force and run the general store on the reservation. Mary arrives, they get married and settle down to live on the reservation. Tianay's little son, Tono, hears that Mary doesn't want Tianay and Tono living under the same roof and decides to run away with his friend Pica to find Geronimo's camp. Geronimo has been to the reservation and is invited to stay as long as he obeys the rules,

Audie Murphy, being introduced to Anne Bancroft's son, Eugene Mazzola, in this scene from WALK THE PROUD LAND

but he wants no part of it. He asks the Apaches to join him and when no one does, he rides away with his braves. Clum and Tianay go looking for the boys and find them the next day.

On their way back to the reservation, they see Geronimo attacking white settlers. As the army comes in and tries to take over again, Clum goes after Geronimo to try to make him surrender. Clum has a plan to capture Geronimo without bloodshed.

Clum meets up with Geronimo and convinces him that more fighting is futile. The Apaches are not strong enough to defeat the army. Reluctantly, Geronimo bows to the inevitable and surrenders. The army takes custody of Geronimo, but Clum is tired of their continual interference and quits as agent. However, the reservation chief, Eskiminzin, pleads with John to stay on since no one else will help protect their interests. Clum has second thoughts and with Mary's encouragement, decides to stay.

BACKGROUND:

This movie presents the true-life story of John Philip Clum, who, at 23, took over the San Carlos, Arizona, Indian Reservation, pacified the Apaches and forced the surrender of Geronimo. He became a famous hero of the Old Southwest. Clum spent the rest of his life fighting for the welfare of the Indians, but his dream of self-government for them was not realized until long after his death. In November 1955, the United States Government turned the administration of the San Carlos reservation over to the Apaches themselves.

In this movie, Audie Murphy, made the critics take serious note of his acting ability, displaying a finesse and maturity far surpassing his former screen efforts. The picture was described as an "interesting, often amusing, and sometimes touching outdoor drama." Its success was predicted on the basis of a "fine performance of the star and fresh, original story material."

One critic wrote: "Audie Murphy proves himself a first-rate actor capable of handling a role fraught with difficulties and potential pitfalls." Another critic said: "Audie Murphy, as Clum, acts it in the quiet, realistic and natural manner which he brings to all his films." A third critic stated: "Murphy is entirely likable as a serious young man. He gives a first rate performance."

Most significantly, a critic pointed out: "Murphy is probably one of the few actors who could successfully carry off this part (Clum). Although he is not a big man, he never implies weakness; and the connotations of his name and career (as a World War II soldier) effectively underscores his determinedly mild behavior."

With WALK THE PROUD LAND, Hollywood finally began to realize that they had been utilizing a genuine acting talent in his movie work. He was no longer a war hero trying to be an actor. His quiet handling of film roles gave them authority. The method was not due to Audie's reluctance to display emotion.

THE GUNS OF FORT PETTICOAT

STUDIO: COLUMBIA

PRODUCER: Harry Joe Brown
DIRECTOR: George Marshall
SCREEN PLAY BY: Walter Doniger
BASED ON A STORY BY: C. William Harrison
TECHNICOLOR COLOR CONSULTANT: Henri Jaffa
PRINT BY TECHNICOLOR
DIRECTOR OF PHOTOGRAPHY: Ray Rennahan, A.S.C.
ART DIRECTOR: George Brooks
FILM EDITOR: Al Clark, A.C.E.
SET DECORATORS: William Kiernan and Frank A. Tuttle
ASSISTANT DIRECTOR: Abner E. Singer
RECORDING SUPERVISOR: John Livadary
SOUND: Franklin Hansen, Jr.
MUSIC CONDUCTED BY: Mischa Bakaleinikoff
ASSISTANT TO PRODUCER: David Breen

DATES OF FILMING: Late April 1956 to May 18, 1956
LOCATION OF FILMING: Tucson, Arizona, area

CAST:

Lt. Frank Hewitt .... Audie Murphy
Ann Martin .... Kathryn Grant
Hannah Lacey .... Hope Emerson
Mary Wheeler.................. Jeff Donnell
Cora Melavan .... Jeanette Nolan
Kettle ....Sean McClory
Hetty ....Ernestine Wade
Lucy Conover .... Peggy Maley
Mrs. Ogden .... Isobel Elsom
Stella Leathem .... Patricia Livingston
Bax ....Kim Charney
Salt Pork .... Ray Teal
Tortilla ....Nestor Paiva
Kipper ....James Griffith
Indian Chief ....Charles Horvath
Col. Chivington .... Ainsile Pryor
Jane Gibbons........... Madge Meredith

RUNNING TIME: 82 minutes
RELEASE DATE: April 1957

SYNOPSIS:

The story is set in the Civil War era in the wake of the infamous Sand Creek massacre. Lt. Frank Hewitt is serving in the Union Army, but hears about the massacre near his home territory in Texas. An order from a headstrong army officer caused the massacre. Frank knows that the Indians will seek revenge and leaves his unit to go back home and help defend the homesteaders. For his concern, he is considered a deserter.

Practically all the men in the territory are away, most of them serving in the Confederate Army. The women left behind are almost defenseless against the Indians. At first, Frank has a hard time convincing the women they must arm and protect themselves for they sense no danger. When a white woman is found dead, apparently killed by Indians, Frank now persuades them to fortify at a nearby mission and to prepare for a possible attack.

Using his military training, Frank organizes the women into a fighting force; he drills them on how to shoot a rifle with accuracy by drawing a target on a wall in the shape of a Comanche Indian.

Another man, Kettle, arrives at the fort. He causes dissension by trying to get the women to leave, taking all the horses. Frank puts him in a makeshift jail, and then decides to let the horse run loose, so no one will be tempted to leave. This is for their own good. However, one of the women has fallen in love with Kettle and gets him out of jail after he promises to marry her. As soon as he is free, though, Kettle steals Frank's horse, which is still inside the fort, and rides out alone.

Kettle meets up with an outlaw gang who threaten to kill him. He tells them of the women in the fort which interests the gang, but they kill him anyway. One of the gang then takes his horse and they approach the fort. The women there welcome the extra guns in the hope that they will help. When Frank sees his horse, however, he knows something isn't right and presumes Kettle is dead. When Frank questions the men about the horse, they knock him unconscious. The women then show their guns to the men, driving them away and thus saving Frank's life.

Audie Murphy instructs Dorothy Crider in the use of a rifle in THE GUNS OF FORT PETTICOAT.

Soon after, Frank sees a dust cloud on the horizon. He guesses that the gang has met up with the Indians, and, like Kettle, tried to bargain their lives by telling them about the women and the fort.

At first, Frank thinks the fort can be made to look deserted to avoid attack. The Indians come but find no one around for Frank has hidden everyone on the roof. The Indians leave thinking there is no one there but Bax, one of the children, trips and his gun goes off accidentally. The Indians hear the shot, come back and attack the fort. It is a standoff, and as some of the women are killed, Frank realizes he must do somthing. As the ammunition starts to run out, the Indians prepare to attack again.

Frank manages to sneak out of the fort before the next attack, kills the medicine man and drags his body back to the mission. He hangs the body at the front gate of the mission as the warriors rush forward. They immediately stop the attack and flee, convinced the enemy is too powerful for them now.

The fort, and the surrounding territory are saved. Frank now faces an army court martial for his desertion, but is acquitted with the help of his "petticoat brigade."

BACKGROUND:

The movie was described by critics as: "an action-full and altogether pleasant Western;" "an amusing and exciting picture that should have more than usual appeal for a historical Western."

A critic wrote: "Audie Murphy does his role likeably;" more significant, another said: "Audie Murphy is an equally fast draw with guns and the boxoffice."

Audie was, by now, quite famous by appearing in many Westerns, which were popular, and usually provided good box office for the studio. In order to get a bigger cut of the profits, Audie and his new partner, Harry Joe Brown, formed a movie production company called, simply enough, Brown-Murphy Productions. THE GUNS OF FORT PETTICOAT was the first and only picture made by the company.

Audie admits his toughest assignment was one he faced in the Arizona desert. In this movie, he combines soldiering and acting; he trained the 40 women in the cast how to handle guns under military discipline so they could help him fight off an Indian attack as the script required.

For a week before the camera rolled, Audie presided over a stiff training regimen in the Arizona location. It involved a 5:30 a.m. rising, roll call, calisthenics, close order drill, hikes (short ones) and then target practice with rifles.

"I split my ladies' platoon in half and pitted them against each other for regular war maneuvers. During these maneuvers, the girls had to throw themselves on the rocky desert ground, crawl on knees and elbows, charge through brush and cactus and learn to load, aim and fire a rifle on the run."

After the first few hours of this, the girls were suffering from bruised and scraped elbows and knees, to say nothing of broken fingernails. So the next time around, the producer issued knee and elbow pads. He also had first-aid men standing by but, fortunately, there was not a single serious injury.

Murphy confessed he had some scares when he found many guns pointed right at him. "First time around," the star recalled, "the girls would turn their heads away and close their eyes when they pulled the trigger, but after drilling an hour or so every day, they learned how to do it properly."

JOE BUTTERFLY

STUDIO: UNIVERSAL-INTERNATIONAL

PRODUCER: Aaron Rosenberg
DIRECTOR: Jesse Hibbs
SCREENPLAY BY: Sy Gomberg, Jack Sher and Marion Hargrove
BASED ON A THREE ACT PLAY BY: Evan Wylie and Jack Ruge
DIRECTOR OF PHOTOGRAPHY: Irving Glassberg, A.S.C.
TECHNICOLOR COLOR CONSULTANT: William Fritzsche
ART DIRECTION: Alexander Golitzen and Alfred Sweeney
SET DIRECTIONS: Russell A. Gausman
SOUND: Leslie I. Carey and Joe Lapis
FILM EDITOR: Milton Carruth, A.C.E.
MAKE-UP: Bud Westmore
ASSISTANT DIRECTOR: Phil Bowles
TECHNICAL ADVISOR: Frank Dorn, Brig. Gen. USA Ret.
MUSIC SUPERVISION BY: Joseph Gershenson

DATES OF FILMING: Mid-July 1956 to August 31, 1956
LOCATION OF FILMING: The entire movie was shot in Japan.

CAST:

Private John Woodley .... Audie Murphy
Sergeant Ed Kennedy ...... George Nader
Henry Hathaway .... Keenan Wynn
Chieko .... Kieko Shima
Colonel E.E. Fuller .... Fred Clark
Sergeant Dick Mason .... John Agar
Sergeant Jim McNulty .. Charles McGraw
Little Boy .... Shinpei Shimazaki
False Tokyo Rose .... Reiko Higa
Father .... Tatsuo Saito
Mother .... Chizu Shimazaki
Major Ferguson .... Herbert Anderson
Sergeant Oscar Hulick .. Eddie Firestone
Chief Yeoman Saul Bernheim . Frank Chase
Colonel Hopper .... Herold Goodwin
Soldier .... Willard Willingham
Joe Butterfly .... Burgess Meredith

RUNNING TIME: 90 minutes
RELEASE DATE: July 1957

SYNOPSIS:

This comedy is set in post-World War II Tokyo. Shortly after VJ Day, the great influx of newly arriving American occupation troops includes the staff of the U.S. Army's weekly *Yank* publication. Their mission: quickly put out a topical issue for the troops coming into Japan. Their job is highly complicated by army brass who insist the correspondents stick to the military rules book, unworkable in this situation.

The story centers around a reporter, Sergeant Ed Kennedy, and Private John Woodley, the *Yank* photographer, who are constantly getting into the hair of the army brass. They are aided by a charming Japanese con man, Joe Butterfly, in accomplishing their mission.

Woodley never consciously plans for bad things to happen, but they seem to anyway. For instance, when he is trying to gain the best angle to photograph the arrival of the Japanese delegation as it boards a battleship, he manages to push well-known civilian reporter Henry Hathaway overboard into the harbor.

Hathaway complains, and Woodley's superior, Colonel Fuller, is almost ready to ship his ace photographer to Siberia. Meanwhile, Woodley and Kennedy continue to make Hathaway (or, as he modestly calls himself, "Hathaway the Great," personal friend to General MacArthur, etc.) miserable in trying to cover the action in the city.

Woodley finally gets the colonel's goat one too many times. Stealing a precious jar of olives from the colonel's private stock, he boldly walks into the office with it (to use with victory martinis). All this just after the colonel has informed the staff that they will share responsibility to keep Woodley out of trouble. The photographer finds himself on board a ship bound for the states.

Kennedy and the other staff need to find a place to put together and print the new issue of *Yank*. They make a deal with Joe for a "nice house in a good neighborhood." Next they need cameras and a photographer to get pictures of the elusive Tokyo Rose. Joe goes out and comes back with 15 cameras and Woodley, who somehow has managed to jump ship in Yokohama and make his way back to Tokyo. Kennedy finds out that Hathaway is also looking for Tokyo Rose.

By accident, Woodley manages to get a picture of Rose, while Joe sets up Hathaway with a fake Rose. Before Hathaway finds out about the deception, *Yank* is able to publish their exclusive scoop. Woodley and Joe turn the real Rose over to the U.S. military authorities.

BACKGROUND:

A critic wrote: "Murphy contributes

Charles McGraw, Fred Clark, and Audie Murphy with the colonel's onion-stuffed olives in this scene from JOE BUTTERFLY

his own special brand of disarming persistence." Another critic said that Audie was "quite satisfactory" in his role. This was his one starring role in a comedy. Another critic described JOE BUTTERFLY as "a lightweight farce with some romantic overtones." The plot was said to be "both original and enjoyable." Burgess Meredith's "Joe Butterfly" is a delightful comic portrayal. Most of the praise went to Meredith, as the Japanese con man was known. But the picture suffered by an inevitable comparison to TEAHOUSE OF THE AUGUST MOON, which had a character, played by Marlon Brando, similar to Joe Butterfly.

Marion Hargrove, one of the three men who wrote the screenplay for JOE BUTTERFLY, was the author of the famed World War II book *See Here Private Hargrove*. It dealt with the humorous experiences of a rookie in the army. With the bombing of Pearl Harbor, America needed a funny book about the military as a morale builder. So *See Here Private Hargrove* was a runaway success. During the war, Hargrove served on the staff of *Yank* magazine in the South Pacific Theater of War.

Here are some little tidbits relating to stories regarding Audie in Japan. Seems he had a state-side habit of falling asleep in taxicabs causing him no little mental anguish and some thousands of yen one day when he was filming JOE BUTTERFLY. Audie tried his hand that day at the native language to tell a Tokyo taxi driver he wanted to go to the Yokohama Camera Store, one of the largest photographic equipment marts in the Japanese capital. He promptly fell asleep in the back seat of the cab and awakened an hour later in the city of Yokohama, thirty miles away. The round-trip fare cost him 8000 yen—roughly $22.

During his stay in Japan, Audie received so many presents from his Japanese fans that he had to rent special storage space for them in the Nikkatsu Hotel, where the movie troupe was quartered. Audie hadn't been in Tokyo a week before his hotel suite was overflowing with chrysanthemums. "It gives you a sort of tug at the heart-strings," Audie remarked. "At home nobody sends you flowers unless you are in the hospital. Over here it's a national complimentary custom."

Next to flowers, the gift that was most popular with Audie's fans was caged crickets. Considered good luck charms by the Japanese, the chirping insects in bamboo and straw cages are to be found in most homes. After Audie had received a score of them and had spent a few sleepless nights, he gave them away to children of hotel employees.

A random survey of other gifts to the popular star revealed more than a dozen pairs of Japanese slippers and wooden sandals, a couple of dozen hand-made silk shirts, two silk kimonos, a complete Japanese skin-diving outfit (Audie's favorite sport), a model of the emperor's palace in teakwood, five sets of china tea services, an honorary first-baseman's uniform, making him a lifetime member of the Nikkatsu Dragons, a half-dozen original water colors by local artists and a small crate of Japanese mechanical toys for his two young sons.

NIGHT PASSAGE

STUDIO: UNIVERSAL-INTERNATIONAL

PRODUCER: Aaron Rosenberg
DIRECTOR: James Neilson
SCREENPLAY BY: Borden Chase
BASED ON A STORY BY: Norman A. Fox
FILMED IN TECHNIRAMA
COLOR BY TECHNICOLOR
DIRECTOR OF PHOTOGRAPHY: William Daniels
TECHNICOLOR COLOR CONSULTANT: William Fritzsche
ART DIRECTION: Alexander Golitzen and Robert Clatworthy
SET DIRECTIONS: Russell A. Gausman and Oliver Emert
SOUND: Leslie I. Carey and Frank H. Wilkinson
SECOND UNIT DIRECTOR: James C. Havens
FILM EDITOR: Sherman Todd, A.C.E.
COSTUMES: Bill Thomas
MAKE-UP: Bud Westmore
ASSISTANT DIRECTOR: Marshall Green
SPECIAL PHOTOGRAPHY: Clifford Stine, A.S.C.
MUSIC COMPOSED AND CONDUCTED BY: Dimitri Tiomkin
"Follow The River," "You Can't Get Far Without a Railroad"
LYRICS BY: Ned Washington
MUSIC BY: Dimitri Tiomkin

DATES OF FILMING: Early October 1956 to November 28, 1956
LOCATION OF FILMING: The Durango and Silverton, Colorado, areas

CAST:

Grant McLaine .... James Stewart
The Utica Kid .... Audie Murphy
Whitey Harbin .... Dan Duryea
Charlotte Drew (Charlie)..Dianne Foster
Verna Kimball .... Elaine Stewart
Joey Adams .... Brandon deWilde
Ben Kimball .... Jay C. Flippen
Will Renner .... Herbert Anderson
Concho .... Robert J. Wilke
Jeff Kurth .... Hugh Beaumont
Shotgun .... Jack Elam
Howdy Sladen .... Tommy Cook
Mr. Feeney .... Paul Fix
Miss Vittles .... Olive Carey
Tim Riley .... James Flavin
Jubilee .... Donald Curtis
Mrs. Feeney .... Ellen Corby
Latigo .... John Day
O'Brien .... Kenny Williams
Trinidad .... Frank Chase

RUNNING TIME: 90 minutes
RELEASE DATE: August 1957

SYNOPSIS:

James Stewart and Audie Murphy play brothers who are quite different. Stewart is a decent, upright man. Murphy, playing his first semi-heavy part, is an outlaw known as The Utica Kid. The story is told against a background of railroad building during the opening up of the West.

The first thing Grant McLaine encounters before riding into the railroad camp, is a boy being chased by a man. He keeps the man from forcing the lad onto his horse and sends him away. The boy is beholden to Grant but declines the offer of his stirrup for a ride to town. Joey explains to Grant that Concho is a part of a gang that robs trains, banks, etc. and that Whitey Harbin is the leader, a real bad guy and almost as crazy as he is bad.

Grant arrives at the camp where the workers are waiting for their pay. Three times the train has been robbed, and if the money doesn't come on the next work train, the men threaten to quit. The wives make them stay on for a little longer in hopes of the payroll getting through. Grant makes his way to Junction City at the request of Ben Kimball, his former boss, who is in charge of seeing that the track is finished.

Grant is offered the job of carrying the next payroll. Ben tells him Whitey Harbin and his gang have held up the last three trains. Years ago, Grant was a trouble shooter for the railroad but had allowed The Utica Kid to get away with a robbery by giving him a horse. When it was found out that the outlaw happened to be his brother, Grant was fired. For five years Grant has been playing the accordion for nickels and dimes. Now, out of desperation, Ben is asking that he carry the payroll once again. Grant accepts. At one time, Grant and Ben's wife Verna, were in love. Grant had asked her to marry him but she wouldn't back him up when he needed help; he left and she married Ben.

Dianne Foster, Audie Murphy, and Brandon deWilde with the railroad payroll in this scene from NIGHT PASSAGE

Grant again meets up with Joey who wants a job at end of track. The two ride together for a while outside for a little fresh air. However, the soot from the train soon has them inside. Concho is also aboard the train whereas Joey gives Grant the lowdown on him.

Meanwhile, Whitey Harbin and his bunch are waiting in an abandoned mining camp to hear from Concho about the payroll train's location. Whitey wants to hit the train again but Utica feels it's too risky since they have robbed three in a row. However, Whitey gets his way. The gang holds up the train but can't locate the money. During the robbery, Grant hides the money in a box in which Joey has a sandwich. Whitey is furious that he couldn't find the payroll, so he decides to take Verna hostage for $10,000. Concho takes revenge on Grant and knocks him unconscious, whereas Utica rides up and takes Joey with him, not knowing Grant was on the train.

Charlie, Utica's girlfriend, rides to the hideout and waits for Utica to return. The gang holds up waiting for the money. Tension builds between Whitey and Utica.

Grant makes his way to the hideout. He sees Charlie and as they are talking, they are surprised by Howdy, another gang member. Grant silences him and ties him up. Before going after Verna, Charlie asks Grant to tell Utica she is waiting for him. Upon his arrival at the gang's hideout, Utica is shocked to see Grant. He certainly did not expect to see his brother show up. Grant asks to join up with the gang but Utica is against it. When Whitey questions his reasons, Utica tells him they are brothers. Now Whitey wants Grant in the gang, just to make The Kid mad, but now Concho speaks up. He has his own reasons for not wanting Grant around. Grant kills Concho in a shootout.

Finally, Grant and Utica have a talk outside. Grant wants Utica to let Joey go but Utica wants him to stay with him. He then tells Utica that Charlie is waiting for him in the barn. Utica tells Grant that they are getting married. Charlie wants to leave that night, but Utica tells her that after tomorrow they will have $10,000. Charlie changes her mind. She won't marry him because he steals things from people. She can't live like that and refuses to go with him. Utica goes back to the hideout where Grant has begun playing an old familiar tune on his accordion. Suddenly Utica shows a sign of sentimentality and recites the words to a childhood song.

Before long, Renner, who is Whitey's contact and who works for Kimball, comes in after hearing the accordion and tells Whitey that Grant was carrying the payroll. Grant tosses the accordion at a lamp and, in the confusion and dark, manages to get away with Verna. They get Charlie and the three of them ride to the mine.

Grant sends Verna out in an ore bucket on a conveyor belt. He wants Charlie to go when the next one comes around but she won't. She and Grant try desperately to hold off the outlaws but the odds are against them. Utica watches from a distance and finally, with Joey's urging, decides to help Grant. The brothers kill all but one gang member, Whitey. Utica, redeeming himself in trying to save Grant's life, is shot by Whitey and with one bullet left in his gun, gives it to Grant, who kills Whitey. Utica is hit hard and reminisces with Grant about their father's favorite tune, then dies in his arms. Grant, Charlie and Joey go to end of track together.

BACKGROUND:

Audie Murphy has become the first top action star in Hollywood history to undergo, at the height of a fabulously successful career, the transition from hero to villain. Grasping an opportunity to change pace which has been consistently shunned by such movie greats as Alan Ladd, Gary Cooper and John Wayne, Murphy co-stars with James Stewart as his bad brother.

"The only thing of importance," said Audie, "is to stay on the screen and I'm here through the whole story. So what's all the fuss about?" The fuss is about a tradition the fans want Murphy to cling to. They want their heroes to do in all the "heavies" and ride off into the sunset with the heroine. They do not relish their favorites biting the dust.

On the other hand, Audie Murphy is not one to walk the line of convention. "I hate to use a cliche," he said, "but variety is still the spice of life. I've been in a rut. Too much sweetness and light. In NIGHT PASSAGE, I'm a bad boy and I love it."

This movie was described as a "top-grade, action-filled outdoor drama," and was a big grosser at the boxoffice. A critic said: "Audie Murphy gives a sound performance as a wild and deadly gunman." A second critic wrote: "Stacked up against the seasoned James Stewart, Audie reveals a sheer talent for acting. He holds his own against Stewart throughout the picture."

THE GLENN MILLER STORY, which starred James Stewart, and TO HELL AND BACK were two of Universal's all-time big money-makers. So Aaron Rosenberg, who produced both pictures, took the star of each, James Stewart and Audie Murphy, and cast them together in NIGHT PASSAGE. The combination produced what Rosenberg expected—a boxoffice winner.

This was the sixth Murphy movie that Rosenberg had produced. Following NIGHT PASSAGE, Rosenberg moved from Universal to the Metro-Goldwyn-Mayer Studio but he retained one agreement with Universal. If that studio ever made the Audie Murphy post-war story, Rosenberg would return to Universal and produce it. This story, titled THE WAY BACK, was never filmed because nobody could come up with a screenplay that was satisfactory to both Audie and Universal. Two screenplays were written and Jesse Hibbs was supposed to direct the movie. Audie finally bought his post-war story from Universal and planned to produce the movie himself but he never got around to doing it.

THE QUIET AMERICAN

STUDIO: UNITED ARTISTS (Release)

PRODUCER: Joseph L. Mankiewicz
WRITTEN FOR THE SCREEN AND DIRECTED BY: Joseph L. Mankiewicz
BASED ON A NOVEL BY: Graham Greene
SETTINGS BY: Rino Mondellini
ASSISTANT DIRECTOR: Piero Mussetta
SOUND RECORDING: Basil Fenton-Smith
CAMERA OPERATOR: John Harris
SET DRESSING: Dario Simon
MAKE-UP: George Frost
CONTINUITY: Elaine Schreyeck
SPECIAL EFFECTS: Rocky Cline
PHOTOGRAPHY BY: Robert Krasker
EDITED BY: William Hornbeck, A.C.E.
ART DIRECTOR: Rino Mondellino
MUSIC BY: Mario Nascimbene
CONDUCTED BY: Franco Ferrara
MANAGER OF PRODUCTION: Forrest E. Johnston
PRODUCTION ASSOCIATES: Michele Waszynski and Vinh Noan
SOUND MIXER: Basil Fenton-Smith

DATES OF FILMING: January 28, 1957 to mid-May 1957
LOCATION OF FILMING: Vietnam and Italy (mostly around Saigon and the Cinecitta Studios in Rome)

CAST:

The American .... Audie Murphy
Thomas Fowler .... Michael Redgrave
Inspector Vigot .... Claude Dauphin
Phuong .... Giorgia Moll
Bill Granger .... Bruce Cabot
Dominguez .... Fred Sadoff
Phuong's Sister .... Kerima
Mister Heng .... Richard Loo
Eliot Wilkins .... Peter Trent
Joe Morton .... Clinton Anderson
Hostess .... Yoko Tani
Yvette .... Sonia Moser
Isabelle .... Phyng-Thi Nghiep
Cao-Dai CommandantVo Doan Chau
Cao-Dai Pope's Deputy .... Le Van Le
Masked Man .... Le Quynh
French Colonel .... Georges Brehat

RUNNING TIME: 120 minutes
RELEASE DATE: February 1958

SYNOPSIS:

Saigon, Vietnam; Chinese New Year, 1952. French troops are fighting against a rebel Communist Army in the northern provinces. However, in Saigon, the New Year is a time of celebration. Amidst the revelry, a man's body is found floating in the river. The police arrive to investigate. It is the body of an American economic adviser.

Fowler, a British news correspondent, is waiting to meet with the American. Also waiting, and worried, is his former mistress, Phuong, who has left Fowler after a two year relationship, to be with the American. They plan to be married. The French police inspector is aware that Fowler and the American are acquainted and asks Fowler to identify the body. He also asks Fowler where he was when the murder occurred. Fowler has an alibi.

At the morgue, Fowler identifies the American's body, and in flashbacks, begins to recall how they met in a restaurant the month before. The American explains his economic mission. It is expected that eventually the French will leave the country, allowing it to be independent. The American wants to promote a free government and economy. Soon, the American invites Fowler and Phuong to dinner. At dinner, the American asks Phuong to dance, leaving Fowler alone and jealous.

Several days later, the men meet again unexpectedly near the war zone. During the conversation, the American tells Fowler he is in love with Phuong and wants to marry her. Fowler is incensed, knowing the American has more to offer her. Fowler is married and his wife will not grant a simple divorce. Fowler also finds out he is being promoted in his news organization, and is to be transferred back to England.

Back in Saigon, the American wants to ask Phuong to marry him, but it is difficult because Phuong understands little English. Although an awkward situation, the American prevails upon Fowler to interpret for him. The scene becomes tense and Phuong breaks off the proposal without answering. Fowler decides to ask his wife again for a divorce.

The American's mission brings him to Tay Ninh, where he confers with the Coadist Commandant, who wants to make Vietnam independent. Fowler arrives to find that the American's car won't start. Both men need to return to Saigon before dark, when the Communists take over the roads.

The American accepts Fowler's offer to ride back to Saigon, but Fowler's car soon runs out of gas. As darkness falls, the men try to hide from the approaching Communists. Fowler breaks his leg, but the American saves him. With help from the French Army, they get back safely to Saigon.

While Fowler recuperates in the hospital, Phuong comes to visit. While she is there, Fowler reads a letter from his wife. She still refuses to grant a divorce. But, he lies to Phuong, telling her the opposite. Fowler feels bad about lying, but is desperate to keep Phuong with him. Fowler tells the American the same lie.

Fowler is informed that the American's trade mission may be more sinister than thought. He is made aware that the American may have imported explosives or weapons for the independence movement.

Phuong finds out that Fowler is lying about getting the divorce from his wife. She tells the American, who soon confronts Fowler. Fowler counters by asking about the "plastics" that the American has imported. The American doesn't understand his concerns.

Fowler returns to his flat to find that Phuong has left him. He is angry and upset. Soon after, a large explosion rocks the center of town. Fowler en-

Michael Redgrave and Audie Murphy, discussing car trouble in this scene from THE QUIET AMERICAN

counters the American and accuses him of smuggling the explosive material for the bombs. The American becomes angry and goes off to help some of the injured.

Fowler is approached by Vietnamese who wish to get rid of the American. With Fowler's help, they can set up a scheme for murder. Fowler invites the American for dinner. They talk about the independence movement again. The American also tells Fowler he is being sent back to the States and is taking Phuong with him.

Fowler had intended to tell the American about the plot against him, but now changes his mind. As the American leaves, he signals to men waiting outside the building. He knows that the American will be killed.

Although Fowler has an alibi, the inspector is still suspicious. Eventually, Fowler confesses that he knew about having the American murdered. However, he is not charged with any crime and leaves to find Phuong. He tries to persuade her to come back to him, but she refuses. Fowler leaves, completely dejected, losing himself in the crowd of New Year celebrants.

BACKGROUND:

The original Graham Greene novel was considered anti-American. *The Quiet American* represented the determined naiveté of American foreign policy in Asia. In adapting the book to the screen, Joseph L. Mankiewicz changed the story enough to make it pro-American. In so doing, some critics thought that he drained the character, played by Audie, of meaning.

One critic predicted that THE QUIET

AMERICAN might well be the best American movie released in 1958. The critics were also divided over the Murphy performance. Most agreed with the reviewer who wrote: "Audie, with his fine war record and quiet charm, seemed perfectly cast in the title role." He was in real-life the quiet American.

One reviewer wrote: "Joseph Mankiewicz gets from Murphy a very interesting and mettlesome performance as the do-good American."

After DESTRY and the phenomenal success of TO HELL AND BACK, the Murphy screen career shot up to an all-time high. Four thousand British exhibitors voted Audie the top Western star with English audiences. He was getting all kinds of movie offers, but his salary remained at $75,000 for starring roles.

A little bit of trivia tells us that Audie smoked his first cigarette, on or off screen. Also, the fifty or so people involved in this film spent three months in Saigon under somewhat less than ideal conditions. They spent several weeks preparing for this journey with a host of inoculations for various diseases. The temperature seldom was below 100 degrees and the hotel accommodations did not include air-conditioning. The ailments, too, were common frequently in the form of stomach disorders from the distinct food variety offered.

Only two hotels housed the crew which offered various forms of entertainment, such as card games and chess. Once the picture started and the cameras began to roll, all energy was focused on one thing—making the movie.

Michael Redgrave and Audie Murphy, having a serious conversation in this scene from THE QUIET AMERICAN

RIDE A CROOKED TRAIL

STUDIO: UNIVERSAL-INTERNATIONAL

PRODUCER: Howard Pine
DIRECTOR: Jesse Hibbs
SCREENPLAY BY: Borden Chase
BASED ON A STORY BY: George Bruce
DIRECTOR OF PHOTOGRAPHY: Harold Lipstein, A.S.C.
ART DIRECTION: Alexander Golitzen and Bill Newberry
SET DIRECTIONS: Russell A. Gausman and Ray A. Jeffers
SOUND: Leslie I. Carey and Donald McKay
EASTMAN COLOR BY PATHE
FILM EDITOR: Edward Curtis, A.C.E.
COSTUMES: Bill Thomas
MAKE-UP: Bud Westmore
ASSISTANT DIRECTOR: William Holland
MUSIC SUPERVISION BY: Joseph Gershenson

DATES OF FILMING: August 26, 1957 to October 7, 1957
LOCATION OF FILMING: Greater Los Angeles area, including Ventura Canyon, Janns Ranch, and Universal Studio

CAST:

Joe Maybe .... Audie Murphy
Tessa .... Gia Scala
Judge Kyle .... Walter Matthau
Sam Teeler .... Henry Silva
Little Brandy .... Joanna Moore
Jimmy .... Eddie Little
Mrs. Curtis .... Mary Field
Pecos .... Mort Mills

RUNNING TIME: 87 minutes
RELEASE DATE: September 1958

SYNOPSIS:

Being chased by a lawman, Joe Maybe rides into town where Judge Kyle is stopping all strangers because there is a bank robber on the loose. Joe is that bank robber but when the judge checks the wallet in the saddlebags, he mistakes Joe for Marshal Noonan. The marshal was the one chasing Joe when he was accidentally killed so Joe took his horse. Since the town has no sheriff, the judge welcomes Joe with open arms and swears him in. Joe doesn't want any part of this charade but really has no choice in the matter. It's either become marshal or go to jail for being a bank robber.

Joe takes on a hot-headed cowboy as his first order of business. This impresses Kyle and they celebrate by getting drunk. The judge is no stranger to whiskey but poor Joe isn't used to liquor and wakes up to the swaying motion of the judge's houseboat when he thinks he's on dry land.

The steamboat docks bringing unsavory characters whom Judge Kyle personally escorts back to the boat. Also on board is Tessa, an old friend of Joe's. She has come to town to meet her boyfriend, Sam Teeler, who is also a bank robber. She is to find out how the bank works then send for Sam so he and his gang can rob it. When she sees Joe, she calls out to him "Maybe!" Joe does some fast thinking and tells her about his role in town. She asks him what he thinks he is doing and he tells her "trying to stay alive." The judge overhears her call him as Joe explains that Tessa is his wife and often calls him "baby." The judge finds this humorous. Joe uses Tessa as a reason to leave town and tells the judge that she wants to go back to New Orleans. The judge, wanting them to stay, takes them to a nicely furnished house to entice Tessa, thus keeping the marshal.

While a celebration is going on, Sam Teeler and his men ride into town. Sam breaks into the saloon. Joe follows him to find out what he wants. Sam knows about Joe and Tessa "playing house" and tells Joe he doesn't like it. Sam wants to hit the bank but Joe persuades him to wait for the trail herds to come in because that's where the big money is. He tells Sam to wait for him out of town and he'll send for him. Sam agrees.

Tessa and Joe go home where she tells him she is tired of the masquerade. Joe informs her that he will be sending for Teeler as soon as they empty the bank; then they will all leave together. While they are talking, they discover that Jimmy, who is an orphan living with the judge, has been in the kitchen and has overheard their conversation. Jimmy knows that they are not really married but pretends that things are on the up and up, especially

Eddie Little, Gia Scala, Audie Murphy, and Walter Mathau, discovering that "Sheriff Noonan" is really Joe Maybe in a scene from RIDE A CROOKED TRAIL

where the judge is concerned. Jimmy believes that the judge would put them both in jail if he knew the truth. Jimmy decides that he is not welcome with Joe and Tessa and moves back in with the judge.

Tessa finds out that Jimmy is missing and tells Joe. During their talk, Joe finds out that Jimmy was born in a saloon (just like Joe) and that his mother died very young. Joe tells Jimmy that he started out that way and after a while, convinces Jimmy to move back much to Tessa's delight.

All through the conversation, Judge Kyle had been sitting outside the houseboat and has heard everything. Jimmy talks with the judge the next day only to find out that the judge is out to get Joe. Jimmy makes good sense when he talks about Joe saying that he's not really a bad guy, but just had some bad breaks. Just then, the deputy comes in to inform the judge that the trail herd is coming.

Jimmy goes along with Joe on the trail drive but accidentally starts the herd running and is caught in the stampede. Joe picks up the boy who has fallen off his horse and takes him back to the house. Joe starts to tend Jimmy's cuts but Tessa sends him for the doctor. While Joe is gone, Sam pays a visit to Tessa to tell her that he is going to rob the bank. He tells her his plan. She is to keep Judge Kyle and the deputy busy late into the night then she is to take them over to the River Palace. While they are all dancing, an explosion is heard. It is in the direction of the bank. Judge Kyle believes that Joe has something to do with it and arrests him. Before the judge can do anything, Jimmy sees what is happening and, from his bedroom window, shoots out the lamp. Joe escapes and heads out after Teeler who is hiding out in the herd. Sam tries to make a deal with Joe but he doesn't want any part of it. After a fight, he brings Sam back to town.

Joe finds Tessa waiting for him at the boat dock along with Judge Kyle and Jimmy. Joe starts to leave, but Kyle stops him. Joe thinks that he's being arrested but the judge knows that Joe has stopped the bank robbery and brought in Teeler. He wants Joe to stay on as marshal and pins his badge back on. Jimmy informs the judge that Joe is going to get a broken back sleeping in the bathtub and that he'd better marry them. The judge orders Joe and Tessa to his chambers at 9:00 sharp the next morning.

BACKGROUND:

This Western movie was called: "fair entertainment for the general public;" also "heartwarming." Audie was complimented for his handling of "salty humor" and for the underplaying of the character he portrayed in his customary fashion.

RIDE A CROOKED TRAIL was originally called BROKEN STAR, then MIDDLE OF THE STREET, before getting its final title.

Audie may well be the world's bravest man, but he still trembles whenever a screenplay calls for him to kiss a girl, an assignment he is called upon to execute with enthusiasm in partnership with the Irish-Italian beauty Gia Scala. Audie, has a number of torrid love scenes with Miss Scala, and to make things worse for the kiss-timid Audie, he had never even met Gia before the picture began shooting.

THE GUN RUNNERS

STUDIO: UNITED ARTISTS (release)

PRODUCER: Clarence Greene
DIRECTOR: Donald Siegel
BASED ON A STORY BY: Ernest Hemingway
SCREENPLAY BY: Daniel Mainwaring and Paul Monash
DIRECTOR OF PHOTOGRAPHY: Hal Mohr, A.S.C.
MUSIC BY: Leith Stevens
IN CHARGE OF PRODUCTION: Herbert E. Stewart
FILM EDITOR: Chester Schaeffer, A.C.E.
ASSISTANT TO PRODUCER: Paul Stone
SONG: "Havana Holiday"
WORDS & MUSIC BY: Joe Lubin and Jerome Howard
ASSISTANT DIRECTOR: Willard Reineck
SOUND: Frank Goodwin and Roger Heman
ART DIRECTOR: Howard Richmond
WOMEN'S COSTUMES: Bernice Pontrelli
MEN'S COSTUMES: Morris Friedman
HAIR STYLIST: Lillian Shore
MAKEUP ARTISTS: Frank Fitz-Gibbon and Vince Romaine
SET DECORATOR: Darrell Silvera
PROPERTY MASTER: Walter Veady

DATES OF FILMING: January 28, 1958 to February 26, 1958
LOCATION OF FILMING: Balboa and Newport Bay, California

CAST:

Sam Martin ....Audie Murphy
Lucy Martin .... Patricia Owens
Hannigan .... Eddie Albert
Harve .... Everett Sloane
Eva Waldstrom ....Gita Hall
Sy Phillips .... Paul Birch
Arnold .... Jack Elam
Pop .... John Qualen

RUNNING TIME: 83 minutes
RELEASE DATE: September 1958

SYNOPSIS:

Sam Martin has a boat called the "Lucy M" where he makes his living taking out big game fishermen. While he and his mate, Harve, are preparing to go out on a charter, they are confronted by two men who want to use Sam's boat for illegal purposes. Sam refuses because if he gets caught, he could lose the boat on which he is still paying. A policeman approaches them, recognizes the men as crooks and draws a gun in an attempt to arrest them. One of the men pulls a knife and kills him. The crooks take off as Sam heads for the boat.

After chartering his boat to a man, Sam tries to collect his money. At the hotel where the man is staying, he finds out the guy has been passing bad checks and has been arrested. Sam needs the money to pay off his creditors. In desperation, he stops by Pop's pawn shop where he hocks his fishing reel. Pop has a gaming room in the back of his store so Sam tries his luck at the slot machine. It pays off. Maybe this will be his lucky day. Unfortunately, he loses everything at the crap table.

The next day, Hannigan whom he met the previous night at Pop's, asks to charter Sam's boat. Hannigan knows of Sam's financial troubles and after a few hours at sea, wants to take a little side trip to Havana. Sam is reluctant and informs Hannigan that he needs clearance to go to Cuba but Hannigan still wants to go. Sam will only go if Hannigan pays him $500. Hannigan agrees.

Upon their arrival in Havana, Sam tells Hannigan and Eva, Hannigan's girlfriend, to be back at the boat by 2:00 a.m. or he's leaving with or without them. He doesn't want to risk getting caught and losing everything. However, by 2:30 they still haven't returned so Sam checks on Harve, his mate, who is sleeping, leaves the boat and goes looking for them. He finally finds Eva in a night club waiting for Hannigan. Unbeknownst to Sam, Hannigan is making a deal to sell guns to a group of revolutionaries.

Driving back to the boat, a Cuban guard asks to see Hannigan's papers. Hannigan kills the guard and the taxi driver and drives back to the boat where Sam is waiting. Sam is unaware that anything is wrong but has a feeling that things aren't on the level.

Lucy, Sam's wife, is waiting as they pull into dock the next morning. Shortly thereafter, the Coast Guard wants to talk to Sam. It seems as though they received a report of a small charter fishing boat having been seen in Cuban waters. When he gets to the station, Harve is being questioned, but since he was asleep, knows nothing about a trip to Cuba. After his interrogation, he asks Sam if they were in Cuba but Sam tells him they were never there. When questioned

Audie Murphy, being questioned by the Commander of Coast Guard in a scene from THE GUN RUNNERS

by the Commander, Sam lies to him telling him that he took out a sportsman and a blonde fishing.

While Sam is on the boat, Eva comes aboard to tell him that Hannigan has another deal and is waiting for him. Sam doesn't want anything to do with Hannigan but his hands are tied since Eva tells him that Hannigan has bought his boat. Sam is very angry and confronts Sy, who holds the deed to the boat, telling him that he thought he was doing him a favor by selling it to his friend. Sam tells Sy that this will put him out of business.

Sam finds out from Harve that a deputy is waiting for him with foreclosure papers. Sam has no choice but to hand over his keys. Not knowing what to do, Sam heads for Pop's and asks to borrow $2,000. Not having that kind of money, Sam goes to the hotel and confronts Hannigan. Hannigan, in turn, blackmails Sam telling him he will go to the Coast Guard and let them know it was Sam who went to Cuba. Sam can't do anything except agree to take Hannigan back to Cuba where Hannigan assures him he will get back his boat and $5,000. However, there are strings attached to this deal. Harve is not to be included on this trip. Lucy, not knowing that Harve isn't going, is worried about Sam and urges Harve to keep an eye on him. Harve sneaks aboard without Sam's knowledge.

As Sam is getting his things together, Lucy gives him a rifle in case of trouble. Sam is securing it as Hannigan boards with one of the revolutionaries. They take off and Hannigan gives Sam a different location then last time. Lucy watches anxiously as they disappear from view.

They dock briefly while Hannigan brings the guns aboard for the rebels. As they are carrying the boxes, one falls and breaks open revealing the weapons. The other crate is carried on board and stored in the cabin. Sam is below when Harve reveals his presence to him. Sam makes Harve stay hidden and not to come out until he tells him.

One of the revolutionaries is curious about the other crate and pries it open. Instead of finding guns, he finds scrap iron. He is angry and tries to kill Hannigan's men, but is killed himself and thrown overboard. Upon hearing the shots, Sam witnesses the killing and stops the boat. Hannigan orders him to start the engine and not to stop again.

Harve tries to sneak up on the other crook but is caught. Hannigan wants to shoot Harve but Sam steps in front of him. Hannigan threatens to kill them both but Sam points out that he's the only one who can steer the boat and read a compass. Hannigan agrees to let Harve go but he must remain below. Sam tells Harve that the next time he stops the boat to jump overboard. He has a plan.

Sam slowly and gradually changes course. Then, he pretends there is something wrong with the engine and stops. He uses this excuse to look for the rifle. However, Hannigan has found it and forces Sam to restart the engine. Harve, obeying Sam's orders, has jumped overboard. As the men try to shoot Harve, Sam makes a hard turn and throws Hannigan's men off balance. This gives Sam the opportunity to immobilize Hannigan and kill the two crooks. As Sam is trying to get Harve back in the boat, Hannigan

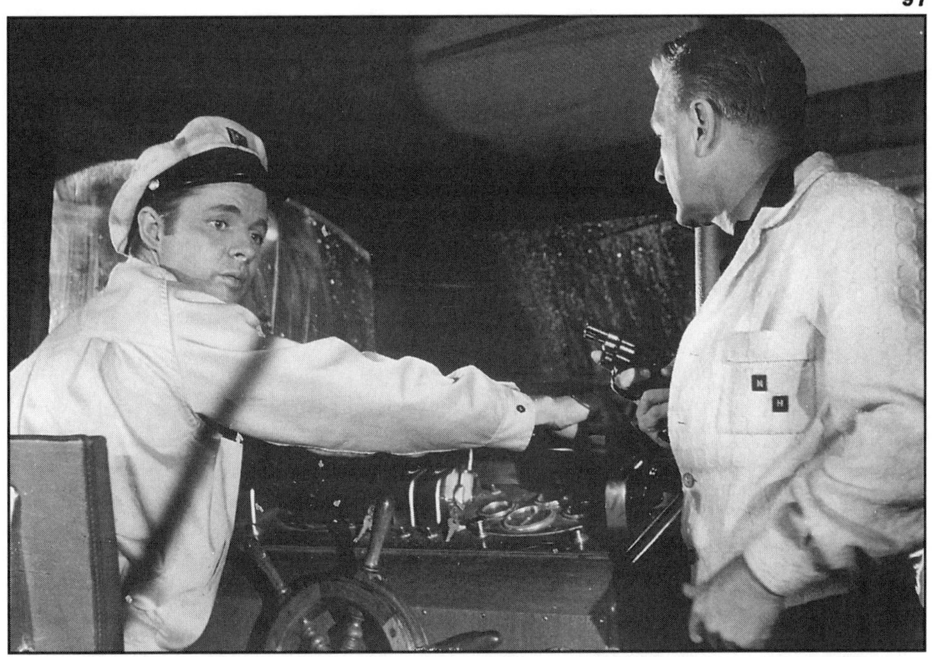

Audie Murphy, under the gun of Eddie Albert in THE GUN RUNNERS

regains consciousness and shoots Sam. Sam kills Hannigan, picks up Harve and they head back home where Lucy is waiting.

BACKGROUND:

THE GUN RUNNERS was described by a critic as "a solid film carefully produced" but admitted that "its main chance at the boxoffice lies in Audie Murphy."

Audie got especially good reviews on his acting job. One critic wrote: "Audie Murphy uses a touch of understanding and a good deal of love in his portrayal of a small boat captain." Another critic called the Murphy performance "strongly appealing." It was also pointed out that "Audie brings an unexpected playfulness to bedroom scenes that is very winning."

THE GUN RUNNERS was a second re-make of the Ernest Hemingway novel titled *To Have and To Have Not*. The original movie version, released in January 1945, starred Humphrey Bogart and Lauren Bacall. The picture made an instant star of Bacall. In it she had the famous line: "If you want anything, just whistle."

Warner Brothers Studio re-filmed the Hemingway story under the title of THE BREAKING POINT. This version starred John Garfield and Patricia Neal. It was released in September 1950. Warner Brothers then sold the story to Eliot Hyman and Ray Stark of Seven Arts Production.

Ernest Hemingway strongly objected to the second re-make because it changed his original story from rum-running to gun-running for Cuban revolutionaries. However, there was little he could do about the alteration as the story had been sold outright.

NO NAME ON THE BULLET

STUDIO: UNIVERSAL-INTERNATIONAL

PRODUCERS: Howard Christie and Jack Arnold
DIRECTOR: Jack Arnold
SCREENPLAY BY: Gene L. Coon
BASED ON A STORY BY: Howard Amacker
DIRECTOR OF PHOTOGRAPHY: Harold Lipstein, A.S.C.
EASTMAN COLOR BY PATHE
ART DIRECTION: Alexander Golitzen and Robert E. Smith
SET DIRECTIONS: Russell A. Gausman and Theodore Driscoll
SOUND: Leslie I. Carey and Frank Wilkinson
FILM EDITOR: Frank Gross, A.C.E.
COSTUMES: Bill Thomas
MAKE-UP: Bud Westmore
HAIR STYLIST: Larry Germain
ASSISTANT DIRECTOR: John Sherwood
MUSIC: Herman Stein
MUSIC SUPERVISION BY: Joseph Gershenson

DATES OF FILMING: Early September 1958 to September 26, 1958
LOCATION OF FILMING: Los Angeles area and Universal Studio

CAST:

John Gant .... Audie Murphy
Luke Canfield .... Charles Drake
Anne Benson .... Joan Evans
Roseanne Fraden .... Virginia Grey
Lou Fraden .... Warren Stevens
Asa Canfield .... R.G. Armstrong
Buck Hastings .... Willis Bouchey
Judge Benson .... Edgar Stehli
Reeger .... Simon Scott
Stricker .... Karl Swenson
Pierce .... Whit Bissell
Sid .... Charles Watts
Chaffee .... John Alderson
Harold Miller .... Jerry Paris
Storekeeper .... Russ Bender
Hugo Mott .... Jim Ryland

RUNNING TIME: 77 minutes
RELEASE DATE: February 1959

SYNOPSIS:

John Gant is a hired killer. His appearance in any town means that someone is going to die. Gant's strategy is always to kill in self defense and his reputation is well known. He has the same pattern. Arriving in a town, Gant checks into the hotel, and by not hinting who his intended victim is, sets up a vicious chain reaction.

Town banker, Thad Pierce and freight line operator Earl Stricker think Gant has come to kill them for stealing a mine from Ben Chaffee. Others have the same feeling that they are being targeted to be killed by Gant.

During his stay in Lordsburg, the townsfolk are getting very nervous, fighting amongst themselves and accusing each other for bringing Gant to town. Each major figure in town has a reason to be afraid for his life. Gant meets Luke Canfield, the town doctor and vet and wind up playing chess together. During the game, Luke is asking Gant questions about why he is in Lordsburg. While Gant pauses for a moment and looks in the direction of the bank, a gunshot rings out. Luke rushes in to find Thad Pierce has committed suicide due to the pressure of Gant's appearance. Pierce had a guilty conscience and couldn't face it. Other townspeople, also with guilty pasts, goad the sheriff into a showdown with Gant. Gant shoots the sheriff but when asked why he didn't kill him, Gant answered that he wasn't paid to. This gives the sheriff a feeling of relief, however, he can't stop Gant with his arm in a sling.

Luke, sensing that Gant is bringing panic to all of Lordsburg, talks things over with his fiance and her ailing, elderly father, Judge Benson. The judge suggests that whomever Gant is looking for, sacrifice his life to make Gant draw first. This will make Gant a murderer, bring him to justice and will hang. Luke, being a physician, does not go along with this theory at all.

Meanwhile, Lou Fraden, one of Stricker's clerks, gets drunk enough from his wife's constant badgering about his manhood to confront Gant in the saloon. Gant calls his bluff and Lou leaves town. Stricker then forms a mob to get Gant to tell them who he's after by threatening to kill him. Gant warns the men that he will get several of them before he is killed. This gives the mob reason to leave since they know that Gant will indeed make good on his threat.

Audie Murphy, being put out of action by the blacksmith's hammer in this scene from NO NAME ON THE BULLET

Gant makes contact with Anne Benson in the general store and walks her part way home. He talks to her about her father at which time she informs him of his terminal illness. As he questions her further about his past, she gets angry at him and walks away. Luke and the judge are horrified to find out that Gant even bothered to speak to her, but the judge now knows that he's Gant's target. Anne finds her father looking through some papers but quickly puts them away as she approaches him.

Anne's curiousity gets the best of her and, after checking to see if her father is around, finds the letters and begins reading one of them. She finds out that Gant is after her father. She goes to see Gant at the hotel and begs him not to kill her father since his doesn't have long to live. When he refuses, she pulls out a gun and threatens to kill him. He tricks her into believing there aren't any bullets in the gun. She looks away briefly and he grabs her arm as the gun goes off. Anne reveals that her father won't defend himself against Gant. She tells him that he won't resist Gant and that if he kills her father, he'll hang. Gant, unruffled by this, rips a portion of her dress, locks her in the closet and checks out of the hotel.

Upon hearing the gunshot, some of the men in the hotel get Luke. He finds Anne hysterical and she tells Luke that Gant is after the judge. Luke and Asa take off after him.

Gant arrives at the house, where he approaches the judge. The judge, not surprised to see Gant, knows that information he has will put him and most of his colleagues in jail for a very long time. He's been dying for a long time, but Gant informs him his associates are impatient. He also tells Gant that he isn't going to resist him and that he will hang for murder if he kills him. He informs the judge that others have tried to resist but they all wound up trying. Since the judge won't defend himself, Gant pulls out the piece of Anne's dress implying he found her to be very pleasant company. The judge is enraged demanding to know what Gant did to her. He threatens to kill Gant. He gets a rifle and follows him outside where he dies of a heart attack.

Luke and his father drive up in the buckboard. As Gant leaves, Luke tries to stop him but Gant shoots him in the shoulder. Luke tosses a blacksmith's hammer at Gant, shattering his gun arm. This will put him out of commission as a gunfighter. When Luke finds out that Gant didn't shoot the judge, he offers to look at the arm but Gant refuses. He rides off not knowing who will be around the bend to kill him.

BACKGROUND:

NO NAME ON THE BULLET was described by a critic: "everything about this film is delightful."

Audie's performance was rated from "routine" to "outstanding." One critic wrote: "Murphy handles his role with his customary easy manner."

This movie has the distinct pleasure of being one of the "shootingest" motion pictures ever filmed. For most outdoor action pictures the studio assigns just one property man to handle guns and bullets, but for this one they needed two.

THE WILD AND THE INNOCENT

STUDIO: UNIVERSAL-INTERNATIONAL

PRODUCER: Sy Gomberg
DIRECTOR: Jack Sher
SCREENPLAY BY: Sy Gomberg and Jack Sher
STORY BY: Sy Gomberg
DIRECTOR OF PHOTOGRAPHY: Harold Lipstein, A.S.C.
EASTMAN COLOR BY PATHE
ART DIRECTION: Alexander Golitzen and Robert Clatworthy
SET DECORATIONS: Russell A. Gausman and William P. Tapp
SOUND: Leslie I. Carey and Joe Lapis
FILM EDITOR: George Gittens, A.C.E.
COSTUMES: Bill Thomas
MAKE-UP: Bud Westmore
HAIR STYLIST: Larry Germain
ASSISTANT DIRECTORS: William Holland and Frank Shaw
SPECIAL PHOTOGRAPHY: Clifford Stine, A.S.C.
MUSIC: Hans J. Salter
MUSIC SUPERVISION BY: Joseph Gershenson
"Touch of Pink" WRITTEN BY: Diane Lampert and Richard Loring

DATES OF FILMING: Late October 1958 to November 13, 1958
LOCATION OF FILMING: Big Bear, California, area

CAST:

Yancey .... Audie Murphy
Marcy .... Joanne Dru
Paul .... Gilbert Roland
Mr. Forbes .... Jim Backus
Rosalie .... Sandra Dee
Uncle Lije .... George Mitchell
Chip .... Peter Breck
Ben Stocker .... Strother Martin
Ma Ransome .... Wesley Marie Tackitt
Mrs. Forbes .... Betty Harford
Pitchman .... Mel Leonard
Kiri .... Lillian Adams
Richie .... Val Benedict
Henchman .... Jim Sheppard
Henchman .... Ed Stroll
Henchman .... John Qualls
Henchman .... Frank Wolff
Dancehall Girl .... Rosemary Eliot
Dancehall Girl .... Barbara Morris
Dancehall Girl .... Louise Glenn
Bouncer .... Stephen Roberts
Townswoman .... Tammy Windsor

RUNNING TIME: 84 minutes
RELEASE DATE: May 1959

SYNOPSIS:

Yancey Hawks works with his uncle as a fur trapper. While the uncle and his wife tend their camp, Yancey is off to the trading post to barter furs for supplies. When he arrives, he discovers the trading post has burned down. Some drunken Indians have accidentally torched the building. Yancey still needs supplies but the closest town is Casper, a two day ride.

Another trader offers his daughter to Yancey in exchange for half his pelts. Yancey is outraged and sends the man away. However, the daughter, Rosalie, is impressed by his refusal. Yancey makes camp nearby for the night. In the morning, Rosalie is waiting for him as he wakes up. She has decided to run away and wants to ride with Yancey. He politely tries to get her to go back home, but she finally convinces him to let her come along.

Upon arriving in Casper, they find the town celebrating the Fourth of July. There is a carnival, dance and band concert. Some of the celebrants have gotten rowdy and Yancey is drawn into a brawl. The sheriff is called and breaks up the fight before it gets completely out of hand.

Yancey and Rosalie head to the general store to trade his pelts. While there, both begin looking for new clothes they could wear for the evening fun. Some of the local dancehall girls come in looking for ribbons. One in particular, Marcy, catches Yancey's eye. Being a naive mountain man, Yancey is unaware of what type of girls inhabit dancehalls. He asks the storekeeper if Marcy is married. He is told, disdainfully, that Marcy doesn't belong to anyone.

Yancey and Rosalie clean up and change clothes at the hotel. He is impressed with her appearance and gives her five silver dollars to enjoy herself with at the carnival. Rosalie is highly disappointed; she wants to go with Yancey, but he has other ideas. The woman who works at the dancehall in partnership with the sheriff, Ma Ransome, comes by, sees Rosalie and offers her a job. Yancey still does not realize what sort of place the dancehall is and encourages

Audie Murphy, on his way to Casper to trade pelts in this scene from THE WILD AND THE INNOCENT

Rosalie to take the job.

Out on the midway, Yancey is suckered into the old shell game by a pitchman. The guy tries to cheat him, a fight ensues and Yancey is once again under a pile of bodies. Rosalie sees the sheriff and asks him to rescue Yancey. A short time later, Yancey tries to ingratiate himself with Marcy, who is not impressed with him and annoyed that the sheriff seems to be very interested in Rosalie. In the course of the festivities, Marcy gets drunk and passes out. Yancey stays with her until she wakes up, tending to her hangover. She decides that maybe this guy isn't so bad after all. The band has begun to play for the town dance, and Marcy teaches Yancey, who "can't dance a lick," a few steps. He now wants to take her to the dance, but she tells him that the women in town don't like dancehall girls around but Yancey doesn't care. He's not about to miss out on all the fun.

A few minutes into the dance, they are suddenly confronted by Chip and some of the men who caused the fight when they first came into town. Chip knows Marcy and demands that she come with him. Yancey steps in to stop him. This leads to another fight where Yancey breaks Chip's hand. Mr. Forbes asks Yancey to take Marcy away as the townswomen tell him she's trash and doesn't belong with decent folk.

After all this, Yancey finally begins to realize what the dancehall is, and what kind of girls work there. Then he realizes that Rosalie is supposed to be working there. He tries to get to her out of the saloon but is beaten up and thrown out into the street. Yancey gets his gun and heads back to the dancehall but is stopped by the sheriff, who owns the dancehall.

Yancey kills the sheriff and rescues Rosalie. The town is now rid of its corrupt official. Yancey is offered the job as the new sheriff, but declines. However, Rosalie has been offered a job clerking in the general store which makes him happy.

As Yancey prepares to leave town, Rosalie comes out of the store in tears. Once again, she wants to go with him. Once again, he can't say no to her. They leave together and make their way back to the mountains where Lije and Kiri are waiting for them.

BACKGROUND:

THE WILD AND THE INNOCENT had two other titles: THE WILD INNOCENTS and THE BUCKSKIN KID AND THE CALICO GIRL. Both were discarded before the movie was released. An interesting bit of information is that Audie also displays another unknown talent to the screen in this picture by really singing in this film with fellow actor, George Mitchell. His voice was not dubbed in.

During the shooting of this film, Audie acquired a new nickname. He was known as the "Prince of Wales." When filming began on location in the mountains of Big Bear, California, Audie was scheduled to do riding scenes aboard a mare who had a four-month-old colt. Unknown to Audie, the mare had not been saddled nor ridden in eight months. A fraction of a second after he occupied the saddle, Audie was treating the movie crew to one of the spectacular "rodeos" of the

Sandra Dee has Audie Murphy tie up her corset in this scene from THE WILD AND THE INNOCENT.

season. The show ended with Audie, one of filmdom's most skilled horsemen, sprawled in the dirt and the mare nuzzling her colt.

Murphy, never one to shun a dare or accept defeat, insisted on remounting the mare and showing her who was boss. Although he managed to do so, the director refused to allow Audie to ride the horse in the scenes, substituting a less boisterous mount.

Also in this movie, Audie, for the first time in his life, had to learn to dance. Brought up on the Texas plains where there's plenty of sagebrush but few ballroom floors, Murphy says he just never got around to studying the finer points of the light fantastic. But now that he's a full-fledged movie star himself, Audie reluctantly allowed himself to be tutored for a dancing scene. Self-conscious about his self-styled "clodhopping," the actor did all his rehearsing behind the locked doors of a studio dance stage. Audie's dancing comes into full flower during an outdoor Fourth of July party in the frontier "city" of Casper, Wyoming.

CAST A LONG SHADOW

STUDIO: UNITED ARTISTS (release)

PRODUCER: Walter M. Mirisch and Audie Murphy (A Mirisch-Murphy Company Production)
DIRECTOR: Thomas Carr
SCREENPLAY BY: Martin M. Goldsmith and John McGreevey
SCREEN STORY BY: Martin M. Goldsmith based on the novel by Wayne D. Overholser
MUSIC BY: Gerald Fried
SUPERVISING FILM EDITOR: Richard V. Heermance, A.C.E.
DIRECTOR OF PHOTOGRAPHY: Wilfrid M. Cline, A.S.C.
ART DIRECTOR: David Milton
PRODUCTION MANAGER: William A. Calihan, Jr.
MUSIC EDITOR: Harold McGhan
SOUND EDITOR: Bruce W. Schoengarth
ASSISTANT DIRECTOR: Austen Jewell
SET DECORATOR: Joseph Kish
SET CONTINUITY: John Franco
SOUND: John Kean
WARDROBE: Sid Mintz
MAKEUP ARTIST: Vincent Romaine
CONSTRUCTION SUPERVISOR: James West
PROPERTY: Ted Mossman
SPECIAL EFFECTS: Milt Rice
DATES OF FILMING: December 1, 1958 to December 19, 1958
LOCATION OF FILMING: 20th Century Fox Studio Lot; Allied Artists Studio; Janns Ranch (all in the Greater Los Angeles area)

CAST:
Matt Brown .... Audie Murphy
Janet Calvert .... Terry Moore
Chip Donohue .... John Dehner
Sam Muller .... James Best
Hortensia .... Rita Lynn
Mr. Harrison .... Denver Pyle
Charlotte Calvert .... Ann Doran
Eph Brown .... Stacy S. Harris
Rigdon .... Robert Foulk
Noah Pringle .... Wright King

RUNNING TIME: 82 minutes
RELEASE DATE: July 1959

SYNOPSIS:
Matt Brown, a saddletramp with a large chip on his shoulder, has spent the past few years drifting through the territory, mostly drinking and gambling. He runs into Chip Donohue, the ranch foreman for a cattle baron who had raised Matt. Chip informs Matt that Keenan has died and left the ranch to him.

Chip figures Matt has no use for the property, since he hasn't been around for four years. He offers Matt $20,000 to sign over the deed to him and the other ranch hands who had stayed on to work the place. Matt's first notion is to accept the offer and take the money. Chip and Matt ride back to town to find the banker who has the deed in his safe. However, since it is

Sunday, the banker has gone on a fishing trip so they will have to wait until the next day. The two ride on to the ranch, where Matt encounters resentment from the ranch hands when they find out he has inherited the old man's property.

Matt's former girlfriend, Janet, comes to see him, but there are still some old, bitter feelings between them. As Matt and Janet talk, they reconsider the idea of getting married, and he changes his mind about selling the ranch. However, Matt soon finds out that the ranch is deep in debt and a large loan payment is due within a few days. The banker will not give up the deed until the payment is made.

Finding himself with some purpose now, Matt decides to reform, stop drinking and take over running the ranch. After much reluctance, he convinces Chip and the hands to help him with a cattle drive and offers them a stake in the ranch as well. Matt also insists that the hands give up drinking while working on the ranch or be fired.

Soon after, Janet argues with Matt because he has made good on his rules,

Audie Murphy and Rita Lynn discuss his future as a ranch owner in this scene from CAST A LONG SHADOW.

firing one of the hands for drinking. Janet does not think this is fair because the hand has a family to support. Matt refuses to change his mind. She feels he is being cruel and hard and tells him she no longer wants to marry him.

Over the next few days, the ranch hands find out that Matt is completely serious about the drinking rule, having fired several of them. Other hands plot to get rid of him. He finds out something is planned and confronts the men in the town saloon. A fight breaks out and Matt is outnumbered four to one when Chip comes and breaks it up. But Chip also challenges Matt by stepping up to the bar and downing a drink. True to his word, Matt fires him.

With a smaller crew of ranch hands, Matt begins the cattle drive. The hands are still planning to get back at Matt and Chip is aware of this. Chip decides to return to the ranch and ask for another chance. Matt relents and rehires him, but thinks that Chip may want to hang around just to see him fail.

The men finally get the cattle to the river, but they are behind schedule. One of the hands accidentally spooks the horses, but Matt and Chip manage to calm them before they cause the cattle to stampede.

Matt decides they need to drive the cattle at night in order to meet the payment deadline. Chip is against this plan. If the cattle cannot be controlled in the dark, the hands could wind up being trampled. The disagreement gets into name-calling where Matt says something to Chip about being Keenan's son. Chip then informs Matt that he is his son, not Keenan's. Matt, outraged, turns on Chip knocking him to the ground. They fight viciously until gunshots are heard. Someone has started the herd running. All the hands try desperately to calm the cattle and round them up. During the stampede, Chip falls off his horse and breaks his arm and is unable to get out of the way of the onrushing cows. Matt sees the fallen foreman and rescues him, thus saving his life. They make the drive on time, and Matt and Chip have patched up their differences; Matt has accepted Chip as his father.

BACKGROUND:

CAST A LONG SHADOW was described by a critic as "a Western of considerable stature and more than juvenile appeal."

Audie got good critical notices such as: "His performance is flexible and sensitive;" "Audie gives a convincing account of himself;" and "a fine performance by Murphy." One critic wrote: "It's fun to watch Murphy in his somewhat plodding movements (a feature of the characterization)."

THE UNFORGIVEN

STUDIO: A HECHT-HILL-LANCASTER PRODUCTION (United Artists release)

PRODUCER: James Hill
DIRECTOR: John Huston
SCREENPLAY BY: Ben Maddow
BASED ON A NOVEL BY: Alan LeMay
DIRECTOR OF PHOTOGRAPHY: Franz Planer, A.S.C.
EXECUTIVE PRODUCTION MANAGER: Gilbert Kurland
EDITOR: Russell Lloyd
ART DIRECTOR: Stephen Grimes
ASSOCIATE: Ramon Rodriguez Granada
ASSISTANT DIRECTOR: Tom Shaw
COSTUME DESIGNER: Dorothy Jeakins
MAKEUP: Frank McCoy and Frank LaRue
SOUND RECORDING: Basil Fenton-Smith
SOUND EDITOR: Leslie Hodgson
PHOTOGRAPHIC LENSES BY: Panavision, Inc.
COLOR BY TECHNICOLOR
MUSIC BY: Dimitri Tiomkin
RECORDED IN ROME, ITALY, with the Santa Cecilia Orchestra

DATES OF FILMING: February 1, 1959 to May 20, 1959 (This unusually long filming time was due to an injury suffered by Audrey Hepburn in a fall from a horse. Shooting on the movie had to be suspended for several weeks until she recovered)
LOCATION OF FILMING: Durango, Mexico, area

CAST:

Ben Zachary .... Burt Lancaster
Rachel Zachary ..... Audrey Hepburn
Cash Zachary .... Audie Murphy
Johnny Portugal .... John Saxon
Zeb Rawlins .... Charles Bickford
Charlie Rawlins .... Albert Salmi
Matthilda Zachary .... Lillian Gish
Abe Kelsey .... Joseph Wiseman
Georgia Rawlins .... Kipp Hamilton
Jude Rawlins .... Arnold Merritt
Hagar Rawlins .... June Walker
Lost Bird .... Carlos Rivas
Andy Zachary .... Doug McClure

RUNNING TIME 125 minutes
RELEASE DATE: April 1960

SYNOPSIS:

The Zachary family owns a ranch near Kiowa Indian territory. Daughter Rachel tends to their hillside sodhouse, with her mother Matthilda, but occasionally likes to go riding on her stallion. During one of her rides, she encounters a strange man who watches her intently. Rachel invites the man back to the house to eat, but he refuses. He seems to know who she is even as he asks her name. Rachel tells him, but he insists she is not really a Zachary by blood or birth. She returns alone and tells Matthilda about her unusual meeting. Matthilda asks Rachel to describe the man, which she does. Matthilda pretends not to know who he is, but in reality, does know. She keeps it a secret from Rachel. Soon after, the man, whose name is Abe Kelsey, appears at the house and confronts Matthilda. She scares him off with a loaded rifle.

Ben and Cash Zachary have been in Wichita finishing a cattle drive. They arrive back at the house, with Ben having brought home a piano for Matthilda. Ben bet a man he could lift it off the ground by himself, which he did, and the man gave it to him. Matthilda is delighted and begins playing Mozart.

The Rawlins family is in partnership with the Zacharys and have come for a visit. Ben's brother, Cash, has become romantically involved with Georgia Rawlins, who has also encountered Kelsey watching her while she is alone. It soon comes out that Kelsey has been to the house. Again, Matthilda pretends she doesn't know who Kelsey is, but Ben can see she is troubled about this.

Later that night, Ben and Cash decide to go out looking for Kelsey. The wind is blowing great clouds of dust making it difficult to see. Kelsey seems to appear like a ghost, first in one direction, then another. Cash spots him and kills his horse but Kelsey gets away. It's impossible to find him in all that dust so Ben and Cash head home.

Soon, there is a round-up of the horses which need breaking to the saddle. Charlie Rawlins, who is interested in Rachel, attempts to ride one of the horses but gets thrown off. One of the ranch hands, a half-breed named Johnny Portugal, is dared by Cash, who is prejudiced against Indians, to break the same horse and succeeds. Rachel is watching. Johnny rides by her slowly, notices a burr in her hair and pulls it out. Ben is very protective of his sister and confronts Johnny. He warns Johnny not to touch his sister again and wants Rachel to return to the house. Rachel goes to the corral but discovers that her horse is missing. Both Ben and Cash know Kelsey stole it to replace his dead animal. They are the only ones who can go after Kelsey because of the secret he carries about Rachel.

Outside the soddy stand three Indians. Ben alerts the family and they secure the house. In the morning, the Indians are still there. In order to find out their intentions, Ben fires a shot over their heads. When the Indians don't leave, Ben goes out to see what they want. They tell him they believe an Indian girl is living in the house and they have come to trade horses for her, to take her back to the tribe. He tells them the woman in the house is white and wants to know who told them this lie. Kelsey has visited the Kiowa and told them about Rachel. Ben says the old man is crazy and returns to the house.

Several minutes later, one of the young braves comes close to the house and throws a lance at the front door. Cash sees it and goes wild. It's the same kind of lance that killed their papa. He runs up to the top of the hill firing recklessly at the departing Indian. Ben finally has to slap Cash to bring him back to reality. Cash finally regains his composure after Ben tells him to take the drive to Wichita. Cash agrees to go.

Another cattle drive is being formed.

The Rawlins men are nervous about the Indian sightings in the area. The rumors about Rachel being an Indian have spread. However, Charlie Rawlins has decided to ask Rachel to marry him. With Ben's permission, she accepts, although she is secretly in love with Ben and disappointed when he gives his blessing. Charlie is delighted and returns home, but along the way is attacked and killed by the Kiowas.

The Zacharys come to pay their respects at Charlie's wake. Rachel tries to comfort Charlie's mother, who lashes out at Rachel. She accuses Rachel of killing Charlie with her 'Injun' ways. Rachel is confused and goes to Matthilda for consolation.

Zeb insists he must know once and for all about Rachel. Ben promises to bring Kelsey back to tell the truth before they hang him. He organizes a posse to hunt for the old man. The trail is picked up as Ben appoints Johnny Portugal to track him down and bring him back to the Rawlins ranch.

Kelsey is questioned at length with a rope around his neck. He finally tells how, in a blind hatred, Matthilda's husband and he had gone to an Indian camp and began killing. They killed almost all the Indians they could find. While they rested, they heard a baby crying. Kelsey was about to kill the baby but Zachary stopped him. "No more killing today," he said and took the baby home to Matthilda. Ben relates that his papa found the baby, whose parents had been killed by Indians, in a settler's camp. Kelsey turns to Matthilda and tells how she

Doug McClure and Audie Murphy, following Kelsey's hanging in this scene from THE UNFORGIVEN

took the baby, washed off the Indian warpaint and kept it as her own. Matthilda has heard enough and whips the horse Kelsey is on. The horse moves away and Kelsey hangs.

Zeb now knows the truth about Rachel. He decides to break off the families' partnership unless Ben can prove Rachel is white. The Zacharys return to their house and discover that Indians had been there in their absence. Ben and Cash find a page from a Kiowa bible. Ben is able to interpret the symbols, which tell of a baby being taken from its cradle some 30 years before. Cash confronts Matthilda for the truth, and she finally confesses. She tells them that their papa brought her the little girl after her own baby girl with golden curls had just died. Her promised name was given to Rachel.

Feeling like an outcast, Rachel locks herself in the bedroom while Ben and Cash argue about her. Cash can't believe that his sister is an Indian and tells Ben to get rid of her. Ben refuses. Cash gets drunk and makes a slurring remark about Rachel which angers Andy, their younger brother. They get into a fight. Ben thinks it best that Cash leave. He goes to Georgia's where he tells her he's left his family because they are Indian lovers.

The Indians come for Rachel again. She offers to go with them to prevent them from going on the warpath. Ben refuses to let her go. She threatens to go first chance she gets. Ben orders Andy to kill one of the Indians, which he does. Now there's no use in Rachel going out. Soon Bens starts talking about fitting Rachel out in veils and the conversation about a wedding comes up. Rachel, Ben and Andy are in the midst of celebrating the upcoming event when the Indians begin attacking the house. Matthilda is wounded and dies shortly thereafter. While Rachel and Andy hide in the root cellar, Ben tries to fend off the newest attack: the Indians try stampeding cattle onto the roof of the sodhouse. Ben sets the roof on fire to scatter the cattle. Andy is wounded and unable to help. It looks hopeless for the three.

Having heard the gunshots at Georgia's, Cash comes back to the house. Ben is trying to defend the house with him, while Rachel tends to Andy. One of the Kiowa braves sneaks in and approaches Rachel. She kills him. Ben and Cash manage to fight off the Indians. Cash and Rachel make peace.

BACKGROUND:

The movie was described as a "Texas-sized Western bursting with action, mystery and romance."

THE UNFORGIVEN could have been the most important movie (with the exception of TO HELL AND BACK) in which Audie Murphy ever appeared. After the successful picture based on his war story, Audie was getting the diversity which he had long sought in his film roles. Murphy, seeking some financial independence from Hollywood, had bought a ranch near Perris, California. He was spending a lot of money on improving the property and investing in Quarter Horses. He was already using the ranch for breeding and raising the horses. He would get good prices when he sold them.

To the end of 1958, Audie needed a

good motion picture in another effort to break from the slightly less than the A-quality Westerns. THE UNFORGIVEN seemed to be the perfect vehicle for him. From beginning to end the movie would get Class-A treatment. The role offered Audie was relatively small, but it would give him his first real opportunity as a character actor. In addition the picture would pay him $75,000. But the great attraction was John Huston. He always did things in a big way. Huston had gotten from Murphy the finest performance of his acting career with THE RED BADGE OF COURAGE.

In THE UNFORGIVEN, Huston again scored with Audie. By many critics Murphy was regarded as doing the best acting job in the picture. One wrote: "Murphy, whose chief film characteristics until now has been a kind of stoic cheerfulness, uncorks a toughness and maturity that is a powerful aid to the story." Another said: "Audie is surprisingly good as Burt Lancaster's hot-headed brother, whose hatred of Indians causes him to abandon his family."

Murphy, after finishing his role in THE UNFORGIVEN, hurried back to Universal to begin work on the television series "Whispering Smith." He was twice pulled from the series to make the Westerns: HELL BENT FOR LEATHER and SEVEN WAYS FROM SUNDOWN.

Another bit of interesting information attached to this film was: in Durango, Mexico, Audie, Albert Salmi and Lillian Gish were out on location. Suddenly, Audie told the driver to stop the car. Murphy leapt out of the car, pulled a handgun out of his pocket, and ran over to a gully. They heard shots. He had killed an animal (which looked like a dog) that was running. He apologized to the people in the car and they resumed their ride to the location site.

Apparently Miss Gish got upset with Audie and asked why he shot that animal. Audie replied that the animal he killed was a coyote and that it could have torn the little children to shreds that were playing outside the hotel or who may have been left alone at some time. After hearing his explanation, the rest of the trip was rather quiet.

A rather unique incident happened during the filming where Audie went duck hunting with another man, Bill Pickens. The vessel they were in capsized and Audie, not knowing how to swim, was caught beneath the boat. He almost drowned but was saved by a young lady roaming through the area looking for objects to photograph.

Audrey Hepburn was injured very badly when she was thrown off a horse during the filming and spent several weeks recuperating. Audie was one of the first to reach her and get her aid.

HELL BENT FOR LEATHER

STUDIO: UNIVERSAL-INTERNATIONAL

PRODUCER: Gordon Kay
DIRECTOR: George Sherman
SCREENPLAY BY: Christopher Knopf
BASED ON A NOVEL BY: Ray Hogan
DIRECTOR OF PHOTOGRAPHY: Clifford Stine, A.S.C.
ART DIRECTOR: Richard H. Riedel
SET DECORATIONS: Russell A. Gausman and Julia Heron
SOUND: Waldon O. Watson and Joe Lapis
FILM EDITOR: Milton Carruth
MAKE-UP: Bud Westmore
HAIR STYLIST: Larry Germain
ASSISTANT DIRECTOR: Phil Bowles
MUSIC: William Lava and Irving Gertz
MUSIC SUPERVISION BY: Joseph Gershenson

DATES OF FILMING: August 17, 1959, to September 11, 1959
LOCATION OF FILMING: Lone Pine, California, area

CAST:

Clay .... Audie Murphy
Janet .... Felicia Farr
Deckett .... Stephen McNally
Ambrose .... Robert Middleton
Moon .... Rad Fulton
Travers .... Jan Merlin
Perrick .... Herbert Rudley
Gamble .... Malcomb Atterbury
Shad .... Joseph Ruskin
Kelsey .... Allan Lane
Old Ben .... John Qualen
William .... Eddie Little Sky
Grover .... Steve Gravers
Stone .... Beau Gentry
Jared .... Bob Steele

RUNNING TIME: 82 minutes
RELEASE DATE: February 1960

SYNOPSIS:
While camped alone on a Western trail, Clay Santell is approached by a cowboy named Travers, who is on foot and desperate for food and water. Clay begins to prepare food, but Travers also has his eye on Clay's horse. He knocks Clay out for a few seconds, grabs the horse and begins to ride away. Clay recovers quickly getting off one shot. He hits Travers in the arm, causing him to drop his rifle. Then Travers is gone. Clay picks up the rifle, but now must walk to the nearest town to get another horse.

In town, a funeral is in progress. An unknown gunman has killed two people, but it is a fact that the killer used the rifle that Clay recovered from Travers. Marshal Deckett is informed and goes to arrest Clay, who protests his innocence but to no avail. The marshal proceeds to take his prisoner to Denver for trial. While en route, Clay escapes and hides out in a nearby barn.

In the barn, Janet is caring for the children of the slain adults. At first, she

Allan Lane, Stephen McNally, and a case of mistaken identity with Audie Murphy in this scene from HELL BENT FOR LEATHER

is afraid but after Clay explains his situation, she decides to help him. She arranges for the children to be taken elsewhere. Deckett has returned to town and formed a posse to catch Clay, who sees Clay and Janet leaving in a wagon. They assume that he is using her as a hostage which makes Deckett more determined to catch Clay.

While Clay hides atop a remote cliff, Janet attempts to go get help from a family friend, but is intercepted by the posse. She tries to convince the marshal that Clay is innocent, but now, enraged at having lost his prisoner, Deckett is "hell-bent" to catch Clay and kill him. Janet is forced to tell where Clay is hiding. As they approach, Clay manages to overwhelm Deckett, free Janet and they both escape from the posse.

With the posse in pursuit, they eventually arrive in another town, where Clay spots his stolen horse tied up in front of the saloon. Clay figures that Travers is in town. While keeping the horse in sight, he waits in the saloon for Travers to come back. As he approaches, the posse rides into town, scaring Travers away. The gunman grabs another horse and rides out of town. Clay and Janet follow Travers with the posse following closely behind them.

Clay catches up with Travers in high country and begins a gun battle with him, dodging between the rocks. Soon, Deckett arrives and it becomes a three-way showdown. Since the marshal is still trying to kill Clay, he leaves himself vulnerable to Travers, who guns him down. Clay then kills Travers and is able to convince the posse that Travers was the real killer.

BACKGROUND:

As the 1950s and the '60s began, Westerns still provided the most popular entertainment on TV. Each of the three networks had top-rated "oaters:" CBS - "Gunsmoke," NBC - "Bonanza," ABC - "Maverick." Most movie studios, Universal among them, still needed an inexpensive product to fill double bills at the theaters. B-Westerns were easy and cheap to churn out and Audie Murphy continued to provide a star attraction for the studio. He made over a dozen Westerns in the 1950s. In the '60s, he would star in 13 more.

HELL BENT FOR LEATHER was described by a critic as "a good straight-line action story, considerably better than the average Audie Murphy Western—one of the screen's rare movies of the West as it really was."

Audie's performance was called "top-notch." A critic also pointed out that the movie gained strength through the fact that audiences knew Murphy really could perform the feats of marksmanship his role required.

Audie's newest hobby proved a valuable asset during the Lone Pine, California, location filming. Murphy flew his new plane to the central California location site and was immediately put to work by the film's director but not in an acting capacity.

Director Sherman climbed into the seat alongside Murphy and the pair went off on an aerial scouting flight. They discovered areas that had never been photographed for films before and the following day the camera equipment and acting personnel had been land-shipped into the isolated spots for filming.

SEVEN WAYS FROM SUNDOWN

STUDIO: UNIVERSAL-INTERNATIONAL

PRODUCER: Gordon Kay
DIRECTOR: Harry Keller
SCREENPLAY BY: Clair Huffaker (BASED ON HIS NOVEL)
DIRECTOR OF PHOTOGRAPHY: Ellis Carter, A.S.C.
EASTMAN COLOR BY PATHE
ART DIRECTORS: Alexander Golitzen and William Newberry
SET DECORATIONS: George Milo
SOUND: Waldon O. Watson and William Russell
FILM EDITOR: Tony Martinelli, A.C.E.
MAKE-UP: Bud Westmore
HAIR STYLIST: Larry Germain
ASSISTANT DIRECTOR: Thomas J. Connors, Jr.
MUSIC: William Lava and Irving Gertz
MUSIC SUPERVISION BY: Joseph Gershenson

DATES OF FILMING: May 2, 1960 to May 26, 1960
LOCATION OF FILMING: Universal Studio and Las Vegas, Nevada, area

CAST:

Seven Jones .... Audie Murphy
Jim Flood .... Barry Sullivan
Joy Karrington ..... Venetia Stevenson
Sgt. Hennessey .... John McIntire
Lt. Herly .... Kenneth Tobey
Ma Karrington.................. Mary Field
Graves .... Ken Lynch
Lucinda .... Suzanne Lloyd
Fogarty .... Ward Ramsey
Duncan .... Don Collier
Beeker............................ Jack Kruschen
Gilda .... Claudia Barrett
Jody .... Teddy Rooney
Dorton .... Don Haggerty
Eavens .... Robert Burton
Chief Waggoner .... Fred Graham
2nd Waggoner .... Dale Van Sickle

RUNNING TIME: 87 minutes
RELEASE DATE: September 1960

SYNOPSIS:

Jim Flood is a killer and has left a trail of dead, wounded and ravaged towns behind him in his wake. He's a charmer who has all the girls in love with him and while doing destructive things, has everyone under his spell.

When Seven-Ways-From-Sundown Jones reports for his new job with the Texas Rangers, he is immediately given the toughest assignment by Lt. Herly, that of bringing in Flood. Sergeant Hennessey is a seasoned ranger, capable of finding Flood. Before they leave, Seven meets Joy Karrington who is very fond of Hennessey and is a good friend. Seven finds Joy to be the right kind of girl for him and tells her they will be careful.

The two men take off in pursuit of Flood. Seven hasn't had much practice in shooting a "revolving gun"—only a rifle. Along the way, Hennessey gives Seven many opportunities to exercise his accuracy with a pistol. The longer they are on the trail, the better Seven becomes.

As they arrive in the town of Sterling for a drink, they meet Lucinda who informs them that Flood has been there and tells them where he was heading. After hitting the trail again, Seven realizes that they are not going in the direction Flood was supposed to be. Hennessey informs Seven that Flood never told a girl the truth about anything.

Hennessey finds a cigar that Flood had thrown away and estimates he's about a day ahead. The sergeant knows a lot about Flood since they have known each other a long time. After several more miles, Seven and Hennessey are ambushed by Flood and Hennessey is shot. He makes Seven promise to go back to town and forget about bringing Flood back to jail. Seven can't make that promise and Hennessey dies.

Seven finds Flood's trail. He gets close enough to shoot Flood and fells him with one bullet. Seven is ready to take Flood back to town, but Flood tells Seven he is about to pass out. However, before he does, he tells Seven of a cabin close by where they can rest and get something to eat. Seems as though it belongs to Flood.

After reaching the cabin, Flood shows much remorse upon hearing of Hennessey's death since Hennessey had saved Flood from a scalping fifteen years before. Seven and Flood spend several days at the cabin while Flood recuperates. They play cards and talk. Flood has a chance to kill Seven but doesn't. Finally, Flood is well enough to travel and they head back to Texas.

Flood keeps telling Seven that he won't go to jail. Several times along the trail Flood has more opportunities to kill Seven, but he hesitates just long enough for Seven to recover and get the upper hand. Both men develop respect for each other, but Seven doesn't let his guard down again in spite of this. Again Flood tells Seven that he won't go back to jail to be hanged.

Audie Murphy, reporting for his first job as a Texas Ranger in this scene from SEVEN WAYS FROM SUNDOWN

The ride back to Texas is long. On their way back to headquarters, they are attacked by Apaches but due to some fancy gunplay by Seven, they manage to get away unscathed. Another night out brings on a conversation regarding Seven's brother Two Jones who was killed because another ranger was a coward. It was the ranger's fault in that he was supposed to be covering Two but that he hid behind a rock. It turns out later that the ranger in question was Lt. Herly.

While in the town of Hobbs for supplies, they stop in the saloon for a drink. Seven doesn't want to go to a town where Flood is known for fear that the people will start protecting him. Naturally, everyone there knows Jim and they try to make Seven let him go. Flood takes Seven's side and they leave Seven alone. Two bounty hunters come in and demand Flood for the reward. When Seven refuses, they try to take him by force whereas Seven kills one of them. Seven tells the other bounty hunter that if he tries to follow them, he'll untie Flood and give him a gun. With this, the bounty hunter high tails it out of the saloon with Seven and Flood close behind.

They set off again and run into a supply wagon. One of the men recognizes Flood and attacks him. Both Flood and Seven fight the men off and they scatter leaving Seven to take the supplies they need. Still more perils occur along the way when they encounter the Handleys, a family of brothers who are after Flood. Flood grabs Seven's side arm and shoots it out, killing some of the men. While Seven is defending himself, Jim takes a pistol from one of the dead men and hides it in his shirt, then gives Seven back his gun.

They finally arrive back in the town of Buckley and Seven puts Flood in jail. Herly wants a full report from Seven in the morning. A reporter is interviewing Jim in jail to get a story for his paper. Jim starts in about the fracas down by the Big Bend where Two Jones gets killed. Herly knows that he was the one to blame and tells Jim that he's going to let him out to say that he broke jail, so therefore, the reason for killing Jim will be legitimate and not murder. However, Herly doesn't know that Jim has a gun.

Meanwhile, Seven is at Joy's having coffee when a shot is heard. Seven sees that Flood is free and has a clear shot but lets him ride past. As Flood is shooting his way out of town, a stray bullet hits Joy, wounding her. She is all right but it's the shock that causes more harm.

Seven knows that he must stop Flood. A few minutes later, Seven hears a horse coming. He goes outside and Jim comes riding up hoping that Seven will join him in a life of crime. Seven tells Jim that he almost killed an innocent girl and tells Flood that he has to stop him. Flood says that he is sorry that he shot her. Seven says he can't go through life being sorry. Finally, it comes down to a shootout between Jim and Seven. Seven outdraws Jim who hesitates for a moment and is killed.

BACKGROUND:

Audie's performance in the movie was described as "excellent" by one critic. "But Barry Sullivan, as a lovable killer, stole the show."

Long regarded as one of Texas' leading citizens, Audie gets his first opportunity to play a Texan on the screen in this film.

POSSE FROM HELL

STUDIO: UNIVERSAL-INTERNATIONAL

PRODUCER: Gordon Kay
DIRECTOR: Herbert Coleman
SCREENPLAY BY: Clair Huffaker (from his novel)
DIRECTOR OF PHOTOGRAPHY: Clifford Stine, A.S.C.
EASTMAN COLOR BY PATHE
ART DIRECTORS: Alexander Golitzen and Alfred Sweeney
SET DIRECTIONS: Oliver Emert
SOUND: Waldon O. Watson and Joe Lapis
ASSISTANT PRODUCER: Willard Willingham
FILM EDITOR: Frederic Knudtson, A.C.E.
MAKE-UP: Bud Westmore
HAIR STYLIST: Larry Germain
ASSISTANT DIRECTOR: Ray Gosnell, Jr.
MUSIC SUPERVISION BY: Joseph Gershenson

DATES OF FILMING: October 31, 1960 to November 29, 1960
LOCATION OF FILMING: Lone Pine, California, and the 20th Century Fox Ranch (near Los Angeles)

CAST:

Banner Cole .... Audie Murphy
Seymour Kern .... John Saxon
Helen Caldwell .... Zohra Lampert
Marshal Webb .... Ward Ramsey
Crip .... Vic Morrow
Capt. Brown .... Robert Keith
Uncle Billy Caldwell .... Royal Dano
Johnny Caddo .... Rudolph Acosta
Jack Riley .... Paul Carr
Burt Hogan .... Frank Overton
Leo .... Lee Van Cleef
Luke Gorman .... Stuart Randall
Hash .... Charles Horvath
Chunk .... Henry Wills
Benson .... James Bell

RUNNING TIME: 89 minutes
RELEASE DATE: May 1961

SYNOPSIS:

The town of Paradise is being terrorized by four outlaws. Webb, the town's marshal has been shot and left for dead. Other townsfolk try to fight the outlaws but aren't a match for their quick guns. After murdering at will, robbing the bank and taking Helen, the niece of the town drunk, they ride off.

Banner Cole, a gunfighter, arrives in town the next day hired to work for Webb as his deputy who is also a friend. He finds the marshal barely alive. Webb tells Banner that Paradise has some good people living there and have been badly wronged. With his last breath, he urges Banner to go after the outlaws and deputizes him. Banner tells Webb that he will do his best to bring the outlaws to justice.

Cole prepares to leave town to conduct the manhunt by himself, but several others want to join him as part of the posse. Cole prefers to work alone but finally gives in. The men riding with him, includes the banker's assistant, who is an Easterner from New York, and Helen's uncle. Reluctantly, Banner agrees to take them but warns them also that there is a good chance some won't come back. He then gives them the opportunity to back out. What started out to be over a dozen men has dwindled down to seven.

Picking up the trail of the outlaws, the posse discovers a piece of Helen's dress in the brush. They surmise that she had tried to escape. Cole is frustrated because the men are poor posse members. He becomes aware that the banker had never before ridden a horse. There is also a young gunslinger who is a showoff and several assorted gun hands. These men aren't posse material and Banner wishes they weren't along.

Further down the trail, they hear a woman screaming. They find Helen bound and a rattlesnake about to strike. Banner diverts the snake where the banker, Kern, kills it. Helen is badly shaken and has been treated brutally by the outlaws. She feels ashamed now and doesn't want to live. Banner finally calms her down and tells her uncle to take her back to town.

The posse presses on. They spot four men and think they may be the outlaws. One of the posse, Brown, a former calvary officer, begins to shoot at them, but Cole realizes that they are only ranch hands. Brown continues firing at the men not realizing that the men aren't the outlaws. Cole tries to get someone to make Brown stop shooting but they can't hear him. Cole finally forces him to stop by shooting him in the leg. The ranch hands tell the posse that the outlaws are holed up at their place. With Brown disabled, the remaining posse members head for the ranch. They are now down to five men and they haven't even seen the outlaws yet.

Cole wants to surround the house, hoping to surprise the gang, but a noise alerts them. They break out through a back door at which time a

Audie Murphy and John Saxon, getting ready to form a posse in this scene from POSSE FROM HELL

gunfight begins. One of the outlaws is killed by a posse member. However, Wiley, the young gunfighter, freezes when confronted by an outlaw and is killed. Another posse member thinks the dead outlaw is the one that killed his brother and feeling that he has avenged his brother's death, leaves. Now three of the posse are remaining: Banner, Johnny Caddo, and Kern.

Banner wants Kern and Johnny to return to town so he can go after the remaining outlaws alone, but they won't leave him. There are three outlaws left—one for each of them. After a short rest and fresh horses, they go after the remaining gang members.

The outlaws double back on their route several times. Cole again tries to get the others to leave so he can take care of business faster. They insist on going with him. Again picking up the trail, they find the gang has gone into a box canyon. As the men ride in after them, they discover that the men have already come out and are heading back to Paradise. As the posse chases after them, they are ambushed. However, Banner mortally wounds one of them and before he dies, says that the two remaining outlaws are going to kill everyone and burn down the town.

These outlaws are getting crazier by the minute. Banner suggests that Johnny ride into town to warn the people while he and Kern keep on the trail. As Johnny heads for town, Banner finds that the outlaws have once again changed direction and that Johnny is riding into a trap. Banner and Kern race after Johnny to stop him but it's too late. A shotgun brings Johnny down and he dies shortly after Banner and Kern reach him.

Kern, by this time, is really feeling the effects of this ordeal. Banner wants to go on alone, but Kern convinces him that he's able to handle it as they start off again. Once more, they find the trail and follow them to a cabin where Helen and her uncle have stopped on the way back to Paradise. Helen still feels ashamed and refuses to go any further. She doesn't want the town's pity. Banner wants them to get out since two of the men are still around. The uncle goes for the buckboard but a few minutes later is killed by a shotgun blast.

Banner and Kern take off after the men. One is killed but the other shoots Kern's horse. He can't jump clear in time and the horse falls on his leg, breaking it. Banner manages to get him out then goes after the last outlaw. Crip is waiting for Banner wounding him with a side full of buckshot. The blast knocks Cole down but he has enough strength to kill Crip. He then goes back for Kern and carries him back to town.

After getting medical attention for Kern, Banner's injuries have been tended to by the doctor and Helen. Banner is asked by the town counsel to remain on and become marshal. There are, however, some people who still think of him as a gunfighter and don't want him to stay. Banner, in thinking it over, recalls some of what Webb told him before he died and he and Helen find that there are some good people left in Paradise.

BACKGROUND:

According to the critics, POSSE FROM

Audie Murphy, trying to convince Zohra Lampert and Royal Dano to go back to town in POSSE FROM HELL

HELL attempted to depict the badmen of the Old West realistically instead of romantically as is often the case. The movie also tried to project social significance. One critic called the picture "an intelligent, serious Western with plenty of action."

Audie got good reviews personally. One critic wrote: "Murphy delivers with his usual understatement, but convincingly. Another said: "Audie Murphy, whose heroic exploits in real life make him ideally suited for and extra believable, does his usual commendably restrained job in super heroic roles."

These points are well taken. Audie's reputation as a super-soldier did add validity to many of the non-military roles he played. As a director, John Huston got the two best performances from Audie in his entire screen career. John explained: "Audie's afraid of making a fool of himself in front of the camera. I assure him that I won't let him make a fool of himself. So he unlimbers for me."

While filming this movie near Lone Pine, California, the area is called Rattlesnake Hill. It is appropriately named because Audie and members of the crew spotted more than 30 rattlers in a single day. The reptiles were removed by a professional herpetologist before the company could get into the mood for their work.

A situation where "hell" actually froze over occurred while on location. While filming scenes for the outdoor color adventure, sub-zero temperatures froze the Meadow Lake area up in the mountains necessitating a shift to lower-level, and ice-free, Echo Lake for water fight sequences of the picture.

BATTLE AT BLOODY BEACH

STUDIO: 20th CENTURY FOX

PRODUCER: Richard Maibaum
DIRECTOR: Herbert Coleman
STORY BY: Richard Maibaum
SCREENPLAY BY: Richard Maibaum and Willard Willingham
MUSIC COMPOSED AND CONDUCTED BY: Henry Vars
DIRECTOR OF PHOTOGRAPHY: Kenneth Peach
SUPERVISING FILM EDITOR: Jodie Copelan, A.C.E.
ART DIRECTION: John Mansbridge
PRODUCTION SUPERVISOR: Harold E. Knox
ASSISTANT DIRECTOR: Francisco Day
PROPERTY MASTER: Wilbur L. Russell
SET DECORATOR: Harry Reif
SCRIPT SUPERVISOR: George Rutter
WARDROBE: Robert Olivas
MAKE-UP: Vincent Romaine
SOUND: Frank McWhorter
SUPERVISING SOUND EDITOR: Jack Cornall
SOUND FACILITIES BY: Glen Glenn Sound Co.

DATES OF FILMING: January 16, 1961 to February 15, 1961
LOCATION OF FILMING: Catalina Island, California

CAST:

Craig Benson .... Audie Murphy
Marty Sackler .... Gary Crosby
Ruth Benson .... Dolores Michaels
Julio Fontana .... Alejandro Rey
Caroline Pelham .... Marjorie Stapp
Jeff Pelham .... Barry Atwater
Dr. Van Bart .... E.J. Andre
Blanco .... Dale Ishimoto
Nahni .... Miriam Colon
Camota .... Pilar Seurat
Delia Ellis .... Lillian Bronson
M'Keever .... William Mims
Tiger Blair .... Ivan Dixon
Timmy Thompson .... Kevin Brodie
Mrs. Thompson .... Sara Anderson

RUNNING TIME: 83 minutes
RELEASE DATE: June 1961

SYNOPSIS:

A submarine arrives near an island in the Philippines. It is World War II during the Japanese occupation. Craig Benson, an American civilian, is bringing supplies to Philippine guerilla fighters. Before the Japanese invasion, Craig was a newly married businessman in Manila. In the confusion of that attack, he became separated from his wife, Ruth, and has been looking for her ever since.

Craig meets up with another American, Marty Sackler, who tells him there are two rival guerilla groups on the island. It is unclear which group they should support against the Japanese. M'Keever, one of the leaders, captures both men, but knowing that

Craig has access to needed supplies, attempts to convince the American that he is fighting the Japanese. However, Craig soon realizes that M'Keever is playing both sides against each other, and, therefore, cannot be trusted.

Benson and Sackler are rescued by the rival leader, Julio Fontana. Fontana's family has been collaborating with the Japanese, but Julio has broken away and has been helping stranded Americans avoid capture. Julio leads the two men to such a group, where Craig finds his wife.

The reunion should be sweet, but there are complications. Ruth was convinced that the Japanese had captured her husband and killed him. She has since begun a romance with Julio.

The Americans trek to the beach where Julio is to receive the supplies hidden in Craig's boat and the rest can be evacuated by the submarine. While waiting for the sub, they are attacked by Japanese soldiers. Well supplied with armaments, they fend off the attack, but are pinned down on the beach. The Japanese badly want to capture the notorious Benson. They propose an offer to Julio. Benson should be turned over to them; the rest can go free. Julio refuses.

Audie Murphy, fighting the Japanese in this scene from BATTLE AT BLOODY BEACH

As the Japanese renew their attack, an SOS is sent to Julio's main guerilla group. Some of the Americans are killed before the guerilla rescue finally routs the enemy. Ruth must choose between the men. The choice is Craig; he vows he will continue his mission until the Japanese are defeated. Julio gallantly strides away (not unlike the ending of the movie CASABLANCA).

BACKGROUND:

A critic said: "Its staunchest ally, from a boxoffice standpoint is the presence of Audie Murphy. He brings his usual authority to the pivotal character." The combat sequences were praised as "brisk stuff."

Audie is completely at ease in pictures of the blood-and-guts school. His authentic characterization of a civilian

Audie Murphy, Dolores Michaels and Alejandro Rey, planning strategy in this scene from BATTLE AT BLOODY BEACH

working with guerilla fighters during the battle of the Philippines, searching for his bride, from whom he has been separated during a Japanese attack; his cool but daring enterprise in combat when he finds her committed to another man, generate the kind of excitement audiences are accustomed to in the screen stories starring this rugged, boyish-looking actor.

Some interesting points of information for this film include: during the lunchbreak one of the mortars was shot accidentally causing the old ship to nearly be completely demolished. The studio carpenters, who are fantastically experienced in working under tremendous pressures and expertly restoring relics to a startling resemblance, worked on the ship for several days, remodeling the boat to its old form. Consequently, everybody had a short vacation while production was halted.

This movie was filmed entirely on location at Catalina, an island in the Pacific Ocean, just 20 miles off the California coast. The most important set in the entire picture was the beached hull of an old submarine chaser which was purchased by the U.S. Navy and towed to the point were it was needed. While the production staff was searching the island for the most rugged beach sites to film the battle scenes, the old sub-chaser sank to the bottom of the ocean. Production was halted while salvage operations lifted the hull back into position. As if that wasn't enough, after the salvage crew had raised the hull, the next scene called for the boat to be completely demolished after a Japanese attack.

SIX BLACK HORSES

STUDIO: UNIVERSAL-INTERNATIONAL

PRODUCER: Gordon Kay
DIRECTOR: Harry Keller
WRITTEN BY: Burt Kennedy
DIRECTOR OF PHOTOGRAPHY: Maury Gertsman, A.S.C.
EASTMAN COLOR BY PATHE
ART DIRECTORS: Alexander Golitzen and Robert Luthardt
SET DIRECTIONS: Oliver Emert
SOUND: Waldon O. Watson and Frank H. Wilkinson
FILM EDITOR: Aaron Stell, A.C.E.
MAKE-UP: Bud Westmore
HAIR STYLIST: Larry Germain
ASSISTANT DIRECTOR: Ivan Volkman
MUSIC SUPERVISION BY: Joseph Gershenson

DATES OF FILMING: August 10, 1961 to September 5, 1961
LOCATION OF FILMING: Las Vegas, Nevada, area

CAST:

Ben Lane .... Audie Murphy
Frank Jesse .... Dan Duryea
Kelly .... Joan O'Brien
Boone .... George Wallace
Mustanger .... Roy Barcroft
Charlie .... Dick Pascoe
Joe .... Bob Steele
Indian Leader .... Henry Wills

RUNNING TIME: 80 minutes
RELEASE DATE: June 1962

SYNOPSIS:

While on his way to town, Ben Lane is on foot and winds up dragging his saddle through the Mexican desert. Totally exhausted, he sees wild horses running, catches up with one and breaks the horse to the saddle. However, he is being watched by the mustangers who accuse him of being a horse thief. Just as he is about to be hanged, Frank Jesse, who is one of the mustangers, rides up and orders the men to release Ben. A short distance later, Ben dismounts wanting to return the horse. Frank convinces him not to because he needs a horse in order to get a job. Also, Frank has never been paid by the group and figures they owe him.

Kelly sees them ride in from her hotel window. They head to the saloon where Frank and Ben talk about their futures. Frank asks Ben if he ever considered hiring out his gun. But Ben isn't interested in this kind of life. On their way to the hotel, they are ambushed by two men but kill them not knowing who they were or why they were shooting at them.

Feeling sorry for the men, they offer to pay for their funerals but don't have enough money. Kelly pays the balance. They go to her hotel room to get some answers. Kelly seems to know who they are. She wants to hire them to take her to Del Cobre to be with her husband. Since Del Cobre is directly in the area of the Coyotero Indians, they are reluctant and for good reason. These Indians are very hostile and are to be avoided.

Kelly offers them $500 apiece and when they hesitate because of the danger involved, she offers them $1000. This time, they agree. Ben figures that if they ride out of the open and away from the skyline, they might make it. Frank knows the territory well and Ben knows the Coyotero.

While resting for the night, Kelly and Ben talk. She asks him what he'll do with the money and he tells her of a place in Montana high country where he would like to build and have a family someday. He wants something he can belong to. She gives Ben the impression that Frank may not make it to Del Cobre and that Ben would get Frank's share of the money. Ben is confused. She leaves as Frank and Ben talk over things. Frank seems to be obsessed with women, in particular, Kelly. Ben warns Frank that he has a funny feeling about the job and about Kelly.

Upon encountering a smoldering cabin, Ben finds a miner who has been killed by the Indians. While they are deciding what to do, a small group of Indians meets up with them wanting to talk. Ben rides to them and in a short while comes back telling them that they want Kelly in trade for a horse. Ben refuses to let her go and the Indians leave. However, they pick up more Indians who begin following the three. Frank tells Ben about a mission a short distance away where they can hold off the Indians if they attack.

They barely make the mission before the Indians begin shooting. As soon as there is a lull in the shooting, Kelly

Audie Murphy, about to be hanged for horse thievery in SIX BLACK HORSES

aims her rifle at Frank intending on killing him. Ben sees this and yells at her. One of the Indians has gotten close enough and throws a lance which pierces her shoulder. Ben kills the Indian, tends to Kelly's wound and watches over her through the night. When she regains consciousness, she asks about Frank. Ben tells her he's still alive. She tells Ben that Frank killed her husband in a gunfight in Del Cobre. She vows to kill Frank and wants Ben's help. Ben rejects her offer especially after Frank saved his life.

Ben thinks that taking Kelly just for the money is wrong but now he wants to take her alone and without Frank because he knows Kelly will kill him when they get there. Frank convinces Ben that he owes him. While Ben is thinking this over, he sees smoke rising from the ridge. They continue on their journey hoping to avoid the Indians.

The next day, Frank and Ben talk about the two men they killed in Perdido. Ben thinks they were paid to kill them; maybe someone crossed them at one time in their lives. Frank tells him that he wouldn't want to go out in a pine box in a flat bed wagon, that when he gets his, he wants six black horses pulling a fancy rig with plumes—the works. A man should go out in style.

Resting for the night, Frank checks Kelly's arm. He tells her that he's sorry her husband is dead. He explains that her husband crossed some men in a card game and he was hired to kill him. These are the men she should be after, not him. If it weren't for these men, her husband would still be alive. After Ben learns that Frank was a hired gunman to kill her husband, he still feels a sense of loyalty to the man who saved his life but is caught between his emotions.

Three men ride up to the camp. Frank knows them as scalp hunters, the lowest kind of human. Shortly thereafter, as the hunters turn to leave, they draw down on Frank and Ben, but one of the hunters is wounded and Frank orders them to leave.

Ben tells Frank that he's not going to try to take Kelly through the Indian territory, but Frank wants to keep going. He knocks Ben out and takes Kelly with him.

Ben goes after them avoiding the Indians along the way. He finds Kelly unconscious with Frank holding a rifle on him. He wants Ben to mount up and ride away but Ben can't do that. Eventually, it comes down to a showdown between the two men. Frank doesn't want it to come to this because he likes Ben. But the draw has Ben killing Frank. The shots bring also the Indians. Ben tells Kelly not to move. The Indians drop off the three scalp hunters' bodies in front of them and ride away. It's all over. Frank gets his fancy funeral with six black horses as Ben and Kelly head for Montana high country.

BACKGROUND:

SIX BLACK HORSES got varying critical notices. One called the movie an "exciting adventure;" another said: "appealing, in spite of unlikely dramatics." Audie's performance was described as "satisfactory." Duryea almost stole the picture with his colorful portrayal of the hired gun.

SHOWDOWN

STUDIO: UNIVERSAL-INTERNATIONAL

PRODUCER: Gordon Kay
DIRECTOR: R. G. Springsteen
DIRECTOR OF PHOTOGRAPHY: Ellis W. Carter, A.S.C.
WRITTEN BY: Bronson Howitzer
UNIT PRODUCTION MANAGER: Robert Larson
ART DIRECTORS: Alexander Golitzen and Alfred Sweeney
SET DECORATIONS: Oliver Emert
SOUND: Waldon O. Watson and Frank H. Wilkinson
UNIT PRODUCTION MANAGER: Robert Larson
ASSISTANT TO PRODUCER: Willard Willingham
TITLES BY: Pacific Title
FILM EDITOR: Jerome Thoms
COSTUMES: Rosemary Odell
MAKE-UP: Bud Westmore
HAIR STYLIST: Larry Germain
ASSISTANT DIRECTOR: Terence Nelson
MUSIC: Hans J. Salter
MUSIC SUPERVISION: Joseph Gershenson

DATES OF FILMING: Early September 1962 to September 25, 1962
LOCATION OF FILMING: Lone Pine, California

CAST:

Chris Foster .... Audie Murphy
Estelle .... Kathleen Crowley
Bert Pickett .... Charles Drake
Lavalle .... Harold J. Stone
Caslon .... Skip Homeier
Foray ....................................L.Q. Jones
Charlie Reeder .... Strother Martin
Hebron .... Charles Horvath
Marshal .... John McKee
Chaca .... Henry Wills
Guard .... Joe Haworth
Buster .... Kevin Brodie
Smithy's Wife .... Carol Thurston
Express Man .... Dabbs Greer

RUNNING TIME: 79 minutes
RELEASE DATE: May 1963

SYNOPSIS:

Two cowboy wranglers, Chris Foster and Bert Pickett, arrive in the small Western town of Adonde to cash their pay vouchers after being on the range for six months. They notice that the sheriff maintains order by chaining any outlaws to an iron maypole in the street. Chris and Bert get their cash at the bank and head for the saloon. Bert is anxious to find a poker game to increase his money to send it on to his girlfriend, Estelle.

The sheriff rides into town with a gang of outlaws as his prisoners. They are chained to the maypole where the gang's leader, Lavalle, vows revenge on the sheriff. Bert gets drunk at the saloon not only that but he is also being cheated at the poker game. Soon, he loses all of his money and picks a fight with the other players who beat him up. Chris, meanwhile, is getting a shave and hears the commotion. He heads over to the saloon and tries to break up the fight. The sheriff arrives, but Bert, not realizing that he is the sheriff, takes a swing at him. Chris tries to smooth things over, but the sheriff wants them to cool off so both boys quickly find themselves also chained to the pole.

During the night, Lavalle has everyone digging to unearth the pole. By daybreak, it is loose enough to bring it down. The gang uses it as a battering ram to break into the express office where the sheriff is keeping their guns. Lavalle kills the sheriff; the gang breaks free of the chains, takes the money from the safe and rides out of town.

Lavalle's men catch up with Chris and Bert, still wearing their collars, taking them to the hideout. One by one, Lavalle's men have the collars removed but Lavalle has other plans for Foster and Pickett and keeps them chained.

Bert tries to bargain with Lavalle, telling him how he managed to grab and hide $12,000 in bonds while the safe was being cleaned out. Lavalle agrees to let Bert go to get the bonds, but keeps Chris as hostage to insure Bert's return. Bert gets the bonds, but decides to send them to Estelle instead. Lavalle's henchmen recapture him and bring him back to the hideout. Lavalle is enraged and tortures Bert about the bonds.

Chris convinces Lavalle to let him go to find the bonds since Bert is in no condition to travel. Lavalle allows Chris to go but has two of his men follow to make sure Chris comes back with the money or he will kill Bert.

Audie Murphy, tending to his friend, Charles Drake, in a scene from SHOWDOWN

Chris finds Estelle. This is her last day singing in the saloon. She plans to take the money and leave. Chris explains the situation to her and tries to persuade her to give the money to him to save Bert's life. She doesn't care and won't give back the bonds.

Again Chris tries to convince her to give the money to him so he can save Bert's life. She tells Chris that she won't give up the money for Bert. Chris has a hard time trying to understand why she feels this way about Bert when he's so much in love with her. Lavalle's men come after Chris but he kills one of them and while he's kept busy with the other outlaw, Estelle grabs the dead outlaw's gun and tries to kill Chris. She rides off on horseback with Chris in pursuit.

Chris finally catches up with her and finds the money. He asks her about her relationship with Bert and she tells him that she was in love with him at one time. He had helped her and her sister when they had a ranch, but Bert had sold it out from under them leaving them with nothing. After Bert had sent her the money, Estelle thought it would be another chance for her and Jenny. Chris sympathizes, but tells her he needs the money in exchange for Bert's life. She reluctantly lets Chris take it.

Chris rides back to the hideout, but insists that Lavalle let Bert go before giving him the money. Lavalle's henchman, Caslon, has grabbed Estelle and also brought her to the hideout. Bert diverts the outlaws' attention, allowing Estelle to escape. Caslon kills Bert as Chris and Estelle escape in the confusion.

They find a place to hide for the night near the railroad, where Estelle tells Chris that she blames herself for Bert's death. While they are talking, Caslon finds them. He fights with Chris and is killed when falling off a high trestle. Chris goes back to Adonde with the money as one of Lavalle's men follows him. Chris approaches a stream, is ambushed, but manages to kill his assailant.

Estelle, meanwhile, has gone into town to tell the marshal about what has happened and they go out looking for Chris. Lavalle has quietly slipped into town and sees Chris coming in wounded. Lavalle takes aims to shoot Chris but is distracted by a young boy. Chris seizes the opportunity and kills Lavalle. Chris and Estelle then go off together.

BACKGROUND:

In SHOWDOWN, critics said that the picture was "interesting and absorbing;" also "well plotted." A critic wrote: "Murphy performs with heroic valor and turns in a good acting job."

More significant was this comment by another critic: "Audie Murphy is the only performer left in Hollywood with personality and following enough to allow him to continue to make modest budget Westerns which exhibitors can count on (meaning to draw enough people into their theaters to make the running of a movie pay off)."

A note of interest: prisoners found themselves attached to the "Iron Maypole" as this unusual jail was called. It consisted quite simply of a tall telephone-type pole set upright in the ground from which hung heavy chains and at the end of each chain, an iron collar. Captives, even those detained overnight, had the iron collars clamped about their necks with sufficient length for prisoners to lie down, walk a few steps or fight. It was outlawed after it was considered inhumane.

GUNFIGHT AT COMANCHE CREEK

STUDIO: ALLIED ARTISTS (release)

PRODUCER: Ben Schwalb
DIRECTOR: Frank McDonald
SCREENPLAY: Edwards Bernds
DIRECTOR OF PHOTOGRAPHY: Joseph F. Biroc, A.S.C.
FILM EDITOR: William Austin, A.C.E.
PRODUCTION MANAGER: Edward Morey, Jr.
MUSIC: Marlin Skiles
ART DIRECTOR: Edward Jewell
ASSISTANT DIRECTOR: Don Torpin
SET DECORATOR: Clarence Steensen
SOUND EDITOR: Marty Greco
SET CONTINUITY: Hazel Hall
RECORDING ENGINEER: Ralph Butler
COSTUME SUPERVISOR: Eddie Armand
MAKEUP SUPERVISION: Wally Westmore, S.M.A.
HAIR STYLE SUPERVISION: Nellie Manley, C.H.S.
CONSTRUCTION SUPERVISOR: James West
PROPERTY MASTER: Max Frankel
FILMED IN PANAVISION and COLOR by DELUXE

DATES OF FILMING: March 27, 1963 to mid-April 1963
LOCATION OF FILMING: Greater Los Angeles area

CAST:

Bob Gifford .... Audie Murphy
Carter .... Ben Cooper
Abbie .... Colleen Miller
Troop .... DeForest Kelley
Nielson .... Jan Merlin
Marshal Shearer .... John Hubbard
Winton .... Damian O'Flynn
Janie .... Susan Seaforth

RUNNING TIME: 91 minutes
RELEASE DATE: November 1963

SYNOPSIS:

A gang, whose members keep their identities hidden, has committed a number of bank robberies in several towns. They have also developed a sideline of breaking known criminals out of jail with the sole purpose of robbing more banks. Because the fugitives are seen on wanted posters when the banks are robbed, the reward money for their capture, dead of alive, is increased. The rest of the gang wear masks to hide their faces so they are not recognized. The gang then kills the wanted men and turns over their bodies for the reward. Soon after, another is selected from another reward poster followed by the same routine.

As this pattern develops and becomes known, a Pinkerton-style detective agency is hired to infiltrate the gang to expose and arrest them. The plan, however, backfires and the detective posing as the outlaw is killed. Another detective, Bob Gifford, is brought in by the agency who then creates the criminal alter-ego, Judd Tanner. He then has himself put in jail near the gang's usual territory. The phony wanted posters are distributed starting out with a small price on his head. Marshal Shearer, who is part of the gang, is not a suspect at this time and is thought to be on the level. Judd gives the marshal all the information about him being a detective and asks for his help in this case. Naturally, Shearer offers to work with him getting this gang and bringing them to justice.

Gifford has now been arrested and thrown in jail. The phony wanted posters work. Marshal Shearer cooperates and gets "Tanner" out of jail, and arranges for him to be brought to the gang's hideout. In order to establish his credibility, Gifford becomes the front man for the gang in a couple

Audie Murphy, capturing the outlaws in the final shootout of GUNFIGHT AT COMANCHE CREEK

of robberies. Naturally, since his face is not covered, everyone knows what he looks like. Since Troop, the leader of this gang, sees that Gifford is working out, he keeps him on to do more robberies. As the banks keep getting robbed and Gifford's face is recognizable, the price on his head gets higher and higher.

As Gifford now has a little leverage with the gang, he signals to his contact with the National Detective Agency who is usually close by. He keeps him informed as to the gang's activities in case anything happens to him. Soon Gifford will signal a contact from the agency to bring in others to arrest the gang.

Gifford befriends a young man who is in the gang against his will and confesses his identity to him. He asks Carter for his help and he is willing to join together with Gifford. He sends Carter into town to get the marshal. Carter tries to tell him what has been happening with the gang and Gifford. Since the marshal doesn't want Carter going back to the hideout and telling Gifford, he kills Carter. The townspeople who hear the shot come to the jail to find out what has happened. He tells them that the boy tried to rob him and that he shot him in self defense.

While Gifford is trying to plan how to get the gang, another fugitive is broken out of jail and brought to the hideout. This puts a different slant on his plan. Meanwhile, Gifford's partner, Neilson, has been captured by one of the gang members. Troop has found out that one of the two men is a detective from the marshal. Troop then challenges Gifford and tells him to kill Neilson to prove that he is indeed an outlaw. Gifford knows he can't kill his partner so Neilson forces one of the gang members to kill him by going after him. Troop is incensed by this act because he still doesn't know which one of the two is the detective.

Troop and the outlaws rob another bank. The marshal has left specific instructions for Troop to kill Gifford and tells him that he is the detective. However, Gifford notifies the agency in time and is saved as the entire gang is arrested, along with the marshal.

BACKGROUND:

GUNFIGHT AT COMANCHE CREEK was a remake of a movie titled THE LAST OF THE BADMEN. The latter picture had starred George Montgomery and was released in February 1957.

GUNFIGHT AT COMANCHE CREEK was described by a reviewer as a "program Western with a fairly good story." In this movie, Audie Murphy played a "Pinkerton-like detective" who infiltrated a gang of outlaws to learn their methods of operation and expose them.

Of the Murphy performance a critic wrote: "Murphy's role was devised and executed with journeyman efficiency." Another reviewer said: "Audie's low-pressure, easy-going histrionic style may not be great acting, but it is ideally suitable to the Western hero mold."

A note of interest to all "Star Trek" fans was that DeForest Kelley, who played the role of Troop in this film was "Bones" McCoy on the Starship Enterprise.

THE QUICK GUN

STUDIO: COLUMBIA

PRODUCER: Grant Whytock
DIRECTOR: Sidney Salkow
SCREENPLAY BY: Robert E. Kent
BASED ON A STORY BY: Steve Fisher
DIRECTOR OF PHOTOGRAPHY: Lester Shorr, A.S.C.
ART DIRECTOR: Robert Purcell
FILM EDITOR: Grant Whytock, A.C.E.
SET DIRECTOR: Frank Tuttle
MAKE-UP SUPERVISION: Ben Lane, S.M.A.
ASSISTANT DIRECTOR: Herbert S. Greene
SOUND SUPERVISOR: Charles J. Rice
SOUND: Josh Westmoreland
MUSIC BY: Richard LaSalle
FILMED IN TECHNISCOPE
COLOR BY TECHNICOLOR

DATES OF FILMING: Mid-September 1963 to October 2, 1963
LOCATION OF FILMING: Columbia Studio Ranch, Burbank, California

CAST:

Clint Cooper .... Audie Murphy
Helen Reed .... Merry Anders
Scotty Grant .... James Best
Spangler .... Ted deCorsia
Tom Morrison .... Walter Sande
Rick Morrison .... Rex Holman
Reverend Staley .... Charles Meredith
Dan Evans .... Frank Ferguson
Cagle .... Mort Mills
Donovan .... Gregg Palmer
George Keely .... Frank Gerstle
Dr. Stevens .... Stephen Roberts
Mitchell .... Paul Bryar
Elderly man .... Raymond Hatton
Mike .... William Fawcett

RUNNING TIME: 87 minutes
RELEASE DATE: April 1964

SYNOPSIS:

In this film, Audie plays a youth turned into a gun-fighter who had taken up with a gang but no longer has ties with them. Spangler tells Clint before he rides out that he plans on robbing the bank and offers him a chance to stay. But Clint is finished and he rides into his former town of Shelby, Montana.

Upon seeing his old friend, Scotty, who is now the sheriff and due to his bad reputation, is told it would be best if he left town. Apparently since Clint left over two years ago, there hasn't been any shooting in Shelby. Clint had killed Tom Morrison's two sons a couple of years ago and Morrison is still seeking revenge against Clint and will kill him at the first opportunity. To show good faith, Clint surrenders his gun to Scotty letting him know he doesn't want any trouble. He does, however, tell Scotty that the gang is planning on robbing the bank.

Morrison's nephew, Rick, has seen

Walter Sande holds a gun on Audie Murphy as nephew, Rex Holman, looks on in this scene from THE QUICK GUN.

Clint ride into town and takes off to his uncle's ranch to let him know that Clint was back. Morrison gathers together some of his ranch hands and heads for town hoping to avenge his sons' deaths.

At Scotty's office, Clint asks about Helen, his former girlfriend. Scotty tells him she is at the school teaching. When she sees Clint, she is quite surprised but tells him that it was over between them a long time ago. They were to be married a little over two years ago but Clint's gunfighting had come between them. Helen then informs Clint that she and Scotty are planning to be married the following week. Clint is visibly hurt but wishes them happiness. He is disappointed that she didn't wait for him.

As Clint enters the saloon, Tom Morrison is there along with Rick. Morrison has had enough time to get drunk and is ready for trouble. Clint sees the state Morrison is in and tries to avoid him. He heads for the door, but Morrison wants a fight. Clint finally takes care of the Morrisons but not without taking a pretty bad pounding. Scotty arrives in time to keep the Morrisons from killing Clint.

Meanwhile, Clint's warning has given the town enough time to set up a trap for the outlaws. A barricade of wagons is put at each end of the street making it impossible for anyone to come through the town.

Tom Morrison is still gunning for Clint and wants him dead. He and Rick grab Clint and plan to hang him. Again Clint is on the defensive and he kills the Morrisons in self defense. However, since there were no witnesses, Scotty has no choice but to put

Clint in jail for murder. Clint tries to convince Scotty to let him out so he can help him when the gang comes into town. But Scotty can't be responsible for Clint's safety, worry about Spangler and protect the town too.

A messenger is sent by Spangler to the jail. Scotty rides out to talk with Spangler in hopes of turning him back. He tries to convince him not to rob the bank and that the streets have been barricaded. The town is ready for him. However, Spangler kills Scotty as he and his men ride into town. Helen gets the women and children to the church. Spangler finds them and takes Helen hostage.

Dan Evans is desperate and lets Clint out of jail so he can help. Now that Scotty is dead, there is no law in Shelby so they are relying in Clint to save them. He sets up a trap for the outlaws and lures them to the hotel where he gets Helen. Then with Dan's and Helen's help, they get the rest of the outlaws. Clint gets the drop on them and ties them up knowing that Spangler will try to get them free with the final shootout being in favor of Clint.

BACKGROUND:

A critic wrote: "Murphy is perfect in this type of role."

Merry Anders watches anxiously as Audie Murphy fights off the outlaws in this scene from THE QUICK GUN.

BULLET FOR A BADMAN

STUDIO: UNIVERSAL-INTERNATIONAL

PRODUCER: Gordon Kay
DIRECTOR: R.G. Springsteen
SCREENPLAY BY: Mary and Willard Willingham
BASED ON A NOVEL BY: Marvin H. Albert
DIRECTOR OF PHOTOGRAPHY: Joseph Biroc, A.S.C.
EASTMAN COLOR BY PATHE
PRODUCTION MANAGER: Howard Pine
ART DIRECTORS: Alexander Golitzen and Henry Bumstead
SET DECORATIONS: Oliver Emert
SOUND: Waldon O. Watson and Joe Lapis
UNIT PRODUCTION MANAGER: Howard Pine
FILM EDITOR: Russell Schoengarth, A.C.E.
COSTUME SUPERVISION: Edward Armand and Olive Koenitz
MAKE-UP: Bud Westmore
HAIR STYLIST: Larry Germain
ASSISTANT DIRECTOR: Phil Bowles
MUSIC: Frank Shinner
MUSIC SUPERVISION: Joseph Gershenson
DATES OF FILMING: Late October 1963 to November 11, 1963
LOCATION OF FILMING: St. George, Utah, area

CAST:

Logan Keliher .... Audie Murphy
Sam Ward .... Darren McGavin
Lottie .... Ruta Lee
Susan .... Beverly Owen
Pink .... Skip Homeier
Diggs .... George Tobias
Leach .... Alan Hale
Tucker .... Edward C. Platt
Jeff .... Berkeley Harris
Sammy .... Kevin Tate
Goldie .... Cece Whitney

RUNNING TIME: 80 minutes
RELEASE DATE: October 1964

SYNOPSIS:

A better-than-average Western exploring the basic theme of good versus evil, dramatized by the divergent careers of two former Texas Rangers. Audie portrays Logan Keliher, retired from the Rangers to marry and settle down to a quiet farming life. A conflict is almost inevitable, since he has married the ex-wife and adopted the son of his one-time partner, Sam Ward, recently released from jail. With his gang, Ward plans to rob the bank in a town near Logan's farm, after which he intends to kill Logan for stealing his family.

Logan is overdue with a mortgage payment to the bank. He travels into town to borrow money from his long-time friend, Goldie, who runs the local saloon. Goldie provides the loan. As Logan walks to the bank, he finds a robbery in progress. A gunfight quickly ensues. Logan shoots Ward but escapes. In the confusion, Logan is unaware that his old partner is the injured crook.

While a posse is being formed in town, Ward rides to Logan's farm, confronting his ex-wife, Susan. He tries to convince her to return to him. She rejects him, which makes Ward more determined to find Logan and kill him.

First, however, Ward reunites with his gang at their hideout. The posse hasn't been successful in finding them yet. After going back to his farm and finding out that Ward has been threatening Susan, Logan finally determines where the hideout is, near Apache Indian territory, and sets out alone to settle the score.

Logan captures Ward. Soon after, the posse arrives. There is an argument about whether to return the stolen bank money or simply divide it among the posse. While they are trying to decide what to do with the money, an Apache war party is spotted nearby. Everyone leaves the hideout to avoid confronting them.

At an overnight campsite, Logan and Ward have the opportunity to discuss

Audie Murphy, taking cover in a scene from BULLET FOR A BADMAN

the good old days in the rangers. Logan tries to convince Ward that Susan was simply trying to pick up the pieces of her life after he went to jail. The McGavin character turned bad, stealing and killing on the excuse that he needed money to give his wife and child a break. He was captured and sent to prison for life. Logan offered to help her, which eventually led to them getting married. Ward, however, still wants to kill Logan who thinks he stole her while he was in jail and couldn't fight for her.

Early the next morning, Ward escapes for a while, but comes back pursued by Apaches. The posse is pinned down but manages to hold off the attack. Further argument about the bank money makes Logan realize he cannot trust the other posse members with the exception of Tucker. He manages to get the money and Ward away from the posse, intending to return both to town. Later, Ward has a chance to grab Logan's gun and is about to shoot him, when the posse catches up and begins shooting at both of them.

Logan and Ward must put aside their differences and fight together to fend off the posse. Ward is shot and wounded again. They finally get back to Logan's farm to rest before going into town for medical help for Sam. While there, Ward sees his young son Sammy. He doesn't know who Ward is because he went to jail shortly after his son was born. One last posse member, Pink, has followed them to the farm. He is about to shoot Logan when Ward sees him and shields him from the bullet. Logan kills Pink as Ward dies in his arms telling Logan what a good job he has done with his son.

BACKGROUND:

During the course of the film, Ward's character is shown repeatedly to be completely corrupt, interested primarily in money, killing and revenge. Toward the conclusion, we begin to see that perhaps Ward is not completely evil, and this point is emphasized by Ward sacrificing himself for his former buddy, who, up to that point, he had been trying to kill. Logan, of course, represents everything that Ward is not, the good guy simply trying to do the right thing, the type of acting role that Murphy usually preferred, particularly in Westerns.

A critic described BULLET FOR A BADMAN as one of the best Murphy Westerns ever made. Credit was given to a "sharply executed screenplay," a good direction, and a "100-proof" cast. Vitality was added to the movie by McGavin, who portrayed "a heartless baddie with an extraordinary sense of humor."

Of the Murphy performance a critic wrote: "Audie now wears these roles (Westerns) as comfortably as his outdoor garb. He is very sincere and has developed solid timing and a fine sense of ensemble playing with regard to fellow actors."

A note of interest comes along with this film. Seems as though Audie contributed more than his performance as the star. He also furnished props for it. In the story, character actor, George Tobias portrays a grizzled old ex-buffalo hunter who does his Indian-fighting with a Sharps buffalo gun. When the studio prop department couldn't come up with the unusual weapon, Audie reached into his personal gun collection and filled the bill.

APACHE RIFLES

STUDIO: 20TH CENTURY FOX-ADMIRAL PICTURES

ASSOCIATE PRODUCER: Grant Whytock
DIRECTOR: William H. Witney
SCREEN PLAY BY: Charles B. Smith
STORY BY: Kenneth Gamet and Richard Schayer
DIRECTOR OF PHOTOGRAPHY: Arch R. Dalzell
SUPERVISING EDITOR: Grant Whytock
ART DIRECTOR: Frank Sylos
COLOR BY DE LUXE
PRODUCTION MANAGER: Joseph Small
ASSISTANT DIRECTOR: Herbert S. Greene
SOUND EDITOR: James Richards
MUSIC EDITOR: Sid Sidney
WARDROBE: Alexis Davidoff
SET DIRECTOR: Morris Hoffman
MAKE-UP ARTIST: Vincent Romaine
HAIR STYLIST: Gladys Witten
PROPERTY MASTER: Max Frankel
SOUND: Lambert Day
MUSIC BY: Richard LaSalle

DATES OF FILMING: May 12, 1964 to May 30, 1964
LOCATION OF FILMING: Mojave, California, area

CAST:

Jeff Stanton .... Audie Murphy
Red Hawk .... Michael Dante
Dawn Gillis .... Linda Lawson
Mike Greer .... L.Q. Jones
Hodges .... Ken Lynch
Victorio .... Joseph A. Vitale
Sergeant Cobb .... Robert Brubaker
Corporal Ramirez ..... Eugene Iglesias
Captain Thatcher .... J. Pat O'Malley
Colonel Perry .... John Archer
Crawford Owens .... Charles Watts
Thompson .... Howard Wright
Captain Green .... Peter Hansen
Sheriff .... Robert Karnes
Arizona Delegate .... Hugh Sanders
General of the Army ... Sydney Smith
General Nelson .... S. John Launer
Miller .... Robert B. Williams

RUNNING TIME: 92 minutes
RELEASE DATE: November 1964

SYNOPSIS:
It is 1879 in the Arizona Territory. Apaches are on the warpath against gold miners who have invaded their lands. The local U.S. Cavalry unit, led by Captain Jeff Stanton, is charged with trying to force the Apaches back to their reservation. Stanton is not sympathetic toward the Apaches because his father, also a cavalry officer, trusted the Indians and half his command got slaughtered. For this, he was court-martialed and cashiered out of the army. Jeff has devoted his army career to make up for his father's troubles by killing Indians when the opportunity arises.

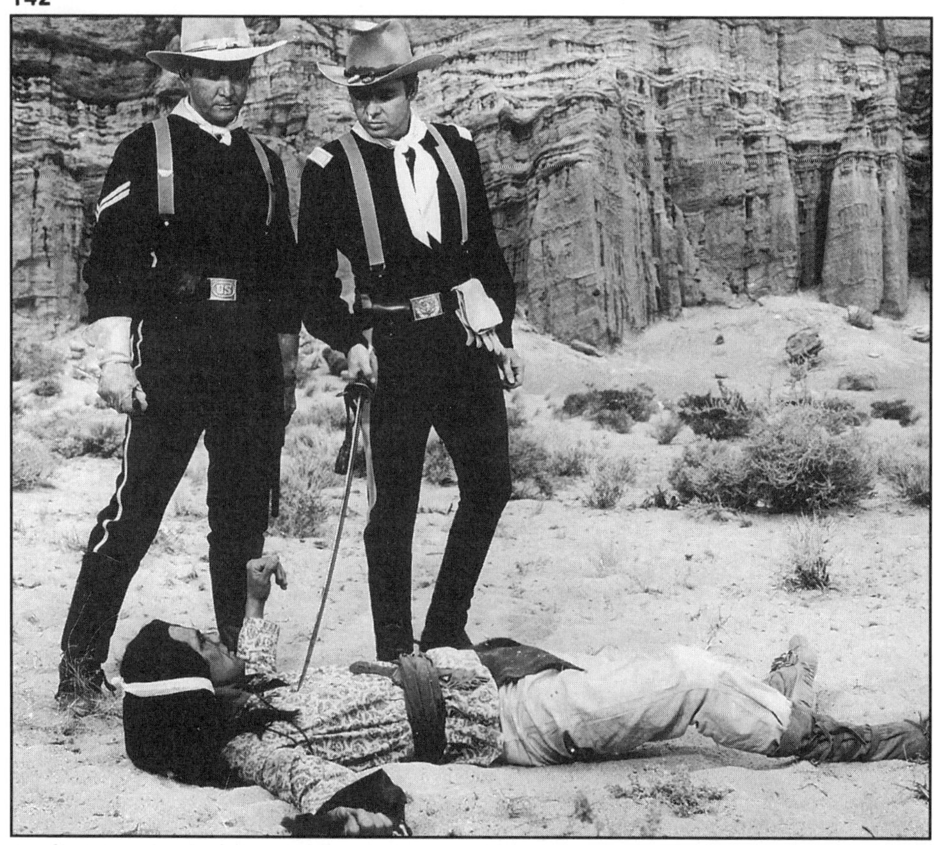

Audie Murphy, holding Michael Dante at bay in this scene from APACHE RIFLES

A small Apache raiding party has killed some local settlers. Jeff decides to set up an ambush, hiding cavalry men inside a supply wagon. The Indians attack, but are soon killed or driven off. One of them, Red Hawk, is wounded and taken prisoner. Red Hawk is the son of the Apache chief, Victorio, one of the most ruthless of all the Apache chiefs. Jeff uses Red Hawk as a bargaining chip to force a powwow with Victorio. Stanton's reputation is well-known among the Indians.

Victorio reluctantly listens to Jeff's demands, thereby gaining the release of Red Hawk. The young Apache tries to kill Jeff, but is stopped by his father. Jeff tells Victorio that a new Indian agent will be sent to look after their interests, but they must return to the reservation. Victorio agrees, but insists that the gold miners must leave all Indian lands. Jeff agrees to this condition.

Before leaving, Jeff notices a white woman among the Indian squaws. He assumes she is a prisoner, and wants to take her back with him. However, he is informed she is not a prisoner, but a missionary, who wishes to stay with the tribe.

Jeff returns to the fort and talks with the army doctor. He wants to know more about his father and what happened to him. The doctor tells Jeff that he knew his father very well. Despite his court-martial, the elder Stanton was not bitter and still had great respect for the Indians. Jeff also meets the new Indian agent, Mr. Thompson. Shortly thereafter, the missionary woman, Dawn, comes to the fort, accompanied by Red Hawk. Jeff asks if there is anything he can do for her. To his surprise, she asks for some Bibles. Jeff agrees to get some for her. After he leaves, Red Hawk wonders why she has neglected to mention that she is half Indian, her mother being a Comanche squaw.

The miners soon find out that the cavalry is supposed to keep them out of the Indian territory where they have their gold claims. They complain to army headquarters in Washington. The army's immediate reaction is that Captain Stanton has overstepped his authority and they proceed to investigate. The miners are sure the ban will soon be overturned. There is open defiance of Jeff's orders, as the miners go back to their digs.

Red Hawk and another brave soon get into a skirmish with two miners. The brave is killed and Red Hawk is captured. He is wearing a gold nugget around his neck. The greedy miners torture him to find out where it came from, but he remains silent. Jeff arrives on the scene, rescues Red Hawk and takes the miners to town to be handled by the sheriff. Jeff then takes Red Hawk to the fort medical dispensary for treatment.

Jeff soon finds out that he is being relieved of command by Colonel Perry and that he has ordered Red Hawk out of the fort. Perry, meantime, has recalled all outpost patrols. The Colonel expects that the Apaches will soon attack.

Thompson, the Indian agent, is found killed with an arrow in the back. The miners now have an excuse to invade the Apache camp. Jeff arrives in camp and tries to stop the killing. Dawn is wounded before peace is restored. Jeff takes her back to the fort and a romantic interest begins to form between them.

After examining the arrow that killed Thompson, Jeff tells Perry he is sure that the Apaches are being framed and the army should defend their interests. Perry refuses to believe him and has Jeff put under house arrest for insubordination. The colonel then leads his troops out into battle with Victorio's Apaches. The cavalry is soon drawn into a trap where Perry is wounded. While the soldiers fight the surrounding Indians, Perry has one soldier sneak out at night to get help from another fort.

Red Hawk comes to take Dawn back to the reservation but she wants to stay with Jeff. Red Hawk reminds Jeff that Dawn is a half-breed, which means that if they married, his children would have Indian blood in them. When Jeff hesitates over this, Dawn becomes upset and leaves with Red Hawk.

Jeff finds out about the attack on Perry's troops. He decides to locate the one who really killed Thompson. He discovers that one of the miners, Greer, killed the agent. Perry, meanwhile, has managed to get back to the fort. Jeff takes Greer to Perry and makes him confess the crime. With his house arrest lifted, Jeff now goes looking for Victorio, in order to stop any further bloodshed.

Jeff encounters Red Hawk, who is

now chief. Victorio is dead. Jeff asks about Dawn, but Red Hawk refuses to discuss her. She is "dead" as far as Jeff is concerned. Jeff now arranges a meeting between Red Hawk and Perry. Red Hawk tells Perry his people will go back to the reservation, as long as there are no reprisals from him or the government. Jeff tells Perry that this request sounds reasonable but Perry refuses to honor it. Instead, Perry orders Red Hawk arrested and he feels betrayed. In his anger, Red Hawk retaliates by throwing his lance at Jeff, severely wounding him.

Jeff recovers in the hospital after three weeks. Perry is transferred back East. The post command is returned to Jeff, along with a promotion to major. However, Jeff insists that the army work out an honorable peace with the Apaches, otherwise he will resign. Red Hawk is released and agrees to go back to the reservation. As he leaves, Red Hawk invites Jeff to visit him someday and bring his children. As Jeff turns to leave, he finds Dawn waiting for him.

BACKGROUND:

The movie was said by a critic to "move at a fast clip." The camera work and the editing were pronounced "exceptionally good."

A reviewer wrote that Audie played his "compassionate officer role with a kind and sturdy conviction."

John Archer with Audie Murphy, pinned down by Indians in this scene from APACHE RIFLES

ARIZONA RAIDERS

STUDIO: COLUMBIA

PRODUCER: Grant Whytock
DIRECTOR: William Witney
STORY BY: Frank Gruber and Richard Schayer
SCREENPLAY BY: Alex Gottlieb, Mary and Willard Willingham
DIRECTOR OF PHOTOGRAPHY: Jacques Marquette
PRODUCTION SUPERVISOR: Harold E. Knox
ART DIRECTOR: Paul Sylos, Jr.
SET DECORATOR: Harry Reif
MAKE-UP ARTIST: Dan Greenway
PROPERTY MASTER: Charles Henley
SOUND: F. Ryan
WARDROBE: Joseph Dimmitt
SOUND SUPERVISOR: Charles J. Rice
MUSIC BY: Richard LaSalle
MUSIC EDITOR: Edna Bullock
SUPERVISING EDITOR: Grant Whytock, A.C.E.
ASSISTANT DIRECTOR: Jack C. Lacey
HAIR STYLIST: Edith Lindon
SOUND EDITOR: Al Bird
SCRIPT SUPERVISOR: John Gannon
COLOR BY TECHNICOLOR
FILMED IN TECHNISCOPE

DATES OF FILMING: November 30, 1964 to December 12, 1964
LOCATION OF FILMING: Tucson, Arizona, area

CAST:

Clint .... Audie Murphy
Brady .... Michael Dante
Willie Martin .... Ben Cooper
Capt. Andrews .... Buster Crabbe
Martina .... Gloria Talbott
Danny Bonner .... Ray Stricklyn
Montana .... George Keymas
Matt Edwards .... Fred Krone
Eddie .... Willard Willingham
Tex .... Red Morgan
Quantrill .... Fred Graham

RUNNING TIME: 88 minutes
RELEASE DATE: August 1965

SYNOPSIS:

During the Civil War, Quantrill's Raiders became infamous for their looting and killing in the West, but were supported by southern sympathizers. After the vicious raid on Lawrence, Kansas, they were soon being pursued vigorously by the U.S. Cavalry as outlaws.

They attempt another raid on a small town, where the cavalry catches up with them. Two of the raiders, Clint Stewart and Willie Martin, are caught robbing the bank. Quantrill is wounded and captured. Clint and

Audie Murphy in a shootout scene from ARIZONA RAIDERS

Willie are tried, convicted and sentenced to 20 years hard labor. Soon after, Quantrill dies of his wounds. Other members of the raiders manage to escape and decide to continue their robbing in a new territory—Arizona.

The governor of the territory calls in Captain Andrews, the former a cavalry officer who captured Quantrill, to pursue the raiders again. Andrews needs to form a unit of rangers for the task. Figuring he needs to have someone infiltrate the raiders' inner circle to find out their plans, Andrews arranges to put Clint and Willie on a prison work detail near the ranger camp. He offers them a pardon for their crimes if they join the rangers and bring the raiders to justice. They agree.

With Andrews' help, Clint and Willie "escape" and take Andrews "hostage." They ride off to the ranger camp where Clint finds that his younger brother, Danny, has also joined the rangers.

The raiders invade a peaceful Yaqui village, which soon becomes a deadly confrontation. Andrews has spread word of the prison break, and, soon after, Clint and Willie find out where the raiders are hiding. They ride to the Yaqui village encountering Montana, one of the raiders' leaders. Clint forces a shootout with Montana and kills him. The other leader, Brady, comes back from robbing a gold train. Brady offers to let Clint and Willie join up again. To Willie's surprise, Clint declines the offer, telling Brady they are on their way to Mexico.

As they leave, Brady has them followed. He doesn't trust them. On Andrews' orders, Danny is also watching the pair. Willie asks Clint if he is serious about Mexico. Clint answers that he never intended to be a ranger. Danny confronts them and tells him he will have to take them back to prison if they try to leave the country. The Mexican border is only a short distance away so Danny stops them with his gun drawn. Brady's men shoot Danny, thinking he is holding them prisoners. Clint tries to comfort his dying brother by promising he will stay in the rangers.

Clint and Willie have a shootout with Brady's henchmen killing one of them while the other is dragged off by Indians. They ride back to the village and when Brady questions them about his men, doesn't believe Clint's story. The two of them appear totally unharmed which seems very suspicious to Brady.

Clint tells Willie he must get to Andrews, to reveal the Raiders hideout. Willie leaves, but is not aware that he is being followed. He is captured, brought back to the village and though badly beaten, doesn't betray Clint's cover. Clint tries to tell Brady that he joined the rangers to get out of prison. Brady doesn't buy this story and kills Willie by shooting him in the back. Clint makes a silent vow to get Brady and make him pay for Willie's life.

Brady decides to break camp and head for Mexico. Clint manages to break away and ride to the ranger camp. The rangers go after Brady and his raiders, who are soon captured, and peace returns to the territory.

BACKGROUND:

The picture was partly based on TEXAS RANGERS, a movie released in 1951.

Critics said that ARIZONA RAIDERS was a "fast-paced Western with good action and rousing fight scenes." As for the star performance, a critic wrote: "Murphy delivers one of his regulation gunman characterizations for plenty of gun-play."

Audie Murphy and Michael Dante, watching for gold shipment in this scene from ARIZONA RAIDERS

GUNPOINT

STUDIO: UNIVERSAL-INTERNATIONAL

PRODUCER: Gordon Kay
DIRECTOR: Earl Bellamy
SCREENPLAY: Mary and Willard Willingham
DIRECTOR OF PHOTOGRAPHY: William Margulies, A.S.C.
ART DIRECTORS: Alexander Golitzen and Henry Bumstead
SET DECORATIONS: John McCarthy and Oliver Emert
SOUND: Waldon O. Watson and Lyle Cain
UNIT PRODUCTION MANAGER: Frank Baur
FILM EDITOR: Russell F. Schoengarth, A.C.E.
MAKE-UP: Bud Westmore
HAIR STYLIST: Larry Germain
ASSISTANT DIRECTOR: Phil Bowles
MUSIC: Hans J. Salter
MUSIC SUPERVISION BY: Joseph Gershenson

DATES OF FILMING: June 2, 1965 to June 17, 1965
LOCATION OF FILMING: St. George, Utah, area

CAST:

Chad Lucas .... Audie Murphy
Uvalde .... Joan Staley
Nate Harlan .... Warren Stevens
Bull .... Edgar Buchanan
Cap .... Denver Pyle
Mark Emerson .... David Macklin
Nicos .... Nick Dennis
Ode .... Royal Dano
Ab .... Kelly Thordsen
Drago .... Morgan Woodward
Hoag .... William Bramley
Mitch .... Robert Pine
Mayor Osborne .... John Hoyt
Emerson .... Ford Rainey
Dr. Beardsley .... Roy Barcroft

RUNNING TIME: 86 minutes
RELEASE DATE: May 1966

SYNOPSIS:

Chad Lucas is the sheriff in a small town which straddles the border of two states. Chad's deputy, Cap Holt, is secretly involved with a gang of bank robbers. Cap ambushes Chad to get him out of the way before the bank is hit again. Thinking Chad is dead, Cap heads back to town. However, Chad regains consciousness and makes his way back, not knowing who shot him or why.

While Cap is planning his strategy with young Mark Emerson and other town members for capturing the robbers, Chad comes walking into the jail. Cap, of course, is surprised to see the sheriff still alive. The doctor treating Chad tells him that he will have blurry vision from his wound on and off for the next few days.

The town is on the brink of bankruptcy and since Chad is not a hundred percent healed, the townsfolk decide to send for a U.S. Marshal to help find the outlaws. However, this will take several days and Chad doesn't want to wait. As the matter is being discussed regarding how to deal with this gang, shots are heard at the bank. When Chad gets there, he finds the teller dead and the banker mortally wounded. He pleads with Chad before he dies to find the murderers and return the money to the town. Chad vows to track down the killers.

Across the street, and the state line, is the town saloon owned by Nate Harlan. Chad has no authority to arrest anyone there, which makes it a haven for criminals. Shooting is heard in the saloon, and Chad goes to investigate. Inside is the gang leader, Drago, who has been identified by a witness coming out of the bank after the robbery. Chad approaches him, but Drago senses he may be in danger. He grabs the singer, Uvalde, and uses her as a shield to escape. Uvalde is Chad's former girlfriend.

Chad forms a posse to hunt Drago, but they run into a band of Apaches, who attack. The posse fights them off. Chad is still having some vision problems and is not aware there is an Indian about to kill him. He is saved at the last second by Nate who has come along to get Uvalde back and also the money stolen from the bank.

The Indians have had enough and leave as the posse continues searching for Drago. A short time later, they find Uvalde riding for her life. Drago has set her loose as a decoy so that the Indians will go after her while he and his gang ride in the opposite direction. Chad rescues Uvalde as the posse goes after the Indians.

Chad and Uvalde reminisce about their old romance. They had planned on getting married at one time but Chad went away on a cattle drive and

Joan Staley and Audie Murphy, talking over old times in a scene from GUNPOINT

got into some trouble. He robbed a bank and went to jail, but since it was his first offense, the judge was lenient and paroled him. After two years, Chad went back to town looking for Bonnie. She changed her name after waiting for him before she ended up working in Harlan's saloon as a singer. Chad decided not to go after her and probably thought it was best for the both of them.

The quest for Drago continues as the posse returns. At one point, they determine he has gotten several miles ahead on the trail. In order to catch up with Drago and cut him off, Chad decides it is shorter to ride over the top of the mountain ridge than go around. Cap sees another opportunity to get rid of the sheriff. He loosens a large boulder which would have killed Chad if his Mexican friend, Nicos, hadn't pushed him out of the way. Nicos is hurled down the mountain to his death. Chad still doesn't realize that Cap is deliberately trying to kill him.

Drago is spotted but he sees a herd of wild horses which he stampedes towards the posse. Chad and Cap hear shots and ride to investigate. Cap draws a gun on Chad and tells him of his partnership with Drago. He also is planning on killing Chad on the spot but the herd of horses are upon them before they know what is happening. Chad manages to jump clear of the stampede but Cap is trampled.

Having lost their own horses in the stampede, Chad, Uvalde and the two remaining posse members, Nate and Mark, walk ahead and find themselves at a settler's camp. As they bed down for the night, Chad senses an uneasiness. Drago and his men invade the camp a short time later resulting in a furious gun battle where Mark is killed.

Chad again starts out after Drago. However, he finds out that Bonnie's brother is running with the gang. She makes Chad promise that Mitch won't get hurt, but he can't make that commitment to her. As he starts to leave, Nate knocks Chad out and takes Bonnie with him to look for Mitch and the money.

Nate and Bonnie get to Drago's shortly before Chad. Bonnie runs to warn Chad but is shot and slightly wounded. Drago tries to escape but Chad kills him. But now, he must fight Nate. Nate is aware that Chad is having trouble seeing and takes advantage of the situation and moves in behind Chad. Bonnie pleads with Nate not to kill Chad, but Nate wants the money all for himself. Realizing that he has a problem, Chad makes a quick move that distracts Nate and he kills him. Chad and Uvalde go off together deciding to renew their romance.

BACKGROUND:

GUNPOINT starred Audie Murphy as a courageous sheriff in a small Western town during the 1880s. One reviewer said the movie involved a train robbery, a dash of romantic interest, and plenty of outlaw-versus-Indian action. A critic rated the picture as "top fare in the outdoor adventure category."

Of the Murphy performance a reviewer wrote: "Audie has always had a quality of sincerity that wears well."

TRUNK TO CAIRO

STUDIO: AMERICAN INTERNATIONAL

PRODUCER: Menahem Golan
DIRECTOR: Menahem Golan
SCRIPT BY: Marc Behm and Alexander Ramati
ASSOCIATE PRODUCER: Michael Kaban
PRODUCTION MANAGER: J. Neuman
EDITOR: Danny Shik
ART DIRECTOR: S. Zafrir
SOUND: Z. Nachtigal
FILM MANAGER: J. Neuman
SET DECORATIONS: K. Sander
SCRIPT GIRL: T. Ordri
DIRECTOR OF PHOTOGRAPHY: Mimish Herbst
MAKE-UP: R. Golun and D. Priver
MUSIC COMPOSED AND CONDUCTED BY: Dov Seltzer

SONG: "Dangerous Woman"
SUNG BY: Geula Bill

DATES OF FILMING: Mid-June to mid-July, 1965
LOCATION OF FILMING: This movie was shot entirely in Israel

CAST:

Mike Merrick .... Audie Murphy
Professor Schlieben . George Sanders
Helga Schlieben .... Marianne Koch
Hans Klugg .... Hans Von Borszodi
Capt. Gabar .... Joseph Yadin
Yasmin .... Gila Almagor
Jamil .... Eitan Priver
Ali .... Bomba I. Zur

RUNNING TIME: 80 minutes
RELEASE DATE: January 1967

SYNOPSIS:
Three people go to the beach expecting to have a day of fun. Instead, a bomb goes off killing the two men. The woman comes out of the water screaming.

The scene shifts to Mike Merrick flying to Cairo, Egypt. He strikes up a conversation with a woman seated across the aisle and introduces himself as Ludwig Bauer, a German scientist. He finds out she is the daughter of the rocket scientist, with whom he will be working.

Mike's first assignment in Cairo is to head for a record store where a coded message is on an album giving him instructions. German scientists are being killed and he is to find out who is killing the Germans and using Israel as a cover.

Back in his hotel room, Mike is attacked by an unknown assailant and almost killed. Captain Gabar, of the police department, enters the room scaring away the would be murderer. While they are having a drink, Mike wants to know from Gabar who is trying to scare the Germans out of Egypt. As they are talking, they are also being watched. Shots are fired but miss them. Gabar tells Mike to stay put as he goes looking for the sniper. Mike, alone at the table, is joined by a woman. He remarks that her voice sounds familiar. Upon his return Gabar hears the conversation, and tells Mike that she is a well-known entertainer. It was her voice Mike heard on the record.

The next day, Mike and Gabar arrive at Professor Schleiben's laboratory where he takes them on a tour of his "little empire." The area is heavily guarded. Inside the lab is a rocket. Schleiben informs Mike he's putting an atomic warhead on the rocket where the "great powers of the West and East will come begging at his door."

Mike is shown his quarters by another worker. A package he was carrying explodes, killing him. Mike remembers an identical package back at the laboratory office. He runs back to the office, takes it outside and carefully disarms the other bomb.

That evening Professor Schleiben is giving a party for his daughter Helga. She begins to flirt with Mike which causes Hans, her fiance´, to regard them with disgust. Helga wants to go for a swim where Mike follows her and they embrace passionately on the beach.

Mike has returned to the record shop where he listens for more instructions. He is to get photos of the rocket plans immediately and must get into the building that night. Under cover of darkness, Mike makes his way to the lab. He finds the plans and begins taking pictures. Engrossed in his work, Mike is surprised by Hans who holds a gun on him and makes him give up the camera. Mike puts Hans off balance for a few seconds and gets the gun. It fires wildly into the rocket's mechanism causing extensive damage. While trying to stop Mike, Hans is killed. Mike then sets fire to the plans and the lab, barely escaping as the sirens wail.

Professor Schleiben surveys the damage, then asks for Bauer. Mike has just made it back when Yasmin locates him. She takes him to Schleiben where Mike is informed that Hans is dead. Schleiben wants Mike to help him repair the rocket.

Mike and Yasmin talk about the assignment ahead. She tells him that the chief wants Mike to leave Egypt at once because the real Ludwig Bauer has been traced to a jail in East Germany where his trial will be in all the papers. Mike tells her he can't leave. They prepare a plan to keep the professor from rebuilding the rocket by kidnapping Helga, the one person he really cares about.

Gabar is suspicious of Mike and wants him picked up. Mike has taken Helga on a midnight sail. He gives her a drink with a sedative in it and takes her to a waiting submarine heading for Tel Aviv. Mike contacts Schleiben telling him if he comes with Mike, he can be with Helga in a matter of hours. Schleiben refuses to go and alarms the guards. Mike goes back to the record shop. Figuring that Mike has a contact, Gabar waits, holding a gun on him. Yasmin comes into the shop to meet Mike, not knowing Gabar is there. She is killed by Gabar while protecting Mike. Mike escapes from Gabar by wounding him but is pursued by guards that are surrounding the shop. The shop owner helps Mike as he seeks help from others. However, these men turn out to be in the resistance and order Mike to be killed. Again, he escapes with some clever tricks and goes back to the shop owner who is still waiting for him.

Mike makes his way to the airport where he steals a plane. He meets up with Gabar who tells him that Schleiben and Helga are both in Rome. They all meet together trying to convince the professor not to repair the rocket and leave with Helga. He refuses and each go their separate ways.

After breaking into the Egyptian embassy, Mike finds Helga. He tries to get her away but is knocked unconscious and put in a trunk headed for Cairo. Some of Mike's men are waiting at the airport, thinking Mike is in the trunk. However, instead of finding Mike in the trunk, they find that Mike has escaped and one of the kidnappers is found inside. He is arrested but they still don't know Mike's whereabouts.

Gabar and Helga drive to the airport where he forces her into the plane. Schleiben tries to go after her but is restrained by Gabar's men. On the plane, Mike is hidden behind Gabar and Helga where he renders Gabar unconscious. Mike and Helga get off the plane where she and her father are reunited.

BACKGROUND:

In a departure from his many Western roles, Audie accepted a part in this low-budget spy thriller, also starring George Sanders. Israeli producer (and director) Menahem Golan, later known for the many action pictures produced by Golan/Globus Pictures, was obviously looking to position this film along the lines of the hugely successful James Bond series.

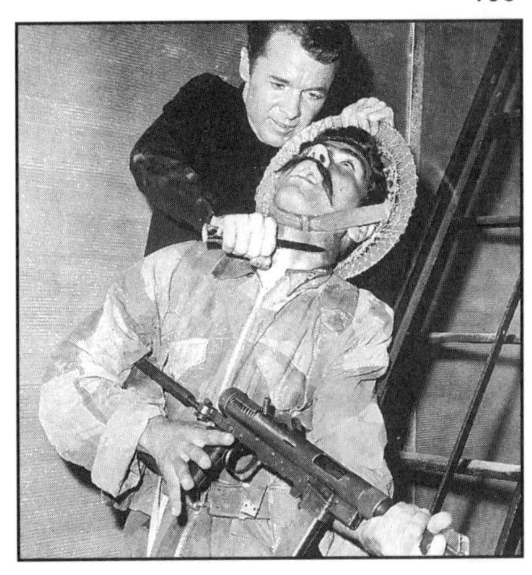

A secret mission has Audie Murphy attempting a break-in at a rocket site in this scene from TRUNK TO CAIRO.

Like Bond, Audie is cast as an intelligence agent named Mike Merrick, apparently American, but employed by a shadowy international spy agency, which is never fully identified. His mission in Cairo seems simple at first, but quickly runs into complications. Sanders' "Professor Schlieben" is an exiled German rocket scientist, ostensibly working on a vehicle designed for lunar travel. In reality, Mike suspects the rockets are to be used as weapons.

Since TRUNK TO CAIRO was shot in Israel and did not receive much publicity in this country, available information on the movie is very limited in Hollywood. It was classified as a mystery.

The song, "Dangerous Woman," in the movie was written by Genia Gil.

THE TEXICAN

STUDIO: COLUMBIA

EXECUTIVE PRODUCERS: Paul C. Ross and Julian Ludwig
PRODUCED BY: John C. Champion and Bruce Balaban
DIRECTOR: Lesley Selander
WRITTEN BY: John C. Champion
DIRECTOR OF PHOTOGRAPHY: Francis Marin
TECHNISCOPE TECHNICOLOR
PRODUCTION SUPERVISOR: Eliseo Boschi
ART DIRECTOR: John Soler
PRODUCTION MANAGER: Mario Berriatua
EDITOR: Teresa Alcocer
CAMERA OPERATOR: Anthony Millan
ASSISTANT DIRECTOR: Joseph Espinosa
CONTINUITY: Lore Meyer
MAKE-UP: Rod Gurrucharri
HAIRDRESSER: Lita Lopez
PHOTOGRAPHER: Max Lopez
SPECIAL EFFECTS: Molina
COSTUME DESIGNER: Ralph Borque
LABORATORIES: Fotofilm - Barcelona
TECHNICOLOR - Rome
FILMED AT: Balcazar Studios, Barcelona
MUSIC COMPOSED BY: Nico Fidenco
CONDUCTED BY: Robby Poitevin

DATES OF FILMING: September 27, 1965 to November 3, 1965
LOCATION OF FILMING: Barcelona, Spain, area

CAST:

Jess Carlin .... Audie Murphy
Luke Starr .... Broderick Crawford
Kit O'Neal .... Diana Lorys
Sandy Adams .... Luz Marquez
Frank Brady .... Antonio Casas
Harv .... Molino Rojo
Gil Rio .... Aldo Sambrell
Eb .... Antonio Peral
Maria Banta .... Helga Genth
Mitch .... Jorge Riguad
U.S. Marshal .... Luis Induni
Elena .... Martha May
Roy Carlin .... Victor Vilanova
Tobe .... Carlos Hurtado
Station Master .... Victor Israel
Miguel .... Jose M. Pinillo
Bounty Hunter .... Cesar Osinaga
Thompson .... Gerard Tichy
Dr. Miller .... Vincente Soler
Townsman .... Juan Carlos Torres
Guitar Player .... Oscar Del Campo
The Gunslinger ..... Manuel Quintana
First Poker Player.... Carlos Miguel Sola
Second Poker Player Angel Lombardi
Mexican Boy .... A. Malla

RUNNING TIME: 90 minutes
RELEASE DATE: June 1966

SYNOPSIS:

Jess Carlin is a disgraced lawman

from Texas law, living across the border in Mexico. However, he arranges with a local border town sheriff to deliver a prisoner from Mexico. The sheriff takes custody of the prisoner, but warns Jess he must stay on the Mexican side of the river or be arrested, reminding him that he, too, is a wanted man. Jess heeds the warning and rides away.

Jess's younger brother, Roy, is a newspaper reporter in Rimrock, who has printed stories about the corruption of the local saloon owner, Luke Starr. Roy is at a relay station with a man who could convict Luke at a trial and send him to jail. The man's testimony would reveal that Luke framed Jess and thereby drove him across the border. Roy's friend is very reluctant to testify, convinced Luke will have him killed.

Luke shows up at the Rimrock waystation where Roy and the man are talking. Luke decides to take care of business right then and kills Roy. At first, Luke is willing to let the other man go, but kills him as he rides away. He plants the gun near Roy, making it look like the two had an argument and shot each other.

Jess finds out about his brother's death and decides to risk traveling into Texas again. He suspects Luke was responsible for Roy's death and must find out the truth. While he is on his way back to Rimrock, two bounty hunters see him and try to bring him in for the $500 reward. Jess defends himself, killing one of the hunters and wounding the other.

Audie Murphy with Antonio Peral, who has the drop on him in this scene from THE TEXICAN

Audie Murphy in the final showdown of THE TEXICAN

them and confronts Luke in the saloon. As usual, Luke knows nothing about it. Later, Luke tells Kit he doesn't like her keeping company with Jess. She tells Luke it's none of his business. Luke then goes to Jess and tells him to be out of town by sunset or he'll be killed.

Jess continues digging into Roy's death. He shows the concho to Sandy, Roy's fiancee. She recognizes it as Luke's. Jess heads for the saloon again. Along the way, he is stopped by three of Luke's gang members but kills them all with some fancy gunplay. Jess tosses the concho at Luke, who pretends he doesn't recognize it. Jess accuses Luke of the killings, and Luke calls Jess a liar. He then informs Jess that there is a .45 pointed at his back. Jess asks if that's how he killed Roy. Luke confesses he killed the two men.

Luke and his henchmen expect that Jess will be looking for them. They try to ambush him, but he gets away. Jess confronts Luke in the saloon, but the outlaw denies he killed Roy and backs away from a showdown. Jess leaves the saloon and is met by Brady, who worked for Roy at the newspaper office. He asks Jess's help to go after Luke and help get rid of Starr. However, Jess's only interest now is who killed his brother.

Jess goes to the waystation to look for clues. He finds a small concho. Later, he meets a man whose life he saved years before. The man tells him that Roy wrote something in the local paper which made Luke angry.

Luke owns half of the Rimrock saloon. The other half is owned by Kit O'Neal, who inherited the share from her father. Jess is interested in her, but Kit thinks Luke is an honest man and Jess a common gunman. She asks Jess to leave her alone. Later, though, Jess rescues Kit from a runaway horse and buggy. She begins to change her mind about him.

Soon after, two of Luke's henchmen try to ambush Jess again. He loses

Luke orders his men to take Jess out and kill him, but Jess moves quickly. With some help from Kit, he kills Luke and the rest of his gang. Jess leaves the saloon, with Kit behind him. She wants to go with him, but Jess knows there is still a price on his head, which he must settle first; then he will come back for her.

BACKGROUND:

"Texicanos" was a name given to drifters and outlaws seeking sanctuary in Mexico in bygone years.

Since THE TEXICAN was filmed in Spain, the Hollywood files contain very little information about the movie.

40 GUNS TO APACHE PASS

STUDIO: COLUMBIA

PRODUCER: Grant Whytock
DIRECTOR: William Witney
STORY BY: Mary and Willard Willingham
WRITTEN BY: Mary and Willard Willingham
MUSIC BY: Richard LaSalle
DIRECTOR OF PHOTOGRAPHY: Jacques Marquette
PRODUCTION SUPERVISOR: Harold E. Knox
ART DIRECTOR: Paul Sylos
FILM EDITOR: Grant Whytock, A.C.E.
SOUND EDITOR: Al Bird
MUSIC EDITOR: Edna Bullock
SET DECORATOR: H. E. Reif
MAKE-UP SUPERVISION: Ted Coodley
WARDROBE: Joseph Dimmitt
PROPERTY MASTER: Max Frankel
ASSISTANT DIRECTOR: Jack Berne
SOUND: Herman Lewis
COLOR BY PATHE
NARRATED BY: Maurice Hart

DATES OF FILMING: May 17, 1966 to May 27, 1966
LOCATION OF FILMING: Lovejoy Buttes near Lancaster, California

CAST:

Captain Coburn ....Audie Murphy
Doug ....Michael Burns
Corporal Bodine ....Kenneth Tobey
Ellen ....Laraine Stephens
Sergeant Walker ......Robert Brubaker
Mike ....Michael Blodgett
Cochise ....Michael Keep
Kate Malone ....Kay Stewart
Harry Malone .. Kenneth MacDonald
Colonel Reed ....Byron Morrow
Fuller ....Willard Willingham
Barrett ....Ted Gehring
Higgins ....James Beck

RUNNING TIME: 95 minutes
RELEASE DATE: May 1967

SYNOPSIS:

In the summer of 1869, Cochise, chief of the Chiricahua Apaches, vows to drive off or kill all white settlers in the southern Arizona territory. Bands of hostile Apaches are roaming the countryside and many settlers have fallen victim to Cochise's bloody oath. A small detail of U.S. Cavalrymen escort survivors to a hastily established outpost at Apache Wells, with Indians in hot pursuit. The cavalry fights them off temporarily, but everyone knows they will return. The cavalry doesn't have enough guns and ammunition to hold off another major attack.

A message is sent to the nearest fort,

and finally they receive the reply that 40 new repeating rifles are being sent, but the cavalry will have to figure out how to get the guns through the mountains and past the Apaches. Captain Coburn asks for volunteers to go out on the dangerous mission.

Under cover of darkness, they ride out to rendezvous with the supply wagons. At Apache Pass, Coburn senses they are being watched and signals some of the men to scout the area. The Indians attack, killing several soldiers before being driven off. Coburn tries to rally his troops, but one of them, Bodine, doesn't trust him and begins plotting against the captain.

The supply wagons arrive at the pass. The troops begin to return to Apache Wells, but Bodine gets the jump on Coburn, knocking him out. The captain's loyal sergeant, Walker, who has been wounded in the fighting, is tied up along with Coburn. Bodine then bribes the rest of the soldiers, including Doug, a young soldier, by offering them the rifles. They leave Coburn and Walker, lighting a dynamite fuse on one of the supply wagons.

Coburn manages to free himself and Walker before the wagon blows up. While the two men try to figure out what to do next, some Indians ride by. Coburn tricks the last Apache and is able to grab the brave's horse. He and Walker ride back to Apache Wells.

Coburn tries to convince the colonel to let him have more men to go out and find the deserters. The colonel refuses, relieves Coburn of his command then orders him confined to the post. However, Coburn must do something to atone for his failure. He

Byron Morrow, giving permission to Robert Brubaker and Audie Murphy to bring back the much needed rifles to fight the Indians, in this scene from 40 GUNS TO APACHE PASS

Kenneth Tobey and Audie Murphy shoot it out in 40 GUNS TO APACHE PASS.

decides to disobey the colonel's orders. With a fresh horse, he rides out alone, hoping to pick up the deserters' trail.

Coburn catches sight of the missing wagon and sees Bodine approaching Cochise's camp under a white flag. He has with him one of the rifles to sell to the chief. Bodine is greedy, he wants the Apaches' gold. Cochise isn't too pleased with the price but the rifles are too valuable to turn down. However, Cochise is interested but refuses to pay until he sees all the rifles.

Coburn sneaks down to the supply wagon and kills one of the deserters who is standing guard. The other guard sees Coburn and fires his gun to warn the troop. Coburn kills the remaining deserters and grabs the wagon and horses. Upon arrival back at the site, Bodine and Cochise find the wagon is gone.

Cochise sends his braves after the wagon, knowing the cavalry can win any fight with his Apaches if they get the new guns. Coburn orders Doug to return to the outpost alone with the rifles, except for a few for Coburn to use as a rearguard.

The Apaches attack. Coburn fights them off, but is running out of ammunition. Just as he is about to be overrun, Doug returns with the rest of the cavalry troop and their new rifles, driving the Apaches away.

Bodine gets caught between the cavalry and the hostile Apaches. While trying to save himself, he encounters Coburn. They fight and Coburn kills him but not before he himself is wounded. Doug finds him and takes the captain back to the outpost where he is reunited with Walker and the rest of his men.

BACKGROUND:

A reviewer described this movie as "good standard cowboy-soldier and Indian affair." It was predicted that the picture would be "popular with the young at heart."

Of Audie's performance, a critic wrote: "Murphy, who still looks like the much decorated hero, plays his role with conviction."

A TIME FOR DYING

STUDIO: A FIPCO PRODUCTION

PRODUCER: Audie Murphy
DIRECTOR: Budd Boetticher
WRITTEN BY: Budd Boetticher
DIRECTOR OF PHOTOGRAPHY: Lucien Ballard, A.S.C.
ART DIRECTOR: Les Thomas
SET DECORATOR: Andy Nealis
COSTUME SUPERVISOR: Eddie Armand
CAMERA OPERATOR: Tom Laughridge
PROPERTY MASTER: Phil Macaluso
PRODUCTION MANAGER: George Tobin
CASTING CONSULTANT: Mildred Gusse
ASSOCIATE TO THE PRODUCER: Willard Willingham
POST PRODUCTION COORDINATOR: Chuck Perry
ASSISTANT DIRECTOR: Bob Farfan
SPECIAL EFFECTS: Herman Townsley
GAFFER: Joe Edesa
HAIRDRESSER: Joan Phillips
GRIP: Richard Moran
MAKEUP: Charles Blackman
SOUND: John Carter
SCRIPT SUPERVISOR: Sandra Nelson
HEAD WRANGLER: Jay Fishburn
MUSIC: Harry Betts
COLOR BY DeLUXE
GLEN GLENN SOUND
TITLE ART: Walt LaRue
TITLES BY: Pacific Title
FILM EDITOR: Harry Knapp

DATES OF FILMING: Late April, 1969 to May 19, 1969
LOCATION OF FILMING: Apache Junction, Arizona

CAST:

Cass Bunning .... Richard Lapp
Nellie Winters .... Anne Randall
Billy Pimple .... Bob Random
Mamie .... Beatrice Kay
Judge Roy Bean .... Victor Jory
Jesse James .... Audie Murphy

IN SILVER CITY

Bartender .... Ron Masak
Ed .... Burt Mustin
Seth .... Peter Brocco
Mayor .... Walter Reed
Blacksmith......................... Louis Ojena
Banker .... Jorge Rado
Shotgun.............................. Walt LaRue
Mamie's Girls .... Maria Desti
.... Betty Rowland
.... Tina Stuart
.... Joanne Shields
.... Miki McDonald
.... Darla Paris

.... Arlette Thomas
.... Nancy Lewis
.... Athena
.... Jo Linn
.... Suzette DeCarlo
Mamie's New Girl . Annette Gorman

IN VINEGAROON

Milton .... Charles Wagenheim
Pepe .... Ira Angustain
Sonny .... Terry M. Murphy
Curly .... Skip Murphy
Cauliflower .... Randy Shields
Rankin .... Bob Herron

JESSE'S MEN

The Southerner .... William Bassett
Southerner's Sidekick ... Casey Tibbs
Frank James .... Willard Willingham
Bob Ford .... J.N. Roberts

BILLY'S BOYS

Dick Spangler, Robert Grever

RUNNING TIME: 72 minutes
RELEASE DATE: None known

SYNOPSIS:

Cass Bunning, a gunfighter with a knack for fancy gunplay, arrives in Silver City. He is soon told that the townsfolk don't like strangers who wear guns. Cass goes into the saloon and is told that the only person allowed to wear a gun is "Billy Pimple" who fashions himself after "Billy the Kid." Cass so impresses the crowd with his gun skills, that the demand to remove his guns ceases.

A beautiful new girl, Nellie Winters, arrives in town on the stagecoach. She immediately attracts a large group of rowdy men surrounding the stage asking if she is the new girl at Mamie's. As the men get more boisterous, Nellie is afraid to leave the coach, so Cass, observing all this, decides to come to her rescue. He swings her up into the saddle and they ride off. A little later on they have a chance to talk and get acquainted.

The ride takes them to Vinegaroon where they encounter Judge Roy Bean who is holding court. Cass and Nellie have been brought before him accused of being together in the same hotel room without being married. This, of course, is a frame up from some of Bean's men. Cass insists that he slept outside Nellie's bedroom. The judge decides, however, that they should be married and performs the ceremony on the spot.

As Cass and Nellie talk over the future, he tells her that he thinks he can make money by being a bounty hunter, bringing to justice such famous outlaws as Jesse and Frank James, Billy the Kid and so on. In fact, he decides that his first capture should be Billy Pimple since he's not so well known. Cass is convinced that because he is good with his guns, he won't have any trouble bringing in these desperadoes.

Nellie is impressed by Cass's fancy gunplay; in fact it attracts several strangers who have also heard the shooting. One of the men, who appears to be the leader, has ordered Cass to drop his pants. This was a custom of the West to keep the man subdued while being robbed, as it was difficult to go after anyone with his pants down. The man rides towards Cass and Nellie and tells Cass that the rhythm of his gunfire had them curious. The stranger offers good advice to Cass, telling him to keep his palms dry especially when drawing his guns. If they are wet with sweat, it could mean the difference between his life or death. The man also warns them to go around Silver City, not through it. Seems there has been some trouble there and he doesn't want to see them get hurt. He also offers Cass a job when he gets finished being a farmer.

Cass is in awe of this man and asks his name. The man apologizes for not introducing himself, his brother Frank, anlong with their friend, Bob Ford. His name is Jesse. He bids Cass and Nellie good day and the men ride away. Cass can't believe that he was just in the presence of Jesse James. He wants to follow them but Nellie feels he is being foolish.

On their way to town, they are met with other gang members who take Nellie with them. They keep Cass from helping her until they are far enough away, then let him go. Eventually, Cass gets to town and helps the people kill several of the gang. Since there is a reward for the James gang, dead or alive, Cass is awarded a portion of the money.

Billy Pimple has heard about Cass's reputation and challenges him to a showdown. Nellie tries to intervene, fearing Cass will be killed. Cass insists on going through with the challenge from Billy. The men draw on each other but Cass's hands are slippery and he drops his guns. Billy takes advantage of this and severely wounds him. With Nellie at Cass's side, Billy finishes the job and kills him. Nellie is taken back to the saloon, grief-stricken, while Billy rides out of town, his reputation intact.

BACKGROUND:

A TIME FOR DYING, with its prophetic title, was the last movie Audie Murphy ever made and the only one he ever produced. For his subject he

Audie Murphy, Budd Boetticher, and Lucien Ballard on the set of A TIME FOR DYING

chose a young gunman of the old West. This was the type of character which he himself had played many times in his twenty-two years of movie-making. However, the young gunman was to live and perish without renown. In a sense, the character represented the countless young men who lived and died by the gun in the early West, but left no legend behind them. No history covered their deeds. In A TIME FOR DYING, the youthful gunman met several famous men of the legendary type. Among them were Jesse James, played by Audie; Frank James, played by Willard Willingham and Judge Roy Bean, played by Victor Jory. In the movie, Murphy introduced his two sons, Terry and James, as actors. Typical of his graveyard humor, Audie, as producer, gave Terry a role that would get him hanged for horse-thievery before the end of the picture.

A TIME FOR DYING was shown to critics in Paris, France. One gave it a rather excellent review that was dated September 30, 1971. *The Daily Variety*, in Hollywood, also ran a favorable review of the movie in its issue of April 23, 1970.

Upon learning of Audie's death, Budd said, "I was devastated with Audie's accident because we had planned on spending the rest of our lives together."

TELEVISION APPEARANCES

Audie's first dramatic appearance on network television was "Incident," appearing on General Electric Theater, in February 1958, playing a Confederate soldier during the Civil War. Next came "The Flight," a Suspicion Theater presentation in July 1959. Audie portrays a pilot involved in South American political intrigue. A third drama, "The Man," aired on the Ford Startime Theater in January 1960.

At about the same time, Audie agreed to do a full season of a Western detective series called "Whispering Smith," also for NBC. It was originally scheduled to go on the air in the fall of 1959, but only seven episodes had been completed when co-star Guy Mitchell was injured. Production was halted until Mitchell recovered. Eventually, a full 26-episode season was completed and the show debuted in May 1961. Only 13 episodes actually aired, as the show was replaced on NBC's 1961-62 schedule.

At a preview party given by Hedda Hopper at the opening of a new hotel in Beverly Hills, Audie appears briefly on the "Colgate Variety Hour" in 1955. During the interview, Audie was asked by Miss Hopper how he got his medals back after giving them away. He replied that the army voluntarily replaced them when they started his newest film TO HELL AND BACK. Apparently, Audie had given the medals away before he had any children of his own.

THE FLIGHT

DIRECTED BY: James Neilson
PRODUCED BY: Frank P. Rosenberg
WRITTEN BY: Halsted Welles and Gene L. Coon
DIRECTOR OF PHOTOGRAPHY: Ernest Haller, A.S.C.
ART DIRECTOR: John Lloyd
EDITORIAL SUPERVISOR: Richard G. Wray, A.C.E.
FILM EDITOR: Lee Huntington
MUSIC SUPERVISOR: Stanley Wilson
SET DECORATOR: James Walters
ASSISTANT DIRECTOR: Willard Sheldon
SOUND: Steve Bass
COSTUME SUPERVISOR: Vincent Dee
MAKEUP: Jack Barron
HAIR STYLIST: Florence Bush
FILMED IN HOLLYWOOD

CAST:

Steve Gordon .... Audie Murphy
Miguel Del Sequiras .. Everett Sloane
Capt. Polendo .... Henry Brandon
Gina Obregon .... Susan Kohner
Newspaperman .... Jack Warden
Vladimir Sokoloff, Joe Perry, Vito Scotti, Harold Goodwin, Freddy Roberto, Susan Ridgway, Albert Carrier, Louis Zito, Alan Lee

SYNOPSIS:

An old man, walking alone down the street at night, is kidnapped by two men and forced into a waiting automobile.

The scene shifts to Steve Gordon, who is a pilot of sorts and also a mechanic working at a tiny airport rental field for people who own their own planes, a type of "puddle jumper" taxi service.

Two men arrive at the airport wanting to speak to Steve. They are introduced as Miguel Del Sequiras and Captain Polendo. The owner of the airport have seen these men before and feels that they are not individuals with which to do business. Steve disagrees with him and goes in and talks with them. They offer him $3000 to fly a charter to Bermuda. Steve asks about what cargo they will be bringing and finds out it is a man who is very ill and quite wealthy who goes to Bermuda for his health. Steve finds this acceptable and within 48 hours, they are ready to leave.

Steve is given half his pay in advance but with it comes a change in plans. The men want to leave at 12:30 a.m. and fly to Tampa instead. This is fine with Steve but he has already put on extra tanks of fuel for the trip to Bermuda. The men tell him that is all right and not to bother removing them. When Steve questions them why the change in plans, they reply that the passenger has changed his mind. Steve is asked to remove some seats as the man must lie down for the trip and rest.

Steve is ready to take off and tests the engines. An ambulance pulls up to

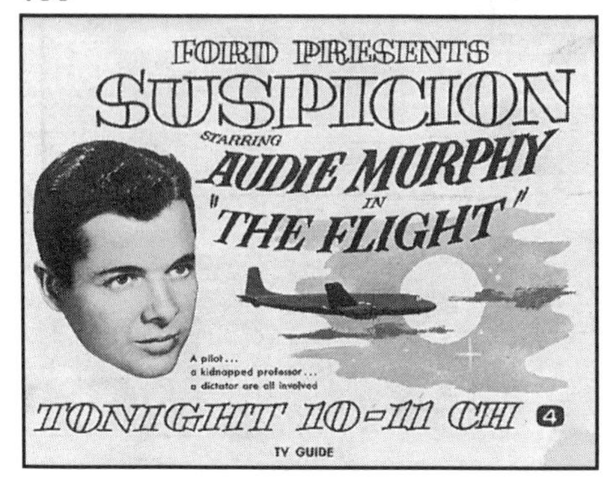

the plane and the passenger is unloaded and brought aboard. We see the face of the unconscious man as the one who was kidnapped.

While in flight, Steve is thinking to himself that there's nothing fishy about taking a sick man south. He's for hire and not doing anything wrong. He doesn't care what kind of a guy he's flying just as long as he's flying. One of the men comes into the cockpit and wants to know where they are. Steve tells him Tarpon Springs and that they'll be in Tampa in a few minutes. Over coffee, they talk and Steve asks where they are from. The man answers Puerto Columbo in South America, which he describes as a beautiful country, a free country. Steve says that it sounds nice.

Steve announces that Tampa is coming up and to fasten their seatbelts. The passenger has awakened and tries to say something whereas the men administer an injection which puts him back to sleep. Steve gets permission to land from the tower. After he lands the plane, he tries to speak with the old man. He is stopped by some different men this time who have come to pick him up telling Steve that the old man couldn't understand him and that he wants to go home to Puerto Columbo. The men insist on leaving Tampa after refueling. Steve finds out that the man is the brother of the president, which they did not tell him before. In New York they could do nothing for him and the president didn't want him dying in a strange country. Steve agrees to take them to Puerto Columbo but only if gets the rest of his money and flies back. The men agree. They are up to no good.

Again, they are in the air and this starts Steve to thinking once more. As the hours go by, he stops worrying and begins to feel great. It all feels good. He gets ready to get landing instructions but is told that they won't be landing at the main airport. He is to just follow the coastline. They will tell Steve where to land, which turns out to be a clearing where they are met by some men with a horse-drawn hearse. "In this country," it is explained to Steve when he looks puzzled at the hearse, "an ambulance draws attention, a hearse goes unnoticed." Shortly after, a group of soldiers in jeeps arrive carrying weapons. They tell Steve to stay in the plane for a few moments. He is curious as to where he will refuel since they are in an open field.

While Steve is taking all this in, the passenger calls to him weakly. He gives Steve a ring and is told to tell Washington about it but to hide the ring from the others. The old man begins to get hysterical as Steve is listening to him. Behind Steve, who is unaware of them, stand two men. He turns around to see who they are and they knock him out.

Steve thinks to himself that he has been in Puerto Columbo for two weeks now, his headache's gone and everything is wonderful. Everything he wants, he gets. He even gets to fly whenever he wants but without the extra gas tanks and he is watched all the time. Every letter he mails, he knows isn't sent. He guesses he's under house arrest or city arrest. There's another American there; he thinks he used to be a newspaper man but now he just seems to drink and sleep.

The American asks Steve if he's a tourist and he invites the man to his table for a drink. They have a conversation and the man warns Steve that for whatever reason he is down there, to be careful.

Gina, the girl at the piano, is teaching Steve Spanish and he feels that she also works for the police. During the Spanish lesson, Gina pronounces various items including the word "ring." She asks if he has a ring and he shows her the ring given to him by the old man on the plane. Gina recognizes the ring and asks Steve where he got it. He tells her that it belonged to his father. Gina cools it for a while and suggests they go to the beach together after siesta and he agrees. Ever since Gina has seen the ring, she has acted strangely; then she kisses Steve without any warning.

On the beach, Steve asks Gina if she works for the police. She denies any involvement with the police. He thinks it odd that before she saw the ring she wouldn't have anything to do with him romantically, then all of a sudden she is in his arms. She confesses that she has an uncle who had a ring just like his but that he has disappeared. Then she sees Steve's ring and believes it belongs to her uncle. Steve tells her that she is lying and that she works for the police. She denies this and starts to leaves. Steve still wants to talk. She asks him why he came to Puerto Columbo in the first place and he tells her about the charter job bringing in an invalid. He was actually someone they were bringing there to kill. She wants to know how he got the ring and he tells her it was given to him on the plane by the old man, knowing that the men who kidnapped him were assassins.

Later that evening, Charlie, the newspaper man, tells Steve he works for a certain faction of the government as a public relations advisor. He places stories in the press telling them what a great little place Puerto Columbo is. He also tells Steve not to trust Gina. He gives Steve an article to read regarding his plane passenger, who is labeled as a sworn enemy and stubborn political foe. His name is Enrique Bartogas, the editor of the Spanish language newspaper. As Steve reads the article he finds that Senor Bartogas had disappeared in New York. But Steve doesn't get to finish the article because at that moment he hears a siren. Senor Sequiras comes over and sits at his table. Charlie leaves and goes over to the bar. Suddenly, two policemen wreck the newspaper stand removing all the magazines pertaining to this particular article. Steve finally realizes that this country is definitely not what's it is described to be—it's a dictatorship.

Steve confronts Sequiras confessing that he has done come crummy things; he's taken their money and had a good time but he doesn't like to think he's a murderer. Sequiras wants him to be happy but Steve wants to know what happened to Bartogas. Sequiras asks Steve what he thinks happened to him and he replies that they have killed him. Sequiras tells Steve that he will take him to see Bartogas. Upon leaving the police station, they drive to a sanitarium where they see Bartogas in a wheelchair. Steve is wary. Bartogas speaks but it is a stilted speech that sounds as though he is being forced to say that he is happy to be back in his beloved country of his own free will. Steve is standing alongside of Bartogas when he lights up a cigarette. The flame from the match sends Bartogas' bandaged hands to his eyes to shield them. Steve inquires about his hands and Sequiras tells him it's a disease that affects the extremities and that he must have rest. Steve says that he has seen enough and they leave.

Sequiras offers Steve a job as a co-pilot in the government airlines and he accepts. Shortly thereafter, he is approached by two men who knock him out and force him into a waiting car. He awakes in the presence of Gina and two men. They want to know where Bartogas is being held. These people are the underground and Steve tells them that's what he was coming for. He tells them where Bartogas is, what's been done to him and how to get him out. If they want him free, they'll have to do it through Steve. He tells them about Bartogas' hands and that he gave Steve his ring on the plane. Steve says that he can get Bartogas out of the sanitarium but the others don't think that he can. Just as he is about to tell them how, there is a knock at the door. They hide Steve in a closet. Upon opening the door, Charlie walks in, goes directly to the closet and tells Steve to come out. He explains that he knew Bartogas quite well since he too is a newspaper man and that he can get him out of El Sol. Steve begins stockpiling gas—stealing it, buying it, getting it wherever he can. Plans are made between the four men. Gina apologizes to Steve for being so cruel, but he tells her he still loves her. Charlie, Steve and the colonel drive to El Sol on the pretense of a story. Steve knocks the colonel out. Charlie, Steve and a guard enter Bartogas' room where Charlie takes his camera pretending to get Bartogas' picture but instead the flash goes off in the guard's face, temporarily blinding him. This gives them enough time to get Bartogas out of the room. However, the colonel revived, takes a shot at Steve and Steve kills him. The shooting brings other guards but the three men get away safely.

Steve gets Bartogas to the boat that is waiting along with Gina and the others. Steve and Charlie stay and head back to the plane. They have Jose posing as Bartogas in a wheelchair as they know they were being followed by Sequiras and his men. Sequiras, alone with several armed guards, instructs them to halt and orders them shot. Jose has a machine gun and kills several of the guards. Charlie is wounded and Steve tries to get him to the plane. Charlie makes him leave him there and tells Steve to get out of there. Jose and Steve make it to the plane but then Charlie is killed. Just as he is about to take off, a bullet from one of the guards grazes Steve's head through the cockpit window, temporarily blinding him. He is so familiar with the plane that he tells Jose that he can fly it blindfolded if necessary. He takes off and flies over the boat carrying Gina, Bartogas and the rest of the men and will meet them at the appointed rendezvous.

THE MAN

FORD STARTIME THEATER

DIRECTOR: Robert Stevens
PRODUCER: Robert Northshield
EXECUTIVE PRODUCER: Hubbell Robinson
ADAPTED FOR TV BY: James P. Cavanagh
FROM THE PLAY BY: Mel Dinelli
PRODUCED ON BROADWAY BY: Kermit Bloomgarden
SCENIC DESIGNER: Don Shirley, Jr.
COSTUME DESIGNER: Guy Kent
TECHNICAL DIRECTOR: Walter Miller
LIGHTING DIRECTOR: William Knight
AUDIO: Phil Falcone
VIDEO: Tony Nelle
ASSISTANT DIRECTOR: Hugh McPhillips
ASSISTANT TO THE PRODUCER: Virginia Raymond
STAGE MANAGER: Chuck Stamps
UNIT MANAGER: Sigmund Bojak
MUSIC COMPOSED BY: Frank Denning
CONDUCTED BY: Al Fanelli

CAST:

Howard .... Audie Murphy
Mrs. Gillis .... Thelma Ritter
Doug .... Michael J. Pollard
Bartender .... Joseph Sullivan
Bill .... William Hickey
The Repairman ... Joseph Campanella
Judy .... Renne Jarrett
Mr. Franks .... John McGovern
A Bowler .... Phil Adams

SYNOPSIS:

A man gets off a bus and places a phone call to a Mrs. Gillis. She is home but when she finally answers it, there is no one on the other end. The bus stop has a bowling alley and bar where the man asks the bartender if he knew of any rooms available. He suggests he try a rooming house. While he is thinking about it, two men come up asking if he would like to bowl a game since they need another player. As they play, he inquires if they know Mrs. Gillis and wonders if she rents out rooms. He finds out her address and goes there.

Mrs. Gillis is cleaning her house when the door bell rings. He asks her if she has any work. He tells her he is doing post graduate work at the university and needs a job. She tells him she doesn't have anything and that she does all her own cleaning.

He returns to the bowling alley where the bartender asks him if he found a room. The man says he wasn't looking for a room. The bartender finds this a little peculiar since this is a complete change from the day before.

Howard goes back the next day again asking for work. Mrs. Gillis insists that she doesn't have anything for him to do. Howard notices that she is polishing her floors and volunteers to finish the job for her. Reluctantly, she lets him stay.

Mrs. Gillis soon has to contend with two personalities in Howard as they appear and disappear but never giving any indication when the two characters come out. Howard's good side suspects he has been mean or done bad things, but can't remember. When he finishes the floor, he wants to see the rest of the house, so Mrs. Gillis shows him around. She tells Howard that one of the rooms was her son's, but he is dead now. Howard likes the room and wants to rent it but Mrs. Gillis tells him that she can't rent it to anyone.

Mrs. Gillis's dog begins to bark, wanting to be let in. Howard tells her he is afraid of dogs and not to let it inside. While Mrs. Gillis is distracted, Howard goes to the front door of the house, locks it and puts the key in his pocket. Soon after, Mrs. Gillis is on the phone ordering groceries. Howard sees her and thinks perhaps she is checking up on him, because he is a stranger. Mrs. Gillis assures him she is only placing a grocery order.

She prepares some food for Howard and asks him where he lives. He tells her "in a room, in lots of rooms, in lots of places." While polishing the floor, he began to pretend he had lived in her house for a long time. She offers the food, but Howard's "bad" side comes out. She asks if he wants something to eat, that he must be hungry after all that work. He tells her "of course he's tired, been working his head off for hours and what did she expect?" He goes upstairs to her son's room. She follows him and suggests that he should go home now, but Howard tells her he's frightened a lot because he forgets what he has done, maybe some bad things. Also, he can't remember where he lives. Again they hear the dog barking and he is afraid. She tells him she'll put her in the kitchen. She can't have the dog disturbing the whole neighborhood.

Mrs. Gillis goes to the front door to let Sarah in but finds that it is locked. The "good" Howard comes down the stairs wanting to know what is wrong. She tells him that the door is locked and the key is gone. She asks Howard for it but he explains that he doesn't have it. Same thing for the back door. Howard even tries to open the door but can't then tries the front door, same story.

While Howard is in the other room, Mrs. Gillis tries to phone the police, but hangs up when he comes in. He has found the keys in his pocket, but can't recall how they got there. He doesn't know why he did it but probably because he wants to stay so badly. He wants to rent the room and can pay for it by working there for her. He begs her to stay, to belong, be safe. He knew about the house from Bob, her son. They were in the same barracks together and he used to talk about the house. He was afraid to tell Mrs. Gillis that he was a friend of her son for fear Bob might have told her about him.

He asks again if he can rent a room but she explains that she already has a boarder but if Howard will come back tomorrow, she will try to arrange something. This seems satisfactory to Howard and he prepares to leave. However, Howard still has the keys and Mrs. Gillis tells him to unlock the door. He suddenly remembers his coat is upstairs. Mrs. Gillis offers to get it for him. As she leaves, Howard goes to the door only to find a man there asking about the boarder, Mr. Armstrong. He tells Howard that he is on vacation and that Mr. Armstrong told him he could rent his room while he was gone. Howard's "bad" side comes out and he tells the man that the room has been taken and sends him away. The man comes back to let the dog in. Howard then silences the dog, permanently.

Mrs. Gillis comes downstairs asking who was at the door since she heard it slam. Howard tells her she is mistaken. She informs him she couldn't find his coat and he says he won't be needing it after all, locking the door. He's not going anywhere!

He tells her he can't trust her because she lied about Mr. Armstrong. He makes her sit down while he finishes the room. The phone rings but he won't allow her to answer. She then asks if she can get the dog's dinner but he tells her the dog won't be needing it. She makes him tell her where the dog is and he takes her to the closet. He tells her that the dog won't hurt anyone ever again. She finds the dead dog and tells Howard that she is sorry she ever had any feelings for him and wants him to get out of her house. He refuses to go and tries to strangle her. Just then the grocery boy comes to the back door. Howard threatens that she says anything, he will kill the boy.

Howard accompanies her to the kitchen and unlocks the door. Mrs. Gillis goes to write a check to pay the boy but Howard pays for the groceries and sends him away. Howard then pulls the phone cord out of the wall and finds Mrs. Gillis writing for help on the back of the check.

Mrs. Gillis's niece, Judy, comes for a visit. He sends Mrs. Gillis upstairs and tells her not to come down or he'll hurt Judy. He lets her in as Judy wonders why the door is locked since her aunt never locks them. She starts upstairs to see her aunt but is stopped by Howard. Judy argues with him but he twists her arm, hurting her. Mrs. Gillis comes downstairs and sends Judy home telling her she doesn't feel well.

Howard tells Mrs. Gillis that he'll never be able to live quietly with her and that he will have to live by himself. He then knocks her out. When she comes to, "good" Howard is there, thinking she has fainted. He decides it's time to leave and asks her if his work was worth the money. She plays along with him and gets the money as he gets his coat. He wants to make sure that she is satisfied with his work and is glad when she approves. He seems very happy at this point.

Before he leaves, he asks her if he has done anything wrong while he was there because he realizes there are times when he does things and then doesn't remember. She tells him he did nothing wrong. He asks again about renting the room or renting a room in the neighborhood. Mrs. Gillis tells him she has no room and knows no one who has a room to rent. He wants to move in and stay with her but she tells him she has a son and that she must fix dinner for him.

Howard finds the door keys in his pocket and realizes that he must have done something wrong. He apologizes to her for the bad things he might have done. At this point, she is very anxious to get rid of him.

There is someone at the door and she insists that Howard open it. Standing there is the telephone repairman. He tells Mrs. Gillis that her phone has been out of order all day. She sends him to the kitchen and tries to tell him about Howard. She asks if he will give Howard a ride to the bus stop. The repairman tells her it is not allowed but will make an exception after she explains that Howard is ill and that he killed her dog. They plan to take Howard to the police station where they will get him the help he needs. "Bad" Howard slips back into the house. Mrs. Gillis goes upstairs for her coat while the repairman calls the police. He then goes to find Mrs. Gillis but instead sees Howard coming down the stairs in a daze. The repairman races upstairs to find Mrs. Gillis's body as Howard stares off into space.

WHISPERING SMITH - STAKEOUT

A WHISPERING COMPANY PRODUCTION

DIRECTED BY: Christian Nyby
TELEPLAY BY: Harold Swanton
STORY BY: Borden Chase and Harold Swanton
PRODUCED BY: Joseph Hoffman
MUSIC SCORE: Gerald Fried
MCA TV EXCLUSIVE DISTRIBUTOR
FILMED IN HOLLYWOOD AT REVUE PRODUCTION INC.
DIRECTOR OF PHOTOGRAPHY: Bud Thackery, A.S.C.
ART DIRECTOR: George Patrick
EDITORIAL SUPERVISOR: Richard G. Wray, A.C.E.
FILM EDITOR: Budd Small
MUSICAL SUPERVISION: Stanley Wilson
SOUND: Melvin M. Metcalff, Sr.
ASSISTANT DIRECTOR: Willard Sheldon
SET DIRECTOR: Perry Murdock
COSTUME SUPERVISOR: Vincent Dee
MAKEUP: Jack Barron
HAIR STYLIST: Florence Bush
PRODUCED IN ASSOCIATION WITH THE NBC TELEVISION NETWORK

CAST:

Whispering Smith ..... Audie Murphy
George Romack .... Guy Mitchell
Chief Richards .... Sam Buffington
Edie .... Joyce Taylor
Richard Devon, John Cliff, Billy McLean, Lyn Thomas

SYNOPSIS:

Two men ride into town looking very much like trouble. All of a sudden come men on horseback and shoot them down. George Romack, of the Denver Police Department, handcuffs one of the men. He tells Steve that he works for him and to let him go.

Voiceover Narrative:

There are nine members of the Denver Police Department, or there were until the night before: the chief, five officers, and two detectives.

One was George Romack who stopped one of the prisoners from escaping. Smith comes into the police office with a pair of saddlebags taken from the bank robbers. The questioning of Garrity, one of the robbers, seems futile.

A collection is taken for the slain detective. Apparently, Romack is taking the death very hard and has not been able to make the prisoner talk. Garrity has been told he will probably hang but he doesn't seem a bit worried.

George and his wife Edie are on the edge over the death of the detective. She tells George how much she needs him right now since she is going to have a baby. As they are talking, a knock at the door brings George to his feet. A man with a large scar running down his face is standing there. George seems to know this man which is a concern to Edie.

A chalk rendering of the man is shown to Smitty and the chief. The bartender drawing the likeness tells them that George had stopped in the saloon that morning and had words with him. Romack had neglected to mention to either Smitty or the chief that they had this meeting. The chief mentions to Smitty that George has been acting a bit out of character but Smitty defends him. He tells the chief that George has a lot on his mind lately with the baby and Edie.

Edie sends for Smitty when he questions her about George's behavior. She tells him that George sent her out of the room while he and Scarface talked privately. She continues that after Scarface left, George sat in the house for a long time and wouldn't speak to her. One of the reasons she is so worried about her husband is because George was supposed to attend the slain detective's wake but never showed.

Smitty finds George drunk in the saloon. He takes him outside and sobers him up. George tells Smitty about the time he rode with Scarface, whose real name is Dugan, once down in Texas over five years ago. Smitty doesn't tell anyone, especially the chief, about this. He has a hunch that Romack has left that part of his life behind. Seems as though Dugan wants George to turn Garrity loose while he's on duty the next night for $1500 in gold. He told Dugan that if he ever showed his face again, he'd break him in half. Romack says he was bluffing and Dugan knew it, and that's why he's so worried. He's afraid something might happen to Edie, and George tells Smitty that he'll quit the department.

The bartender comes to the office where he finds George and Smitty talking. He tells them that Dugan has just come into the saloon. George starts to go in after him but Smitty stops him. He has a plan. He tells the bartender to stall Dugan for as long as he can. George thinks Smitty is crazy to try anything, but Smitty asks George where he thinks Garrity would go if he were to be turned loose. George thinks he would ride back to his boys and the hideout. Smitty agrees.

Dugan is still there when George enters the saloon. The bartender did his job well. They sit down and George tells he can't let Garrity out. He still works for Chief Richards and he gets paid for doing it even though he doesn't like it much. Smitty walks into the saloon and he and Romack put on their charade in front of Dugan. They pretend to be on the outs with each other whereas Romack pretends to get drunk and Smitty comes in after him. They have words and Smitty forces George to leave.

Smitty tells the chief about Romack's past in Texas, but when confronted by the chief for not telling him this sooner, Smitty says he would have fired him if he had known.

Romack comes into the office with a bag of $500 in it and he will get the rest when Garrity is delivered to Dugan. The jail break will happen sometime between midnight and one o'clock in the morning where Dugan will have horses waiting. The chief isn't going to fire George but he tells him his plan had better work or he'll be swinging beside Garrity if he gets lynched. George leaves to see Edie before she leaves to visit her mother for a little while.

Upon his arrival at home, George finds Dugan waiting for him and that Edie is missing. Dugan tells him that they have her and will let her go as soon as Garrity is handed over to them. Seems as though Garrity isn't one for taking any chances. George approaches Dugan, incensed, demanding to know what they've done with her, beats him up and takes him back to headquarters.

Smitty and the chief are studying a map trying to determine where the hideout might be located. Just about then, George brings Dugan into the office, battered and bruised, and has him confess to them that Edie's at the Plum Creek Church. The chief wants to get more men to help but Smitty tells him that if they ride in with an army, they'll kill her. He suggests that they might make a deal with Dugan and Garrity.

The outlaws are waiting at the church when four riders are seen. Smitty tells Dugan that if they turn Edie safely over to them they will let Garrity go. Dugan wants to meet half-way— he will have Edie and Smitty will have Garrity, and they will exchange in the middle.

Garrity tries to make a run for it but Smitty knocks him out. Since he is unconscious, Garrity is of no use to them. Smitty has an idea and puts Romack in Garrity's clothes. As they walk to the middle, Edie realizes that George is in Garrity's clothes but doesn't give it away to the outlaw who is with her. However, one of the outlaws is suspicious because Garrity had a bad leg and Romack is only walking with a slight limp. The outlaw shouts to the man with Edie to stop. As shots are fired, Edie shoves the outlaw while she takes cover with Smitty and George. Smitty heads for the church, scattering the horses and takes the outlaws into town. George takes Edie home and Smitty knew there would never be any questions about George's past again.

BACKGROUND:

"Whispering Smith" first went into production in the summer of 1959, headed for the Monday at 7:30 p.m. time period on NBC that fall. After filming seven episodes, co-star Guy Mitchell broke his shoulder and production had to be postponed. After finding a substitution show, "Whispering Smith" was moved out of the Monday night spot. Meanwhile, Audie had a picture commitment to fulfill and production again was postponed. It was then rescheduled for Friday nights. Actually, it ended up on Monday nights because the "Smith" series had to be scheduled to fill the void left by the cancellation of "Acapulco."

"If the show is a success and they decide to make more," Murphy said at that time, "I guess I'm hooked to go back. I really don't want to be a failure. But I'm not really looking forward to its being a smashing success, either. Because I think my contract is firm for something like 86 episodes and I just don't think I could stand that."

Despite his feelings about the show,

Audie rushed to its defense when the Senate Juvenile Delinquency Subcommittee in Washington deemed that it was "not only bad for children; it's bad for adults" and issued this statement: "Apparently some people were shocked by what they considered violence in the first episode of "Whispering Smith." My feeling is that this episode had an extremely high moral value, which has been overlooked. The story was about a policeman who was willing to risk his life in order to rehabilitate a juvenile delinquent.... Smith was interested in helping youngsters and avoided violence for violence's sake.... In a half-hour TV show, the bad must be established fast and with impact or the entire show would dwell on this subject. If even extreme violence is part of good drama, it is never criticized. Unfortunately, I have learned that a half-hour TV program cannot present drama at its best."

This new series presents stories in authentic settings and are enacted against the background of the Denver Police Department—first in the West to adopt methods of tracing and apprehending criminals that are now standard in modern criminology—in the 1870 period.

Presented in semi-documentary style, the stories feature guest stars and are based on dramatizations of real cases from the files of the Denver Police.

Monday evening, May 8, 1961, at 9:00 p.m. "Whispering Smith" was to have taken to the NBC airwaves. Unfortunately, it was not shown due to an NBC News special that night.

Audie Murphy in a scene from "Whispering Smith"

The TV debut starred Audie Murphy as Whispering Smith, Guy Mitchell as Detective George Romack and Sam Buffington as Chief John Richards as regulars. The guest cast included Jan Merlin as Thad Janeck; Robert Osterloh as Ben Avery and Earl Hansen as Rex Avery. The filmed series is set against the background of the Denver Police Department during the 1870s. The first story is entitled *The Blind Gun* and the synopsis is as follows:

Bandit Thad Janeck, sightless as the result of a gunfight in which he was captured, agrees to turn over his booty in exchange for reward money—which he intends to spend for an operation on his eyes.

Episodes 1 through 20 of "Whispering Smith" are described here briefly.

1. "The Blind Gun" (May 8, 1961) with Jan Merlin, Earl Hansen and Robert Osterloh.
2. "The Grudge" (May 15, 1961) with Robert Redford, June Walker and Gloria Talbott.
3. "The Devil's Share" (May 22, 1961) with Clu Gulager, Rosemary Day and James Lydon.
4. "Stakeout" (May 29, 1961) with John Cliff, Troy Melton and Joyce Taylor.
5. "Safety Value" (June 5, 1961) with Della Sharman, Less Tremayne and Harry Carey, Jr.
6. "Stain of Justice" (June 12, 1961) with Richard Chamberlain, Patric Knowles and Nancy Valentine.
7. "The Deadliest Weapon" (June 19, 1961) with Aline Towne, Paul Lees, Bartlett Robinson and Don Keefer.
8. "The Quest" (June 26, 1961) with Ellen Willard and John Harmon.
9. "Three for One" (July 3, 1961) with Richard Crane, Ken Mayer, Roscoe Ates and Pamela Duncan.
10. "Death at Even Money" (July 10, 1961) with Marc Lawrence, Robert Lowery, John Day, Sandy Sanders and Sherwood Price.
11. "The Hemp Reeger Case" (July 17, 1961) with James Best, Patricia Medina and Edward C. Platt.
12. "The Mortal Coil" (July 24, 1961) with Henry Brandon and Hugh Sanders.
13. "Cross Cut" (July 31, 1961) with Audrey Dalton, Colin Male and Jim Hayward.
14. "Double Edge" (August 7, 1961) with Myron Healey, Lori Nelson and Read Morgan.
15. "The Trademark" (August 14, 1961) with Marie Windsor, Donald Buka, Forrest Tucker and Andrew Winberg.
16. "The Jodie Tyler Story" (August 21, 1961) with Rachel Fougler, Read Morgan and Jimmy Carter.
17. "Poet and Peasant Case: (August 28, 1961) with Alan Mowbray, Jack Catron and Yvonne Adrian.
18. "Dark Circle" (September 4, 1961) with E. J. Andre, Diana Millay, Carleton Young and Adam Williams.
19. "Swift Justice" (September 11, 1961) with Monte Burkhart, Minerva Urecal and William Tannen.
20. "The Idol" (September 18, 1961) with Joan O'Brien, Alan Hale, Jr., and John Stephenson.

MILITARY HERITAGE - WAR YEARS

Audie's roots in America go back into eighteenth and nineteenth century Virginia, North Carolina, Tennessee and Louisiana, before the transplant to Texas. One of the most interesting of Audie's ancestors was John Berry, a paternal great-grandfather. He fought in a Virginia company in the Revolutionary War. As a member of a Kentucky militia company, Berry fought in the Battle of Tippecanoe (November 7, 1811) under General William Henry Harrison. Upon the outbreak of the War of 1812, Berry enlisted in Colonel Samuel Hopkins' regiment and saw action at the Battle of the Thames (October 5, 1813). Berry, succumbing to the call for men to colonize Texas, headed southwest in 1826.

Following the Texas War for Independence (1835-1836), Berry moved his family to land granted to Berry for his service to the Republic of Texas.

Curtis Gill, Audie's maternal great-grandfather, served in the Confederate Army enlisting in April 1861 in the Third Tennessee Mounted Infantry Regiment. The unit, as part of Kirby Smith's Brigade, fought in the first Battle of Bull Run. During the winter of 1861-1862, the Third Tennessee was engaged in sporadic fighting in East Tennessee, taking part in the siege of Cumberland Gap in the summer of 1862. The unit participated in General Braxton Bragg's ill-fated invasion of Kentucky in the fall of 1862. The unit also participated in the defense of Vicksburg, Mississippi. Gill died under unknown circumstances on his way home from Vicksburg to Tennessee.

Audie Murphy's military heritage was solid and deeply rooted in America's past. A great-great-grandfather fought in the American Revolution, a great-grandfather participated in the war of 1812, three great-half uncles were in the Texas Revolution, one great-half uncle fought in the Mexican War, and he could count at least six ancestors in the Civil War—a great-grandfather, three great-uncles and two great-half uncles; all were in the Confederate Army. Five of his uncles—three of his father's brothers and two of his mother's brothers, fought in World War I. Besides Audie, two of his brothers, Richard and Eugene, fought in World War II. Thus, the Texas farm boy's affinity for military service and his patriotism came naturally—it was inherited. Few Americans can boast of such military background credentials. (*Audie Murphy, American Soldier*)

Before his 21st birthday, and after more than two years overseas (most of it front line duty), Audie Murphy returned home at the end of World War II with every decoration for valor this country could bestow. He participated in nine battle campaigns including participation in the assault landings at Sicily and Southern France. His fame earned him the title of "The most decorated combat soldier of World War II."

Audie's string of decorations began on 2 March 1944 with the Bronze Star Medal with "V" device for valorous conduct in action against the enemy on the Anzio Beachhead, in Italy. This was followed with the First Oak Leaf

Cluster on the Bronze Star Medal for exemplary conduct in ground combat on or about 8 May 1944. Also at this time, Audie was awarded the Combat Infantryman Badge.

After landing near Ramatuelle in Southern France, Audie earned the Distinguished Service Cross on 15 August 1944. Audie advanced inland with his squad but was halted by intense machine gun and small arms fire from a boulder-covered hill to his front. Acting alone, he obtained a light machine gun and in the ensuing duel, he was able to silence the enemy weapon, killing two of its crew and wounding a third. As he proceeded further up the draw, two Germans advanced towards him. They were quickly killed. Still alone, Audie then dashed further up the draw toward the enemy strongpoint, disregarding the hail of bullets directed at him. Closing in, he wounded two Germans with carbine fire, killed two more in a fire-fight, and forced the remaining five to surrender. But it was this action that took the life of his dear friend, Lattie Tipton. So devastated by this loss, Audie co-dedicated his autobiographical book *To Hell and Back* to Pvt. Lattie Tipton and to Pvt. Joe Sieja, who was killed in action on the Anzio Beachhead in January 1944.

On the morning of 2 October 1944, near the Cleurie Quarry, France, Audie inched his way over rugged terrain towards an enemy machine gun which had fired upon a group of American officers on reconnaissance. Getting to within fifteen yards of the German gun, Audie stood up, and disregarding a burst of enemy fire, flung two hand grenades into the position, killing four Germans and wounding three more and thus destroying the position. For this action, Audie was awarded the Silver Star. Just three days later, on 5 October 1944, on a hill in the Vosges Mountains near Le Tholy, France, he earned an Oak Leaf Cluster for his Silver Star. Carrying an SCR 536 radio, and alone, Audie crawled fifty yards under severe enemy machine gun and rifle fire, to a point 200 yards from a strongly entrenched enemy. For an hour Audie directed artillery fire upon the enemy killing fifteen Germans and inflicting approximately thirty-five casualties.

Audie's three Purple Hearts recognize wounds received on 15 September 1944 in action near Genevreuville, France; 26 October 1944 in action near Les Rouges, Eaux, France and on 25 January 1945 in action in the Colmar Pocket.

But it was on 26 January 1945 that Audie Murphy earned the nation's highest tribute for action in the Riedwihr Woods near Holtzwihr, France. The Third Division was engaged in fierce fighting in the Colmar Pocket which consisted of a heavily fortified bulge stretching from the Rhine into France. At midnight on January 25, Company B moved through the Riedwihr Woods, but fierce fighting reduced the company to two officers and about 28 men. Despite five replacements, the company remained critically under strength. As the senior ranking officer, Audie was placed in charge of the company and was ordered to advance to the edge of the forest and hold the line until relieved. Company B was supported by two tank destroyers from the 601st Tank Battalion which were attached to the 15th Infantry, but they were soon out of action.

The frozen ground was covered with 10-12 inches of snow; it was impossible for the men to dig in. Audie's company was strung along a three hundred yard front at the edge of woods. Company B was in a defensive position when, at 2:00 p.m. on January 26, the Germans began a savage attack from Holtzwihr. This assault consisted of six heavy Jagdpanther tanks supported by approximately 250 German infantry attired in white snow capes. The first tank destroyer slid into a drainage ditch and could not extricate itself. The second TD received a direct hit from a German 88 killing the commander and gunner. Seeing that the situation was desperate, Audie ordered his men to fall back to an alternate position. At this time, Audie began calling in artillery support by a field telephone through Battalion Headquarters. With his ammunition depleted, he decided to mount the burning TD and employ its 50 caliber machine gun.

After removing the dead TD commander, Audie sprayed deadly fire upon the German infantry. With the TD in danger of blowing up any moment, the Germans gave it a wide berth. The black smoke streaming from the TD made it difficult for the Germans to see Audie, but it also reduced his view of the advancing infantry. At this point, Audie called in more artillery support even though it was dangerously close to his own position. For an hour, Audie managed to kill or wound approximately 50 to 100 Germans and confused them as to the source of the deadly fire. The German tanks, lacking infantry support, were forced to withdraw. Audie jumped from the burning TD only to hear it explode seconds later. Thus ended one of the most famous Medal of Honor actions of World War II.

Army recruiting poster used to recruit for the "Audie Murphy Platoon" in February 1973

Following the presentation of the Medal of Honor on 2 June 1945, at an airfield near Werfen, Austria, Audie was also awarded the Legion of Merit. In addition to the U.S. awards, Audie received the French Legion of Honor (Grade of Chevelier); the French Croix du Guerre with Silver Star; the French Croix du Guerre with Palm and the Belgium Croix du Guerre 1940 with Palm. Despite the weight and burden of his medals, Audie always stated that "the real heroes were the ones with the wooden crosses."

Audie's Medal of Honor action reads as follows:

Second Lieutenant Audie L. Murphy, 01 692 509, 15th Infantry, Third Infantry Division, on 26 January 1945, near Holtzwihr, France, commanded Company B, which was attacked by six tanks and waves of infantry. Lieutenant Murphy ordered his men to withdraw to prepared positions in a woods, while he remained forward at his company Command Post and continued to give fire directions to the artillery by telephone. Behind him, to his right, one of our tank destroyers received a direct hit and began to burn. Its crew withdrew to the woods. Lieutenant Murphy continued to direct artillery fire which killed large numbers of the advancing enemy infantry. With the enemy tanks abreast of his position, Lieutenant Murphy climbed on the burning tank destroyer which was in danger of blowing up at any instant, and employed its 50 caliber machine gun against the enemy. He was alone and exposed to German fire from three sides, but his deadly fire killed dozens of Germans and caused their infantry attack to waver. The enemy tanks, losing infantry support, began to fall back. For an hour the Germans tried every available weapon to eliminate Lieutenant Murphy, but he continued to hold his position and wiped out a squad which was trying to creep up unnoticed on his right flank. Germans reached as close as ten yards only to be mowed down by his fire. He received a leg wound but ignored it and continued the single-handed fight until his ammunition was exhausted. He then made his way to his company, refused medical attention, and organized the company in a counterattack which forced the Germans to withdraw. His directing of artillery fire wiped out many of the enemy; he killed or wounded about fifty. Lieutenant Murphy's indomitable courage and his refusal to give an inch of ground saved his company from possible encirclement and destruction, and enabled it to hold the woods which had been the enemy's objective.

Audie dressed for combat. The pistol hanging from his belt shows Audie is an officer (1st Lieutenant).

All in all, Audie received credit for participating in nine battle campaigns, entitling him to wear nine Bronze Stars (battle stars).

The list of Audie's awards is most impressive:

MEDAL OF HONOR
Distinguished Service Cross
Silver Star with First Oak Leaf Cluster
Legion of Merit
Bronze Star Medal with "V" Device and First Oak Leaf Cluster
Purple Heart with Second Oak Leaf Cluster
Good Conduct Medal
Distinguished Unit Emblem with First Oak Leaf Cluster
American Campaign Medal
European-African-Middle Eastern Campaign Medal with One Silver Star, Four Bronze Service Stars (representing nine Campaigns) and one Bronze Arrowhead (representing assault landing at Sicily and Southern France)
World War II Victory Medal
Army of Occupation Medal with Germany Clasp
Armed Forces Reserve Medal
Combat Infantryman Badge
Marksman Badge with Rifle Bar
Expert Badge with Bayonet Bar
French Fourragere in Colors of the Croix de Guerre
French Legion of Honor, Grade of Chevalier
French Croix de Guerre with Silver Star
French Croix de Guerre with Palm
Medal of Liberated France
Belgian Croix de Guerre 1940 Palm

Audie wrote in his book on the dedication page:

If there be any glory in war, let it rest on men like these.

SONGS AND POETRY

Audie wrote a number of country-and-western songs, recorded by artists such as Roy Clark, Dean Martin, Jerry Wallace, Eddy Arnold, Porter Waggoner, Teresa Brewer, Charlie Pride, and Jimmy Dean, among others.

"Shutters and Boards," co-written with Scott Turner, was recorded by Wallace in 1962, and became his biggest hit, selling at least 600,000 copies.

An album of ten songs on which Audie and Scott Turner collaborated has been recorded.

While still serving in the Army, Audie began writing poetry. Understandably, much of the early material dealt with the war that surrounded him, and memories of his fallen war buddies. The most famous of the three remaining poems is as follows:

Dusty old helmet, rusty old gun,
They sit in the corner and wait —
Two souvenirs of the Second World War
That have withstood the time, and the hate.

Many times I've wanted to ask them —
And now that we're here all alone,
Relics all three of a long ago war —
Where has freedom gone?

Mute witness to a time of much trouble,
Where kill or be killed was the law —
Were these implements used with high honor?
What was the glory they saw?

Freedom flies in your heart like an eagle,
Let it soar with the winds high above
Among the spirits of soldiers now sleeping,
Guard it with care and with love.

I salute my old friends in the corner.
I agree with all they have said —
And if the moment of truth comes tomorrow,
I'll be free, or by God, I'll be dead!

Two other poems he wrote in 1948 again tell of the terrible war and the deaths of his comrades. Audie had a deep respect for the soldiers and his buddies. He never forgot that they made the ultimate sacrifice, their lives, so we can be free. This particular poem is in Audie's book, *To Hell and Back,* but has the character of Johnson doing the writing.

Oh, gather 'round me, comrades; and listen while I speak
Of a war, a war, a war where hell is six feet deep.
Along the shore, the cannons roar. Oh how can a soldier sleep?
The going's slow on Anzio. And hell is six feet deep.

Praise be to God for this captured sod that rich with blood does seep.
With yours and mine, like butchered swine's; and hell is six feet deep.
That death awaits there's no debate; no triumph will we reap.
The crosses grow on Anzio, where hell is six feet deep.

The final poem is very pensive and reflects the reverence to God and man. Audie opens his heart and soul to let us know his true feelings.

Alone and far removed from earthly care
The noble ruins of men lie buried here.
You were strong men, good men
Endowed with youth and much the will to live.
I hear no protest from the mute lips of the dead
They rest; there is no more to give.

So long my comrades,
Sleep ye where you fell upon the field.
But tread softly please
March o'er my heart with ease
March on and on,
But to God alone we kneel.

PHOTO GALLERY

BEYOND GLORY

BAD BOY

THE KID FROM TEXAS

SIERRA

KANSAS RAIDERS

THE RED BADGE OF COURAGE

THE CIMARRON KID

THE DUEL AT SILVER CREEK

GUNSMOKE

RIDE CLEAR OF DIABLO

COLUMN SOUTH

DRUMS ACROSS THE RIVER

TUMBLEWEED

DESTRY

TO HELL AND BACK

WORLD IN MY CORNER

WALK THE PROUD LAND

THE GUNS OF FORT PETTICOAT

JOE BUTTERFLY

NIGHT PASSAGE

RIDE A CROOKED TRAIL

THE QUIET AMERICAN

THE GUN RUNNERS

THE WILD AND THE INNOCENT

NO NAME ON THE BULLET

CAST A LONG SHADOW

THE UNFORGIVEN

POSSE FROM HELL

HELL BENT FOR LEATHER

BATTLE AT BLOODY BEACH

SEVEN WAYS FROM SUNDOWN

SIX BLACK HORSES

THE QUICK GUN

SHOWDOWN

GUNFIGHT AT COMANCHE CREEK

BULLET FOR A BADMAN

APACHE RIFLES

THE TEXICAN

ARIZONA RAIDERS

TRUNK TO CAIRO

GUNPOINT

40 GUNS TO APACHE PASS

Audie with his sons, James Shannon and Terry Michael, on the set of RIDE A CROOKED TRAIL

Tourists lean from sightseeing bus to greet Audie Murphy on Universal's set.

Audie reads some of his fan mail on the Universal back lot.

Band singer Abbe Lane rehearses with Audie between scenes of RIDE CLEAR OF DIABLO.

Susan Cabot with Audie and Terry on the set of Universal Studios

COMPLETE FILMOGRAPHY

FILM	YEAR	PRODUCTION COMPANY
BEYOND GLORY	1948	Paramount
TEXAS, BROOKLYN AND HEAVEN	1948	United Artists
BAD BOY	1949	Allied Artists
THE KID FROM TEXAS	1950	Universal-International
SIERRA	1950	Universal-International
KANSAS RAIDERS	1950	Universal-International
THE RED BADGE OF COURAGE	1951	Metro-Goldwyn-Mayer
THE CIMARRON KID	1952	Universal-International
THE DUEL AT SILVER CREEK	1952	Universal-International
GUNSMOKE	1953	Universal-International
COLUMN SOUTH	1953	Universal-International
TUMBLEWEED	1953	Universal-International
RIDE CLEAR OF DIABLO	1954	Universal-International
DRUMS ACROSS THE RIVER	1954	Universal-International
DESTRY	1954	Universal-International
TO HELL AND BACK	1955	Universal-International
WORLD IN MY CORNER	1956	Universal-International
WALK THE PROUD LAND	1956	Universal-International
THE GUNS OF FT. PETTICOAT	1957	Columbia
JOE BUTTERFLY	1957	Universal-International
NIGHT PASSAGE	1957	Universal-International
THE QUIET AMERICAN	1958	United Artists
RIDE A CROOKED TRAIL	1958	Universal-International
THE GUN RUNNERS	1958	United Artists
NO NAME ON THE BULLET	1959	Universal-International
THE WILD AND THE INNOCENT	1959	Universal-International
CAST A LONG SHADOW	1959	United Artists
THE UNFORGIVEN	1960	United Artists
HELL BENT FOR LEATHER	1960	Universal-International
SEVEN WAYS FROM SUNDOWN	1960	Universal-International
POSSE FROM HELL	1961	Universal-International
BATTLE AT BLOODY BEACH	1961	20th Century Fox
SIX BLACK HORSES	1962	Universal-International
SHOWDOWN	1963	Universal-International
GUNFIGHT AT COMANCHE CREEK	1963	Allied Artists
THE QUICK GUN	1964	Columbia
BULLET FOR A BADMAN	1964	Universal-International
APACHE RIFLES	1964	20th Century Fox
ARIZONA RAIDERS	1965	Columbia
GUNPOINT	1966	Universal-International
THE TEXICAN	1966	Columbia
TRUNK TO CAIRO	1967	American International
40 GUNS TO APACHE PASS	1967	Columbia
A TIME FOR DYING	None	Fipco

SELECTED BIBLIOGRAPHY

Simpson, Harold B., Col., *Audie Murphy, American Soldier*, (Hill College Press, Hillsboro, Texas, 1975).

ABOUT THE AUTHOR

Born in Newark, New Jersey, Sue began going to movies as a teenager, enjoying the Saturday afternoon matinees at The Royal Theater in Bloomfield, New Jersey. In 1954, at the age of 13, she saw her first Audie Murphy movie and started collecting on the baby-faced movie star.

The love for movies and the theater she comes by honestly, as that's how her parents met back in the 1930's. Into the early 1940's, Sue's father was one of the founders of The Little Theater in East Orange, New Jersey. Not only was he a talented actor, but also a very accomplished director. Although Sue never saw her mother act, she too, was an actress, who later did a lot of backstage preparations such as props, make-up, etc. Being the shy one in the family, Sue's only acting was a small part in a high school play.

Sue Gossett

After graduating from high school, Sue joined the United States Navy where she met her future husband, Dave, in Washington, D.C. They were married in 1960 and have two wonderful sons and daughters-in-law and four beautiful grandchildren.

For eight years Sue was a member of the world champion Gem City Sweet Adelines, a barbershop chorus for women. After a short course, Sue has done small amounts of professional modeling and acting.

Sue has also written a book entitled, *Audie Murphy: Now Showing,* which celebrates the movie career of Audie Murphy. It contains 200+ pages and more than 500 photo illustrations of advertising materials used to promote the 44 films given to Audie's credit.

Sue and Dave have lived in the Dayton, Ohio, area since 1972.

Other Movie / TV Books Available from Empire Publishing:

ABC's of Movie Cowboys by Edgar M. Wyatt

An Ambush of Ghosts, A Personal Guide to Favorite Western Film Locations by David Rothel

Audie Murphy: Now Showing by Sue Gossett

Back in the Saddle: Essays on Western Film and Television Actors edited by Garry Yoggy

Bill Elliott, The Peaceable Man by Bobby Copeland

Bob Steele, Stars and Support Players by Bob Nareau

Bonanza, A Viewer's Guide to the TV Legend by David R. Greenland

B-Western Actors Encyclopedia by Ted Holland

Buster Crabbe, A Self-Portrait as told to Karl Whitezel

B-Western Boot Hill: A Final Tribute to the Cowboys and Cowgirls Who Rode the Saturday Matinee Movie Range by Bobby Copeland

The Cowboy and the Kid by Jefferson Brim Crow, III

Duke, The Life and Image of John Wayne by Ronald L. Davis

The Films and Career of Audie Murphy by Sue Gossett

The Films of the Cisco Kid by Francis M. Nevins, Jr.

The Films of Hopalong Cassidy by Francis M. Nevins, Jr.

From Pigskin to Saddle Leather: The Films of Johnny Mack Brown by John A. Rutherford

The Gene Autry Reference-Trivia-Scrapbook by David Rothel

The Golden Corral, A Roundup of Magnificent Western Films by Ed Andreychuk

The Hollywood Posse, The Story of a Gallant Band of Horsemen Who Made Movie History by Diana Serra Cary

Hoppy by Hank Williams

In a Door, Into a Fight, Out a Door, Into a Chase, Movie-Making Remembered by the Guy at the Door by William Witney

John Ford, Hollywood's Old Master by Ronald L. Davis

John Wayne—Actor, Artist, Hero by Richard D. McGhee

John Wayne, An American Legend by Roger M. Crowley

Last of the Cowboy Heroes by Budd Boetticher

The Life and Films of Buck Jones, the Silent Era by Buck Rainey

The Life and Films of Buck Jones, the Sound Era by Buck Rainey

More Cowboy Movie Posters by Bruce Hershenson

More Cowboy Shooting Stars by John A. Rutherford and Richard B. Smith, III

Peggy Stewart, Princess of the Prairie by Bob Carman and Dan Scapperotti

Quiet on the Set, Motion Picture History at the Iverson Movie Location Ranch by Robert G. Sherman

Randolph Scott, A Film Biography by Jefferson Brim Crow, III

Richard Boone: A Knight Without Armor in a Savage Land by David Rothel

Riding the (Silver Screen) Range, The Ultimate Western Movie Trivia Book by Ann Snuggs

Riding the Video Range, The Rise and Fall of the Western on Television by Garry A. Yoggy

The Round-Up, A Pictorial History of Western Movie and Television Stars Through the Years by Donald R. Key

Roy Barcroft, the King of the Badmen by Bobby Copeland

Roy Rogers, A Biography, Radio History, Television Career Chronicle, Discography, Filmography, etc. by Robert W. Phillips

The Roy Rogers Reference-Trivia-Scrapbook by David Rothel

Saddle Gals, A Filmography of Female Players in B-Westerns of the Sound Era by Edgar M. Wyatt and Steve Turner

Saddle Pals: A Complete B-Western Roster of the Sound Era by Garv Towell and Wayne E. Keates

Silent Hoofbeats by Bobby Copeland

Singing in the Saddle: The History of the Singing Cowboy by Douglas B. Green

The Sons of the Pioneers by Bill O'Neal and Fred Goodwin

Television Westerns Episode Guide by Harris M. Lentz, III

Tex Ritter: America's Most Beloved Cowboy by Bill O'Neal

They Still Call Me Junior by Frank "Junior" Coghlan

Those Wide Open Spaces by Hank Williams

Those Great Cowboy Sidekicks by David Rothel

Tim Holt by David Rothel

The Tom Mix Book by M. G. "Bud" Norris

Trail Talk, Candid Comments and Quotes by Performers and Participants of The Saturday Matinee Western Films by Bobby Copeland

Western and Frontier Film and Television Credits, 1903-1995 by Harris M. ***Lentz***

The Western Films of Sunset Carson by Bob Carman and Dan Scapperotti

Western Movies: A TV and Video Guide to 4200 Genre Films compiled by Michael R. Pitts

Westerns Women by Boyd Magers and Michael G. Fitzgerald

Whatever Happened to Randolph Scott? by C. H. Scott

White Hats and Silver Spurs, Interviews with 24 Stars of Film and Television Westerns of the 1930s-1960s

Audie Murphy: NOW SHOWING

by Sue Gossett

To celebrate the movie career of Audie Murphy, Sue Gossett and Empire Publishing are delighted to present, for the first time, this volume of *Audie Murphy: Now Showing*. It contains 200+ pages and more than 500 photo illustrations of advertising materials used to promote the 44 films given to Audie's credit. The contents include photos of movie 1-sheet posters, lobby and window display cards, half sheets, publicity items, author's comments, and more.

A must-have for the true Audie Murphy fan!

Author Sue Gossett is a true Audie Murphy historian, having followed his career since 1954. She is the author of another Empire publication, The Films and Career of Audie Murphy.

Contents include:

- The movie magic of this legendary giant as illustrated via theatrical promotional materials.
- 200+ pages
- More than 500 photo illustrations
- Complete filmography
- Foreign items and testimonials
- Interviews with actors who appeared in his films
- Locations where movies were filmed
- Brief synopsis of each film
- Much more!

ALL BOOKS GUARANTEED . . . YOU WILL BE SATISFIED!